Obsession, Aesthetics, and the Iberian City

Obsession, Aesthetics, and the Iberian City:
The Partial Madness of Modern Urban Culture

Benjamin Fraser

Vanderbilt University Press
Nashville, Tennessee

LIBRARY OF CONGRESS CATALOGING-IN-PUBLICATION DATA

Names: Fraser, Benjamin, author.
Title: Obsession, aesthetics, and the Iberian city : the partial madness of
  modern urban culture / Benjamin Fraser.
Description: Nashville : Vanderbilt University Press, [2020] | Includes
  bibliographical references and index.
Identifiers: LCCN 2021033642 (print) | LCCN 2021033643 (ebook) | ISBN
  9780826502377 (paperback) | ISBN 9780826502384 (hardback) | ISBN
  9780826502391 (epub) | ISBN 9780826502407 (pdf)
Subjects: LCSH: City and town life—Spain. | Cities and towns—Spain. |
  City and town life—Portugal. | Cities and towns—Portugal.
Classification: LCC HT145.S7 F47 2020 (print) | LCC HT145.S7 (ebook) |
  DDC 307.760946—dc23
LC record available at https://lccn.loc.gov/2021033642
LC ebook record available at https://lccn.loc.gov/2021033643

CONTENTS

ACKNOWLEDGMENTS

This book draws from three previous article-length publications but adapts them to a new context. Material from the article "Obsessively Writing the Modern City: The Partial Madness of Urban Planning Culture and the Case of Arturo Soria y Mata in Madrid, Spain," published by Liverpool University Press in the *Journal of Literary and Cultural Disability Studies* 13, no. 1 (2019): 21–37, figures into the first part of Chapter 3 and is largely unchanged. I am grateful to David Bolt, the editor of that journal, and to the anonymous reviewers he contacted for feedback that set me on the course to finish this book. The third section of Chapter 2 repeats some material from "Architecture, Urbanistic Ideology, and the Poetic-Analytic Documentary Mode in *Mercado de futuros* (2011) by Mercedes Álvarez," in *Architecture and the Urban in Spanish Film*, edited by Susan Larson (Bristol: Intellect, 2021), but introduces a new argument centered on disability aesthetics. Material from "Madrid, Histological City: The Scientific, Artistic and Urbanized Vision of Santiago Ramón y Cajal," published by Taylor and Francis in *Symposium: A Quarterly Journal of Modern Literatures* 67, no. 3 (2013): 119–34, figures into the third section of Chapter 3, but it has been recast and expanded to deal with disability aesthetics. I thank those publishers and their journal editors for allowing the re-use and adaptation of that previous material here. I am grateful to the three anonymous reviewers and Zachary Gresham at Vanderbilt University Press for suggestions leading to a stronger volume.

Introduction.
Our Urban Obsessions

We are obsessed by the modern city. This obsession may very well be, in fact, a defining element of urban modernity. The chapters of *Obsession, Aesthetics, and the Iberian City* explore the need to obsessively reconstruct and represent the city by examining urban aesthetics in the cultural production of selected figures from planning, architecture, science, prose and poetry, documentary film, and the graphic novel. Yet neither are those who consume and study literature or film immune to this obsessive fascination with the urban environment. The city is a collective obsession to which all of us contribute. The fact that the book you are reading exists is further proof of the point.

Although many depictions of the city in prose, poetry, and visual art can be found dating from earlier periods in human history,

Obsession, Aesthetics, and the Iberian City emphasizes a particular phase in urban development. This is the quintessentially modern city that comes into being in the nineteenth century. In social terms, this nineteenth-century city is the product of a specialist class of planners engaged in what urban theorist Henri Lefebvre has called the bourgeois science of modern urbanism. One thinks first of the large scale and the wide boulevards of Baron Georges von Haussmann's Paris or the geometrical planning vision made concrete in Ildefons Cerdà's Barcelona. Certainly not restricted to these specific European centers of power, the modern science of urban design famously inaugurates and disseminates a new way of thinking the city. Urban modernity comes to be defined by the triumph of exchange-value over use-value, and the lived city is eclipsed by the planned city as it is envisioned by capitalists, builders, and speculators. The present book explores this tension between planners and urbanites as it is expressed in a broadly Iberian social imaginary. Thus urban plans and architecture, literary prose and poetry, documentary cinema, and comics art all serve as windows into our modern obsession with urban aesthetics. Each of these examples are artistic texts requiring close cultural readings. By examining their structure, images, and meaning, and by seeing the modern city itself as a cultural text of sorts, the chapters that follow chart our collective cultural obsession with the urban environment from the late nineteenth century through today.

This book is neither encyclopedic nor comprehensive in terms of its scope. It does not pursue an archival history of medicine in the urban Iberian world; nor does it single out the European planning tradition for extended critique, though that is perhaps yet another worthy project.[1] Instead, it is content to investigate obsession and obsessive thinking as hallmark aspects and even social values of urban modernity through texts selected from four cities that are broadly representative of the cultural heterogeneity of the Iberian peninsula. Each chapter introduces but moves well beyond an identifiable urban area in a given city, noting the cultural obsession implicit in its reconstruction as well as the role of obsession in its artistic representation of the urban environment. These areas are Barcelona's Eixample district, Madrid's Linear City, Lisbon's central Baixa area, and Bilbao's Seven Streets, or Zazpikaleak. The theme of obsession—explored below as synonymous with the concept of partial madness—provides a point of departure for understanding the interconnection of both urbanistic and artistic discourses.

On one hand, the urbanistic thinking of such figures as Ildefons Cerdà (Barcelona), Arturo Soria y Mata (Madrid), the Marquês de Pombal (Lisbon), and Pablo Alzola, Severino Achúcarro, and Ernesto Hoffmeyer (Bilbao) reveals an obsessive drive in line with the hallmark tropes of a partially mad modernity outlined by disability studies scholar Lennard J. Davis in his book *Obsession: A History* (2008). On the other hand, an engagement with both the city and the obsessive aspects of modernity is crucial for understanding the work of architect Antoni Gaudí and documentary filmmakers Mercedes Álvarez and Hiroshi Teshigahara (Barcelona); prose authors Emilia Pardo Bazán and Santiago Ramón y Cajal (Madrid); poetic writers Fernando Pessoa and Cesário Verde (Lisbon); and two collaborations by comics artists: Josep Busquet, Pedro J. Colombo, and Aintzane Landa, and also Kike Infame and Sr. Verde (Bilbao). These texts have been selected because they are markedly urban and because they manifest a quintessentially modern theme of obsessive thinking, but not because they are somehow unique. Other urban texts that indulge in obsession as a response or reaction to modernity are no doubt plentiful. The range of creative genres, urban contexts, and time periods here has been calibrated to showcase the way obsession has become a widespread cultural value of an urbanized modernity. It is not just that the creative energy motivating geometrical planning is obsessive, not just that literary authors create, and readers eagerly consume, obsessive characters, or even that modern critics have praised sprawling, obsessive works. It is that there is a certain everydayness and even banality to this obsession. Though it is seldom recognized as such, obsession is a mode of cognition valued by the modern urbanite.

This book brings together two heretofore relatively distinct bodies of knowledge, urban cultural studies, on one hand, and literary and cultural disability studies, on the other. As with my previous books, this book attends to the representation of the city in cultural production.[2] Yet it also draws on an ongoing interest in disability studies.[3] These two bodies of knowledge overlap somewhat in the sense that both the quintessentially modern understanding of the city and the socially constructed category disability were forged during the nineteenth century. That said, this overlap is not a clean one, and the result is neither a true disability studies project nor a systematic investigation of urban cultural history.

In approaching the Iberian city, a vital disciplinary tradition of cultural studies has yielded no shortage of investigations into cultural representations, space/place, and urban modernity.[4] One can take as a touchstone Joan Ramon Resina's publication of the volume *Iberian Cities* (2001), which sought to expand beyond interest in Castilian literature and culture to encompass analyses of Catalan, Galician, Portuguese, and Basque cultural production. Many twenty-first-century studies of Iberian urban culture dialogue with the insights of prolific Marxian thinker Henri Lefebvre, who theorized nineteenth-century urban modernity as a product of capitalist socio-economic relations. Some Iberian studies scholars make this connection directly, referencing widely influential works by the French theorist such as *The Production of Space* (1991), *Critique of Everyday Life* (1991), *The Urban Revolution* (2003), and *The Right to the City* (1996).[5] Others draw on Lefebvre more indirectly, sustaining connections with thinkers he influenced or with whom he had contact, perhaps most notably David Harvey, but also Edward Soja, Manuel Castells, Guy Debord and the Situationists, Andy Merrifield, and Barcelona-based theorist Manuel Delgado Ruiz. Still other scholars construct arguments that are indebted implicitly to the line of urban critique that Lefebvre forged.

Collectively, such approaches trace the cultural representations of the modern Iberian city from the nineteenth into the twentieth and twenty-first centuries. The present book draws inspiration from this rich tradition of Iberian urban critique, but also attends to important work from the interdisciplinary field of literary and cultural disability studies.

In order to establish the main through line of *Obsession, Aesthetics, and the Iberian City*, it is necessary to include the figure of the urban planner alongside the list of specialists—artists, scientists, and writers—at the core of an argument made by disability studies pioneer Lennard J. Davis. The fact is that his book *Obsession: A History* (2008) may perhaps too easily be regarded as marginal when read against the scholar's other pathbreaking contributions to disability studies. In the latter category one may consult such volumes as *Enforcing Normalcy: Disability, Deafness and the Body* (1995), the *Disability Studies Reader* (1997), *Bending Over Backwards: Disability, Dismodernism and Other Difficult Positions* (2002), and *The End of Normal: Identity in a Biocultural Era* (2013). Yet it was the proposed composition of *Obsession: A History* that notably earned its author a Guggenheim Fellowship in 2002–2003. The finished product was not explicitly urban in conception. Nevertheless, its argument is predicated on the existence of a certain modern European urban setting and its corresponding urban circuits of cultural exchange. Davis himself drew attention to urban considerations in passing during key moments of the book, and those references prove to be quite significant for our present purposes. As pursued in the theoretical chapter that follows this introduction, it is by emphasizing those urban elements already present in Davis's text and by thinking through the considerable entanglements of obsession with urban modernity that we reach a greater understanding regarding the presence of cognitive difference in modern urban life.

This book seeks to make innovative contributions to two distinct areas of research. It moves beyond the confines of traditional

Castilian (Spanish) cultural studies, and it works to globalize concerns pertinent to disability studies. The focus on Barcelona, Madrid, Lisbon, and Bilbao is consistent with turns within Iberian studies that emphasize commonalities across the variegated cultural and linguistic landscapes of Spain and Portugal. Thus it attends not merely to Spanish cultural production but acknowledges the variations that both connect and distinguish Castilian Spanish from other linguistic cultures present on the Iberian peninsula, here Catalan, Portuguese, and Basque. Although cultural studies of cognitive difference are still infrequent outside of English-dominant areas of the academic realm and the globe, Davis's focus on broader trends in Europe pushes us beyond some of the persisting Anglophone borders of work on disability and the city.[6] This examination of representations of four Iberian cities thus follows up on the calls for global disability studies scholarship launched in the *Journal of Literary and Cultural Disability Studies* through two co-written editorials, one by David Mitchell and Sharon Snyder, and the other by Stuart Murray and Clare Barker, both published in 2010. In the more narrow selection of work focusing on disability and the city, this tendency to investigate Anglophone areas of the globe is perhaps even more pronounced. The chapters that follow trace out a novel path that is not synonymous with, but rather adjacent to, contemporary disability studies.[7] Still, the result draws more from disability studies approaches than it does from the long history of literary mashups on madness and modernism.[8] There is a wealth of theory and literature relevant to understanding the social construction and material experience of cognitive difference, not least of all Michel Foucault's *History of Madness* and *The Birth of the Clinic*, from which I drew in my previous book *Cognitive Disability Aesthetics: Visual Culture, Disability Representations and the (In)Visibility of Cognitive Difference* (2018). Here, however, given the wide variety of possible subthemes implicated in a study of this nature, I have preferred to gravitate more closely toward the selected cultural

texts themselves, with references to disability scholars Davis, Mitchell and Snyder, Tobin Siebers, Joseph Straus, Henri-Jacques Stiker,
Rob Imrie, Jos Boys, Tanya Titchkosky, and others where possible.

While global interest in disability themes increases, there still
remains a disconnect between work from the subdisciplines com-
prising Iberian and Latin American Studies, on one hand, and
Anglophone disability studies, on the other.[9] Yet there are numerous scholars who have studied Iberian and Latin American cultures within a critical framework explicitly indebted to disability
studies—Susan Antebi, Madeline Conway, Beth Jörgenson, Encar-
nación Juárez Almendros, Matthew Marr, Raquel Medina, Julie
Avril Minich, Ryan Prout, and Victoria Rivera Cordero, for example.
Such authors broaden the global reach of disability studies as a
discipline. More can still be done, however, to bring the work of
these Iberian and Latin American studies scholars to the attention of the wider interdisciplinary field of humanistic approaches
to disability.

The first chapter, "The Partial Madness of Modern Urban Culture," covers some necessary theoretical ground. By developing points that Davis left largely implicit in *Obsession: A History*,
it underscores the central urban metaphor through which he
explained the concept of partial madness. Stating these points
in advance can help to contextualize the arguments made in this
book's chapters. The first is that modern urban planners and their
work can be understood within a framework of obsession in much
the same way as Davis approaches the lives and artistic careers of
prolific literary and scientific authors. The second is that obsession also becomes prized within urban culture and urbanized
consciousness, which develop in tandem with the construction of
the modern urban built environment. As a consequence, the varied cultural and artistic representations of urban life tend to rely
on the trope of obsession as a crucial element in their narrative
and visual forms of composition. Importantly, too, as Davis notes,
the concept of partial madness was a modern idea. It displaced

totalizing all-or-nothing characterizations from the premodern era regarding social assessments of sanity. A grey area was introduced, one in which a person could be judged as being neither completely insane nor completely of sound mind, but instead somewhere in between. The use of the Latin-derived word *obsessio* for this new category relies on an imagery of fortifications, walls, and cities, one that remains understated in Davis's book but that is deeply relevant to understanding how cognitive difference is implicated in modern urbanism and the production and circulation of city images. As these two points and the urban metaphor underlying Davis's approach to obsession suggest, it is necessary in this project to dialogue more extensively with the history of cities and urban theory. Modern planners were obsessive figures, and the urbanistic and architectural legacy that continues to influence contemporary city building remains obsessive.

A brief comment on methodology is in order. When contrasted with previous urban work centered on the theme of disability, the present book is concerned not with sensory and mobility disability, but instead with cognitive difference. Here, the argument is that the social construction of cognitive difference is present but unacknowledged within the modern planning tradition. This constitutes a direction complementary to existing scholarship, such as that advanced by Rob Imrie and Jos Boys, that critiques the absence of attention to mobility and sensory disabilities in ableist architecture and urban design. As a matter of course, this argument finds more common ground with the work of scholars of disability aesthetics such as Tobin Siebers and Joseph Straus than it does with the existing and emergent forms of scholarship linking urban space with the disability rights movement's important focus on access. Asserting the relevance of cognition to urban aesthetics requires the development of a new frame, one that sustains a theoretical challenge to the social construction of normalcy and nonetheless still complements the struggle for practical social gains. This endeavor outlines the convergence between the disability scholarship of Lennard J.

Davis and the urban theory of Henri Lefebvre. Davis's argument contains a few striking comments that help us to acknowledge the connections between the modern urban environment, industrialization, the democratization of mental illness, and the emergence of the construction of partial madness. These connections are crucial to understanding how urban planners were quintessentially modern. They were, like scientists, artists, and writers of the nineteenth century, obsessive thinkers whose partial madness became synonymous with the art of urban design.

Chapter 2, "Disfiguring Barcelona: Geometry and the Grid" highlights architecture through an exploration of documentary cinema. Its starting point is the geometrical obsession of engineer and urban planner Ildefons Cerdà (1815–1876), renowned for his nineteenth-century design of Barcelona's Eixample district. Cerdà famously constructed beyond the city's medieval walls using an ornamental grid pattern, large cross-cutting diagonal streets, spacious squares, and tree-lined avenues. He is particularly known for his creation of the *xamfrà* or truncated corner. While previous research has emphasized his accomplishments, social commitment, and the enduring visual resonance of his project in contemporary culture, this chapter casts him as an obsessive thinker and writer in line with the arguments made by Lennard Davis. In particular, at some seven hundred pages per volume, his two-tome *Teoría general de la urbanización* (1867) is characterized as an obsessive— and at once even literary—text due to the particular way he fixates on geometrical form, employs organic urban metaphor, and obsesses over the concept of perfection. Here the work of Tobin Siebers—and particularly the disability theorist's return to Erich Auerbach's *Mimesis*—establishes a way of reading visually that can be applied to Cerdà's urbanistic writing.

Each of the next two sections takes on an intriguing documentary film whose impact hinges on what Joan Ramon Resina (2008) has called Barcelona's urbanistic "vocation of modernity." Both directors pursue the modern obsession with the urban environment,

leading them at once to obsessively intriguing forms of metanar-
rative and visual and sonorous estrangement. The case of Hiroshi Teshigahara's *Antoni Gaudí* (1985) has often escaped extended
critical attention from scholars of Iberian film, despite the visibility
it has gained as a part of the Criterion Collection. Beyond Teshigahara's own entrancing and obsessive approach, here an extra
layer of obsession is introduced through the urban architectural
works of obsessive artist Gaudí, whose creations adorn and sur-
round the Eixample district. Joseph Straus's concept of disablist
hearing is—following in the line established by Siebers—equally
relevant to understanding the film's presentation of Gaudí's work.
Also centered on Barcelona's urban environment, Mercedes Álvarez's *Mercado de futuros* (2011) takes on the construction fever of
the beginning of the twenty-first century, prioritizing the margins of the Eixample and the Els Encants market situated under
the shadow of the Torre Agbar. Her film poses the question of
whether there is room for the nonproductive human mind, for
human figures and feelings, and for the everyday in the speculative obsessions of modern urbanism. In each case study, a cultural
studies approach to each film balances close reading, cinematic
language, and urban context.

In Chapter 3, "Madrid Mania: Linearity and the Zig-Zag," seeing the modern city as the outcome of urbanism's obsessive thinking and partial madness allows us to account for the contradictory
struggle that emerges between two distinguishable social groups.
On one side are the urbanists themselves, a special class of modern planner empowered to treat the fabric of the city as their personal canvas. The first section delves into the urbanistic work and
thought of Arturo Soria y Mata (1844–1920), the creator of the
Ciudad Lineal, the Linear City, in Madrid, as a paradigmatic case
study in obsessive modernity. Fixated on the nineteenth-century
technology that Wolfgang Schivelbusch (1986) has called the railway ensemble, Soria y Mata (1892) famously imagined the Linear
City plan—a city to be built along a single line that would cover

vast distances and in theory extend infinitely over the earth. After forming the Compañía Madrileña de Urbanización (Urbanization Company of Madrid) in 1894, he was able to begin a short stretch of his plan in the Spanish capital, where it still can be visited today. Soria y Mata demonstrates the monomaniacal thinking typical of modernity in his fixation on the infinite extension of the straight line, and the conceptual violence of his resulting plan banishes urban spontaneity to the margins.

On the other side are those modern figures who might be considered more typically obsessive in the sense outlined by Lennard Davis—writers and scientists such as Emilia Pardo Bazán and Santiago Ramón y Cajal. Through their literary prose, these two authors are obsessed not with imposing a plan, but rather with recovering a different kind of urban order. Their fictions depict the Lefebvrian city whose streets have a spontaneous use-value for its inhabitants. This is the urban as a site of play, recreation, wandering, and perhaps even wonder, and not merely the city as the locus of industrial productivity or a normative order. The literary spirit of Charles Baudelaire, with his reputation for extolling the virtues of urban wandering, echoes strongly in Pardo Bazán's "La gota de sangre" (1911) and Ramón y Cajal's "El pesimista corregido" (1905). While these works were published during the period in which the Ciudad Lineal was being constructed, this chapter does not pursue any specific literary representations of Soria y Mata's project but rather contrasts the urban values implied in these texts with the principles governing Soria y Mata's urbanistic thinking. The goal is to distinguish two types of contemporaneous obsession with the city that are developed in parallel, and which continue to be the focus of this book's Chapters 4 and 5.

From an urban perspective, each of these literary works can be seen as a Baudelairean zig-zag, one whose affirmation of the use-value of the city streets contrasts with and challenges the linear excesses of urban modernity. Both laud the spontaneity of urban experience that persists despite the staid aestheticization of the modern planning tradition. The neurasthenic main character in Pardo Bazán's mysterious tale becomes obsessed by a possible murder. Believing he is the only one who can solve it, his mono-mania turns the city streets into the site of an imaginative flight of fancy. The transformative moment for the pessimist of Cajal's story is carried out through a visual distortion rooted in scientific obsession, this time in the public green space of Madrid's Retiro Park. While urban planners are complicit with the phobia of the everyday—as exemplified by the stifling linearity of Soria y Mata's vision—these literary texts demonstrate the persistence and use-value of spontaneity as their protagonists zig, zag, and forge an urban experience that suits their own whims.[10]

Chapter 4, "Shattering Lisbon: Destabilization and Drudgery" takes as its starting point the year 1755, when the central area of Lisbon, Portugal, suffered a devastating earthquake. The ensuring destruction prompted Sebastião José de Carvalho e Melo (1699–1782) to carry out a complete reconstruction of the city's central Baixa area, or lower city, which assumed even greater importance as the modernized center of commerce in the Portuguese capital. Carvalho e Melo, more commonly known as the Marquês de Pombal, served as a statesman under José I of Portugal and was not himself an urban planner. His adoption of a blank-slate approach to the Baixa's redesign led to standardized blocks, certain building features, and what has been called the "Pombaline street." The Marquês de Pombal's urbanistic response to the Lisbon earthquake of 1755 continues to echo in the tropes of rupture and urban shift examined in the urban prose of Fernando Pessoa (1888–1935) and explored much more briefly in the poetic verse of Cesário Verde (1855–1886). Pessoa's *Livro do desassossego* (1982; *Book of Disquiet* [2017]), which was written over the first third of the twentieth century but published only after his death, returns obsessively to Lisbon's Baixa. The city itself becomes intertwined with details from what might seem to be the author's autobiography and ultimately comes to reflect and resonate with his interior mood and obsessive thoughts. What is more, the book foregrounds Pessoa's character-istically complex layering of narrative voices. The *Book of Disquiet* is presented to readers as the product not of the author's voice per se, but rather that of Bernardo Soares, a bookkeeper living in the Baixa, or else one Vicente Guedes. Centuries later, in line with Pessoa's sustained pattern of using what he called semi-heteronyms, the urban ruptures of the earthquake resonate in the rupture—or fragmentation, even multiplication—of a poetic self in the text. This is an obsession not only with the city but with the repetitive act of self-creation in which Pessoa indulges through his writing.

Notably, Pessoa was himself a champion of Cesário Verde's poetic work, which provides a brief but still interesting point of comparison in thematic and narrative terms. Verde lived and died in Lisbon, and though he spent time living in and writing about the rural countryside, he was equally an urban poet. In "O senti-mento dum ocidental" and other poems, this so-called Portuguese Baudelaire engages not with the city's monumental grid but with its remaining winding streets. As a flâneur he is concerned with feelings and moods rather than architecture, with the use-value that the city holds for the stroller rather than its buildings. This is a destabilized self constantly in movement. Verde's poetic voice is never still, and his obsession is as much with the lived city as with the dissolution of the self into it. Where Pessoa's narration multiplies the self, Verde's dissolves it into the urban environment. In both cases, however, this rewriting of self relies on and gains strength from the poetic re-creation of Lisbon's urban modernity.

The first section of Chapter 5, "Bilbao Rebuilt: Urban Fixations and the After-Image," focuses on the discourse of Bilbao's urban modernity, referencing the central Seven Streets or Zazpikaleak of the Casco Viejo and covering in quick succession a number of nineteenth-century plans for the city's expansion: Nicolás Lore-do's plan of 1786, the failed plan of 1861 crafted by Amado Lázaro, and the eventual definitive plan of 1876 by Alzola, Achúcarro, and Hoffmeyer. Here the modern planning of the city emerges as a collective fixation that concertedly neglects a close topographic consideration of the city's needs. The consequences of this neglect are exacerbated by severe flooding of Bilbao's iconic and central segment of the Nervión river in 1983, and further apparent in a new wave of urban design beginning in the 1990s. The city was catapulted to global recognition as a result of isolated projects designed by international star architects, including Frank Gehry's construction of the Guggenheim Museum on the river's bank. The marketable potency of the so-called "Bilbao effect" or "Guggenheim effect" in fact suggests the way—according to the central argument of Joan Ramon Resina and Dieter Ingenschay's edited volume *After-Images of the City* (2003)—the modern urban image becomes subjected to an excessively malleable idea-form that can be endlessly manipulated. This "after-image" of the city can itself be meaningfully approached as a modern obsession.

Two divergent forms of modern urban obsession are revealed in a pair of twenty-first-century Bilbao-centered graphic novels. *En segundo plano* (2015), by collaborators Josep Busquet, Pedro J. Colombo, and Aintzane Landa, narrates a young man's obsession with a woman he has seen in a photograph. Recalling the central conceit of more shocking tales of photographic obsession—such as Julio Cortázar's "Las babas del diablo" and Michelangelo Antonioni's *Blow-Up*, a loose filmic adaptation of that same story—the comic emphasizes its protagonist's monotonous life, reflecting a banalization of the urban mystery theme. His interest in photography is subdued by the drudgery of work in a photography store but piqued by figures he photographs in his flâneur-like urban wanderings along the Nervión and throughout Bilbao. His is a diminished neurasthenic response to urban modernity that never quite rises to the level of Emilia Pardo Bazan's amateur detective protagonist. The second graphic novel, *Morirse en Bilbao* (2018), by Kike Infame and Sr. Verde, imagines a future Bilbao of the twenty-second century that is partially underwater and under threat of multiple apocalyptic threats. Here the destabilizing anxiety of the modern obsessive thinker is rendered allegorically as a social reality. More important, the way architecture figures—and does not figure—in the pages of the comic connects with Resina and Ingenschay's reading of the contemporary urban after-image. An initial two-page spread of a partially submerged Bilbao catalyzes persisting anxieties stemming from the 1983 flooding of the Casco Viejo, and a later two-page sequence featuring the Basílica de Begoña can be read in terms proposed by Resina and Ingenschay. The graphic novel reveals how urban images become detached and abstracted from the everyday experience of the city at ground level. The visual and tactile dimensions of architecture thus turn into a collective obsession with the city, more as a mere object of cognition than as a lived space.

The conclusion returns to Davis's central arguments in order to sum up the contributions of previous chapters. The regularization to which the modern urban environment has been subjected and the monotony of modern urban life are not inconsequential outcomes, but instead the natural consequences of forms of obsessive thinking. Quintessentially modern reactions to such obsessive urban thinking emerge through tropes of blurred boundaries, endlessness, fragmentation, irregularity, clutter, fixation, and instability. To attend to these aesthetic elements as manifestations of cognition is at once to consider how regularized and monotonous modern urban life is both reproduced and contested through obsessive patterns of thought. Whether it goes by the name of partial madness, monomania, neurasthenia, or obsession, the notion of cognitive difference is central to the way we think about the city, and it is implicated in the social value we attribute to urban aesthetics. Understanding this may ultimately help us to think about cities in a more capacious, and more expansively human, way.

Chapter 1
The Partial Madness of Modern Urban Culture

Obsession, Aesthetics, and the Iberian City builds on pioneering work linking disability, architecture, and cities sustained over three decades (1990s, 2000s, 2010s). A whole scholarly tradition has already applied disability studies methods to analyses of the urban built environment. This existing tradition asserts that constructions of disability and urbanity are co-constitutive forces that have shaped, and continue to shape, the lived experiences of people with disabilities. Rob Imrie's landmark publication *Disability and the City: International Perspectives* (1996) conveys well the value and scope of this branch of disability scholarship. That book was steeped in the hallmark critique of disability studies, and it grappled just as deeply with key thinkers from urban studies. In the introduction, Imrie declared in no uncertain terms that

> building form and design are inscribed with the values of a society which seeks to project and prioritize the dominant values of the 'able-bodied'. From the shattered paving stones along the high street, to the absence of induction loops in a civic building, people with disabilities face the daily hurdles of negotiating their way through hostile environments which the majority of us take for granted. Using a range of empirical material, the book documents how the environmental planning system in the United Kingdom is attempting to address and overturn the inaccessible nature of the built environment for people with disabilities. (viii)

Imrie's approach was thorough and far-reaching through time. He considered the arguments made by Richard Sennett in *Flesh and Stone* (1994) as a way of addressing the ableist orientation of classical architecture, and thus he implicated the roots of Western city planning (16). Despite what the subtitle of Imrie's book might suggest, however, the "international perspectives" foregrounded there are largely limited to UK and US contexts.

The foundational focus on access to the built environment in Imrie's book is echoed and expanded in a number of post-1996 publications that are indebted to his investigations (see, for example, Gleeson 1997, 2001; Hamraie 2012; Imrie 2000a, 2000b, 2003, 2007, 2017; and Titchkosky 2011). One might use the term "access literature" as an apt descriptor for much of this research. In linking disability with geography, many scholars have also turned explicitly toward the works of urban thinkers such as Henri Lefebvre, David Harvey, Lewis Mumford, Jane Jacobs, and Richard Sennett, or else the urban figure of the flâneur (see especially Imrie 1996; also see Dolmage 2017; Serlin 2006, 2012). The volume *Mind and Body Spaces: Geographies of Illness, Impairment and Disability* (1999)—edited by Ruth Butler and Hester Parr and based on a session delivered at the conference of the Royal Geographical Society (with the Institute of British Geographers)—represents a particularly important contribution to the intersection of disability and geography. Yet while this tradition has looked closely at the ableist nature of discourse surrounding the production of the built environment, it has tended to focus largely on the scale of individual buildings, of curb cut-outs, of architectural form and its associated ableist ideology, rather than engage the larger scale of urban planning on its own terms or the wider realm of urban aesthetics. Of course, buildings, architecture, and the access literature that analyzes them in seeking to impact ableist spatial policy are important. However, applying disability approaches to the large-scale urban planning that coalesced in the nineteenth-century in European cities—for example, Haussmann in Paris, Cerdà in Barcelona, or Soria y Mata in Madrid—is also valuable. In Lefebvrian terms, this specific book project is concerned more with space as conceived and represented than space as lived.[1] Of course, as evident in Lefebvre's triadic model of space, these are interconnected dimensions of spatial practice, and the lived experience of city life is an important touchstone for the cultural analyses in later chapters. Yet privileging the conception and representation of urban space contributes to a discourse adjacent to those frameworks of disability theory that already exist.

Cripping the Cultures of Urbanism

In terms of its global reach and cognitive emphasis, *Obsession, Aesthetics, and the Iberian City* carves out a relatively unique space of inquiry. Because of how far this book's argument diverges from Imrie's concerns, for example, there are a few baseline assumptions that require further explanation. First, while previous work on disability and the city has attended to mobility and sensory disabilities, it is still somewhat novel that this book emphasizes cognitive difference. In truth, cognition did not figure as prominently in disability studies as a whole as did physical disabilities until the twenty-first century (see Fraser 2018a). The result is that psychiatric disability, madness, and cognitive difference in general remained comparatively undertheorized. David T. Mitchell and Sharon L. Snyder wrote in *Narrative Prosthesis* (2000) that, "while most of the work in the humanities to date has centered upon physical disability as its grounding object of study, one of the major new areas of research in disability studies will need to be that of cognitive disabilities" (39).[2] That change signaled by Mitchell and Synder has only recently emerged as a core element of disability studies. It was still possible for Alison Kafer to write in *Feminist Queer Crip* (2013) that "Many expressions of crip pride or crip politics often explicitly address only physical impairments, thereby ignoring or marginalizing the experiences of those with sensory or mental impairments" (15–16; see also McRuer 2017). In asserting the value of addressing cognitive difference within the context of disability studies one must attend to a somewhat different subset of problems. In his essay "Autism as Culture," Joseph Straus (2013) has identified what he calls "the problem of narration" and "the problem of community" (462) which are more broadly applicable to populations living with cognitive disabilities. This approach identifies a contradiction central to discussions of cognitive difference. Neoliberal ideology and the rules of representational democracy require a member of a minoritized social group to "to resist medicalized discourse by speaking for him or herself," and yet complicating this matter is the fact that, as Straus emphasizes, "a group of people who have problems with communication and social relatedness may find it difficult to forge . . . a self-aware community" (462; see also Mitchell and Snyder 2015; Fraser 2018a).

Due to its focus on urban aesthetics, subsequent chapters of this book do not seek to advance any convincing narratives related to disability advocacy. They do, however, contribute to the cognitive turn in disability studies in less tangible but equally important ways. Along with scholarship challenging the centrality of cognitive ableism, significant contributions exist, in increasing numbers, to the scholarship on psychiatric and cognitive disability. Some examples would be the volume *Mad Matters: A Critical Reader in Canadian Mad Studies* (2013, edited by LeFrancois, Menzies, and Reaume) as well as several special sections of the *Journal of Literary and Cultural Disability Studies* and *Disability Studies Quarterly*. In the latter category readers may be interested in consulting special issues on cognitive impairment, edited by Lucy Burke (2008); on emotion and disability, edited by Elizabeth Donaldson and Catherine Prendergast (2011); on disability and madness, edited by Noam Ostrander and Bruce Henderson (2013); on autism and neurodiversity, edited by Emily Thornton Savarese and Ralph James Savarese (2010); and on learning disabilities, edited by David J. Connor and Beth A. Ferri (2010). Yet while these and other works of scholarship address the inclusion of populations with cognitive disability in modern life more concertedly, the present book is focused more specifically on what might be called cripping the narrative of modern urbanism.

Second, while previous scholarship has underscored the absence of disability in ableist architectural diagramming and urban design, this book asks whether it is possible to discern the presence of cognitive difference within ableist planning traditions. These are very distinct, if ultimately complementary, research questions. When scholarship addresses how ableist planning excludes and does not consider disability in the construction of building architecture or large-scale design, it seeks to reform that architectural and planning tradition. That branch of disability studies research seeks to crip architectural and planning activity, either through an appeal to the broad narrative of universal design or through the more targeted but equally important narrative of the inclusion of specific concerns and identifiable populations living with disabilities in urban areas. These valuable approaches acknowledge that disability is understood as a lack by ableist planning and design narratives, and it thus seeks to reshape those narratives through the integration of disability into the planning of urban life. Yet it is somewhat a different matter to suggest that ableist urbanism already involves cognitive difference in certain ways. To ask how cognitive difference already figures as a presence in ableist narratives of the modern city necessitates a deeper questioning of the standard binaries of disability/ability that are a necessary component of disability advocacy in the political sphere. This questioning can be quite productive if one wants to acknowledge the way the categories of disability and ability are each implied in the other. Disability studies as an academic project requires analyses that destabilize the notion of normalcy as much as it does those that advocate for people with disabilities by emphasizing inclusive social and conceptual practices.

The risk of pursuing only the mode of advocacy, inclusion, and redesign is that scholarship becomes too instrumentalist. It may even risk reifying the notion of disability so that it becomes identified with the reality of the material experience of impairment, rather than being implicated more broadly in the construction of social relationships. For example, advocating for an inclusive urban design or an architectural practice based not on the construct of the able-bodied male but on a seated wheelchair user is potentially emancipatory (see Boys 2017). Changing the way space is produced and experienced is a necessary part of social change. Consider Henri Lefebvre's dictum that *no revolution can be successful that does not transform space* (1991, 54). Yet changing a specific location in space alone is not sufficient for changing the myriad ways the disability/ability binary influences social practice and adheres in urban life. As theorists such as David Mitchell and Sharon Snyder (2015) and Jasbir Puar (2007) have explored, the discourse of inclusion, while valuable in the short-term, risks disability's long-term assimilation into the neoliberal circuits that perpetuate the construction of alterity and the reality of minoritized, stigmatized categorization. The risk of pursuing only the destabilization of the notion of normalcy itself is that analysis becomes too abstract and is effectively decoupled from the push for tangible social change. Texts that are too philosophical or too theoretical risk being critiqued for their lack of practical application. Yet the individual monograph is not a monad but instead part of a complex system of intellectual exchange; when pursued in tandem these theoretical and practical approaches are mutually constitutive. This is exactly the dual pathway that has already been pursued by feminist and queer theory.

This brings us to the third component of the motivation behind *Obsession, Aesthetics, and the Iberian City*, which is to help ensure that cognitive difference, in the form of obsession, is considered more broadly relevant to critical theory and cultural aesthetics. Jos Boys makes a compelling and related point in her edition of *Disability, Space, Architecture: A Reader* (2017), which collects significant essays in this tradition, mostly from the 2000s and 2010s. On the first page of the book's introduction she writes, "within the discipline of architecture disability remains predominantly framed by design guidance and building regulations on the one hand, and by a 'common sense' language of accessibility and inclusive/universal design on the other." She goes on to express the hope that emerging scholarship can correct for the prevailing assumption that disability is "unable to bring any kind of criticality or creativity to the discipline of architecture" (1). While the present book is not focused on architecture—with the exception of Chapter 2's discussion of Antoni Gaudí—it does, however, echo Boys's hope that theory might approach the intersection of disability and the city in novel ways. There is certainly great value in advocating for design regulations and accessibility, but also, as Boys suggests, in expanding how disability is used in cultural and critical theory. By thinking cognitive difference through urban aesthetics, we do bring it closer to "the feminist, post-colonial and queer studies which underpin associated scholarship and debate" (1). The present book is thus motivated by the idea that making the case for the broad relevance of the disability studies project entails an extension of its critical premise into adjacent areas of research.

Cognitive Disability as an Aesthetic Presence in Modern Urbanism

To understand urbanism in aesthetic terms does not mean that urbanism and architectural design should be severed from the discourses related to policy, governmentality, access, regulation, and inclusion within which they are necessarily imbricated. Far from it. Still, the understanding that urbanism is in fact an aesthetic practice is both accurate and productive.

It is accurate because the city at any given moment is more than a set of static structures or a string of monuments related to ableism's self-representation. It is also an image, a metaphor, a work of art, an idea, and even an ideal. As a collective social ideal there is no doubt that the city has been produced in certain interests and not others. That said, however, the urban is a complex cultural product and cannot be reduced to being merely a set of objects whose existence can be taken at face value. Embedded in the city's constantly changing fabric there are sets of contradictions and potentialities. Considering—as this book's Chapters 2 and 3 do, for example—the way metaphor and aesthetics impact and shape the urban thinking of planners like Ildefons Cerdà in Barcelona or Arturo Soria y Mata in Madrid is important because these exercises reveal that there is much more to be investigated in the work of urban design than its convergence or divergence from ableist functionalism. Understanding urbanism as an aesthetic practice helps us recognize its complexity and its broadly social nature by considering its connection with metaphorical tropes of beauty, harmony, and health that are deeply rooted in modern culture and also implicit, if not explicit, in disability studies research. It is productive to foreground the aesthetic elements of urbanistic thinking, in that once the city is understood as a collective social product, rather than just the set of buildings fashioned by a specialist class of modern designers, it can be understood as multivocal and multivalent rather than univocal or uniform.

This book asks readers to consider the degree to which disability is not solely an absence in modern urbanism, but also an unacknowledged presence. To consider modern urbanism as an aesthetic realm in which cognitive difference is already implied can be understood as an extension of the scholarship that has shown disability to be a presence indicative of the prestige of modernist music or modern visual art. The former case is made in *Broken Beauty: Musical Modernism and the Representation of Disability* (2018), where Joseph Straus asserts the relevance of disability for making sense of modernist music's "fractured forms, immobilized harmonies, conflicting textual layers, radical simplification of means in some cases, and radical complexity and hermeticism in others" (1). The latter case is made by Tobin Siebers in *Disability Aesthetics* (2010), wherein the scholar argues that disability is what causes "the beauty of an artwork to endure over time" (5). Straus's scholarship is indebted to Siebers's work, and the spirit of both is harnessed here to advance scholarship prompting a confrontation between disability studies and the urban humanities.

The main argument of *Disability Aesthetics* is instructive. Therein Tobin Siebers provides evidence that disability is a core element of modern painting, sculpture, and visual art. In this realm, it is a presence, rather than an absence. He writes, "what I am calling disability aesthetics names a critical concept that seeks to emphasize the presence of disability in the tradition of aesthetic representation" (2). In Siebers's work on the dis/abled body, the theorist articulates a dual goal that can also be adapted for analyses of the presence of cognitive difference in modern urbanism. He states that "it is not a matter of representing the exclusion of disability from aesthetic history, since such an exclusion has not taken place, but of making the influence of disability obvious.

This goal may take two forms: 1) to establish disability as a critical framework that questions the presuppositions underlying definitions of aesthetic production and appreciation; 2) to establish disability as a significant value in itself worthy of future development" (2017, 58). By following this line of thinking further we can tie other aesthetic practices into the disability studies project. If modern art, painting, sculpture, and music are entwined with disability, and if the city has been seen as "a work of art," it is time for disability studies scholars to consider the relevance of cognitive difference to the aesthetics of the modern city.

Echoing Siebers's argument about visual art, a good starting point is to provisionally accept the premise that cognitive difference has not in fact been excluded from aesthetic urban history. There can be no doubt that disability has been left out of the city as a practico-material fact, and of the urban as a social relationship—it is for this reason that the push by scholars such as Imrie, Boys, Dolmage, Gleeson, Hamraie, Serlin, and others must continue. But the paradox remains that cognitive difference is nonetheless still there, implicated in the aesthetics of modern urban life, just as disability is already there, expressed through the aesthetics of modern visual art and modernist music. Aesthetics are often dismissed as inconsequential by certain invocations of social science methodology, but as humanists such as Siebers and Straus demonstrate, they are fundamental. The investigation of urban aesthetics is crucial to challenging ableism in that this area of experience reveals the way ableist society excludes conceptually at the same time that it does so materially. This is a theoretical move with practical consequences. With time, as the future development of the urban humanities is able to show disability as a presence in both the creation and enjoyment of the modern urban environment, it should become easier to crip Henri Lefebvre's goal of ensuring that all who live within it can claim their "right to the city."

The evidence that this disablist aesthetic reading of urban space is long overdue is quite easy to identify in classic texts of urbanism.

As explored in this book's chapters, the modern city is planned and constructed according to a linear, geometrical set of coordinates and a reductive way of thinking. Discourses of use and function outline the proper use of the city streets, such that it becomes possible to claim the streets by "misusing" them. Because the nineteenth-century construction of the modern city represents the triumph of urban exchange-value, all that is necessary if one wants to misuse the streets is to assert their use-value. To practice such misuse is to challenge the perceived and normative function of the streets. This is why Henri Lefebvre underscores the spontaneous energies of the urban festival. It is also why the figure of the flâneur emerges as a crucial component of the work of Michel de Certeau. These points are echoed in Manuel Delgado Ruiz's celebration of the quotidian figure of the pedestrian. When the Situationists and the participants of the movements of 1968 sought to subvert the restrictive norms of modern bourgeois society, they simultaneously turned to the urban practices of the *dérive* and the spontaneity of street protest. In each of these urban critiques, something as simple as undirected wandering poses a challenge to the functionalist idea that cities are produced and maintained solely to facilitate the circulation of traffic, goods, and services. In these cases, the aesthetic field serves as a critique of the limitations and exclusion inherent in functionalist aims of certain forms of architectural and planning activity.

There is also the aesthetic metaphor of the city as a body to consider. A privileged point in the development of this conceptual equivalence can be found in the discovery of the circulation of blood in the human body, often attributed to English physician William Harvey in the seventeenth century. After this discovery, urban roads were explicitly envisioned as a circulatory system, such that the city by extension became an organism. As an organism, the city was conceived as a body with organs. Baron Georges von Haussmann (1809–1891) famously referred to the sewers of Paris as its bowels. Literature has been particularly important in extending this metaphor. The posthumous publication of prose poet Charles Baudelaire's *Le spleen de Paris* in 1869 also contributed to notions of the organic city. Imagined against the background of this widespread metaphor of the city as a body, urban parks and green spaces came to be understood as the lungs of the city. This form of metaphorical thinking has become so entrenched that it is used by both urbanists and anti-urbanists alike. Nineteenth-century planners considered it their task to restore health to a sick city. Ildefons Cerdà (1867), for example, saw himself as a surgeon who wielded the art of urban planning as a scalpel, excising illness from the urban social body.[3] In a very different spirit, but using the same organic metaphor, twentieth-century anti-urbanist Jane Jacobs (1992) called attention to the city as a complex problem similar to those studied by the biological sciences (433). Her goal was not to extol the virtues of modern urban planning but rather to denounce its large-scale errors and critique the triumph of the planned city over the lived, human city.

To recognize urban planning as an aesthetic practice is to understand fully the social importance of its appeal to metaphorical thinking, whatever form that thinking takes in relation to tropes of corporeality, health, or harmony. The matter of beauty is crucial to modern urbanism, whether one considers, for example, the symmetrical geometries of modern city grids, the harmonious integration of nature into the nineteenth-century city, or the more complex aims of the parks movement or the city beautiful movement at the turn of the twentieth century. It is worth pointing out for twenty-first-century readers that the beauty historically ascribed to urban green space in particular is not merely rooted in practices of visually consuming nature but is also related to the connections identified between rural spaces and health discourse. Miasmic theories of health impacted the development of nineteenth-century planning and led to the development of open green spaces where sick air could be diffused and dispersed in favor of healthy air (see P. Hall 2002). This handful of details outlines how urbanism's aesthetics might be closely compared with the aesthetics of modern art.

Both urban aesthetics and the aesthetics of visual art are deeply grounded in bodily representation and/or corporeal metaphor. In "Disability Aesthetics," Tobin Siebers (2017) wrote that "Modern art continues to move us because of its refusal of harmony, bodily integrity and perfect health" (59). The theorist explores the Nazi rejection of this form of what might be considered as a "perfectionist," and thus ableist, modernism as a way of proving the point. Nazi aesthetics demonstrated "the inability to tolerate any human forms except the most familiar, monochromatic, and regular," such that modern art was considered "degenerate and ugly" (59). Modern art, at least in the sense privileged in Siebers's text, is quite visual, and what the Nazis saw as degenerate and ugly becomes a prized attribute for artistic modernism—even if the connection to disability was not always recognized socially. Joseph Straus's work in *Broken Beauty* and *Extraordinary Measures* (2011) shows how the notion of disability aesthetics can also be applied to nonvisual, aural, musical texts. A modern composition's beauty hinges more and more on complexity, on breaks, ruptures, and fractured forms of classical harmony, melody, and rhythm. The "disfiguring" of modern visual art and the "disfiguring" of modern musical form thus have something in common, and this commonality can be extended to considerations of urban aesthetics.

Urban plans and urban images are notably "readable" as visual texts. Yet the notion that the city is a body should give us pause. Cities are not visual representations of human bodies. They are not shaped like bodies, and they cannot represent the body as visual art can. Beyond the convincing nature of certain metaphors, perhaps the circulation of traffic in the urban body being chief among them, cities are not concerned with bodily shape as a compositional figure. Nonetheless, in urbanistic thought the borders between inner/outer, self/other, tidy/chaotic, figurative/disfiguring continue to be relevant, as discussed further in Chapter 2.

The notion that cities grow, as does organic life, is another point of connection with corporeal thinking. But in other ways the bodily metaphor in urbanism is less representational than in visual art; it is more conceptual, as it is with Straus's analyses of modernist music. Still, prompted by Siebers's forays into establishing a visual way of analyzing writing, the bodily metaphor can be identified in urbanistic texts and also in urbanism's writing of the city itself. The nature of urbanism as a conceptual practice means that we must be attentive to bodily metaphor, but also to corporeality's indirect presence in metaphorical thinking. In Nazi sculpture one can visually identify, as Siebers does in his analyses, the presence of ableist bodily representations. In modernist music one can hear, as Straus does, fractured musical forms that link with the social discourse of disability. But—to anticipate a question posed in Chapter 3's discussion of Arturo Soria y Mata's Linear City project—what does it mean to disfigure a line? This question brings us closer to Straus's notion of "immobilized harmony" in modernist music than it does to Siebers's visual critique of bodily representations. It is the projected extension of the linear city over time that raises questions about the normal or the abnormal growth of organisms, just as it raises questions about the particular way that obsession disfigures a work of art. An infinite line is obsessive in modern urban aesthetics, just as it would be in modern visual art. It demonstrates excessive fixity, an inability to respond to changing conditions, a fear of spontaneity in both design and use. And what does it mean—as in the case of Cerdà's Barcelona in Chapter 2, for example—that the twisted streets in the city's central core are maintained even as medieval walls are demolished and a straight geometrical grid established? Note too, that Cerdà's imposition of the harmonious and fixed geometrical grid is not total; aesthetically, the planner retains the spontaneity of the city's messy central core. While these specific questions are investigated in subsequent chapters, here it is essential to continue at a more general level.

The way disability figures in modern urban planning poses a challenge to accepted understandings of cognition and art. In cannot be avoided that in discussing the topic of urbanist aesthetics we encounter the cognitively ableist bias ingrained in questions regarding who can make art and what art even is. A quotation from "Disability Aesthetics" can help us by highlighting some of these more general matters:

> The appreciation of the work of art is a topic well rehearsed in the history of aesthetics, but rarely is it considered from the vantage point of the disabled mind—no doubt because the spectacle of the mentally disabled person, rising with emotion before the shining work of art, disrupts the long-standing belief that pronouncements of taste depend on a form of human intelligence as autonomous and imaginative as the art object itself. Artistic production also seems to reflect a limited and well defined range of mental actions. Traditionally, we understand that art originates in genius, but genius is really at a minimum only the name for an intelligence large enough to plan and execute works of art—an intelligence that usually goes by the name of "intention." Defective or impaired intelligence cannot make art according to this rule. Mental disability represents an absolute rupture with the work of art. (Siebers 2017, 62)

Taken in the context of his larger work, this passage challenges the cognitive ableism implicit in the idea and the industry of modern art. This ableism presents an obstacle, for example, for the social recognition of the value of art produced, say, by Judith Scott, a noted fiber artist that Siebers addresses specifically in his book. As I explored in an essay published in *Cultural Studies* in 2010, Judith Scott—who was a person with Down syndrome, cognitive impairment, and profound deafness—was the subject of *¿Qué tienes debajo del sombrero?* (2006; What's under your hat), an intriguing Iberian documentary that testifies to the international attention Scott's artwork has received. I share with Siebers the understanding that it is difficult to sustain the position that cognitive impairment is antithetical to art. Moreover, as I argued in a chapter of *Cognitive Disability Aesthetics* where I emphasized the case of a 2015 graphic novel by María and Miguel Gallardo, to accept that artistic production can also be a collaborative project is a further move away from cognitively ableist understandings of art as the effort of individuals who, reproducing the ableist myth of the independent human being, may be stigmatized and reduced to their interdependent relationship with others.[4]

In approaching the legacy of nineteenth-century urbanism in terms of aesthetics, however, there are two distinct problems to consider. First there is the matter of whether a city is or is not a work of art. Consider that an affirmative response to this question has become a commonplace. It is enshrined in a book authored by Donald J. Olsen titled *The City as a Work of Art: London, Paris, Vienna* (1986). One must also account for the ease with which one can now buy aesthetic urban objects: paintings, glassware, puzzles, and so on, bearing plans, maps, or photographs of specific cities. Admittedly the fact that the city is a common subject of both high and commercial forms of art does not necessarily mean that the city is itself seen as art. On the other hand, however, if modern society were not so thoroughly saturated by this notion, Jane Jacobs would not have felt it necessary to contradict it. In *Death and Life of Great American Cities* (1992), a work that she referred to as an attack on urban planning, Jacobs also wrote defiantly that "The city is not a work of art" (372). There is no question in my mind that the continuity between slum tours at the turn of the twentieth century and the vast proliferation of architectural urban tours at the turn of the twenty-first is consistent with the increasingly popular acceptance that the city is a work of art. This acceptance is, no doubt, illustrative of an internalization of the ideology of capitalist urbanism—what Lefebvre referred to as the city's exchange-value, that is, the fact that it becomes yet another object of consumption not so different from others. This fact is splendidly brought to life and critiqued in a documentary film by Mercedes Álvarez, analyzed in Chapter 2. The point is this: beyond the fact that the city is reproduced as an aesthetic product, it is also received as such by those who live within it. The urban form and the urban experience both have an aesthetic component that merits careful consideration.

The second problem concerns whether or not the notion of disabling urban modernity requires one to name planners who identify as or who can be identified as cognitively disabled. I prefer to follow the method used by Joseph Straus in his musical studies and thus to discuss the presence of disability in the aesthetics, the discourse, the product, and the representation of urbanism and the urban experience. Beyond urban plans themselves, that is, I am equally interested in the presence of cognitive disability in the urban aesthetics of specific literary, filmic, architectural, and cultural products. Both of these two problems become fused, and in my judgment justified, as we explore the argument presented by Lennard J. Davis in *Obsession: A History*. Davis's examination of obsession as modern state synonymous with the idea of partial madness forces a confrontation between the city as planned and the city as experienced. In adapting his argument, I intentionally avoid any strong identification of urban planners as being themselves cognitively disabled, but I also stress the expansive nature of cognitive difference as a social construction. In the end, it is sufficient to demonstrate that the planners and architects, the literary authors, the filmmakers, and the comics artists discussed in this book were obsessive thinkers, and/or that their cultural production examines or derives its significance from an engagement with urban obsession.

The Urban Planner as Archetypal Obsessive Figure

Obsession: A History offers readers an argument consistent with the core commitment of disability studies as both an academic and a political project.[5] Davis's book shares with other landmarks of disability scholarship the central assertion that the very idea of normalcy is an ableist creation. That is, both what Rosemarie Garland-Thomson, in *Extraordinary Bodies: Figuring Physical Disability in American Culture and Literature* (1997), called the normate and what is referred to as disability are equally social constructions. Theorist Tanya Titchkosky invokes this understanding of disability as a social relationship in *The Question of Access: Disability, Space, Meaning* (2011) when she writes that "One cannot be disabled alone" (5). It is the social context of a given time and place that shapes narratives about ability and disability, and that brings stigmatized social significance to the material experience of impairment. Thus, Titchkosky explains, "without mass literacy demands there is no dyslexia; with dyslexia, there arises something other than a person fully at one with literate culture" (21). Similarly, advocacy for ramp access to buildings becomes necessary only in the context of a built environment produced by an ableist social imaginary. Following in this tradition, Davis crafts the intriguing argument that obsession and obsessive thinking emerge only as such within the context of modernity. Though he does not allow this fact to take center stage in his book, his argument is grounded in the very context of an urban modernity.

Here it is necessary to cull from *Obsession: A History* a handful of spatial and urban references that provide compelling reason to urbanize Davis's argument. Once it is established that his exploration of obsession gains social significance only within the context of urban modernity, I blend Davis's approach with insights from Henri Lefebvre's urban theory. The end result is that obsession becomes an essential component of both urban planning narratives themselves and also of the way the urban experience is engaged by artists and creators from the nineteenth through the twenty-first centuries. As obsession becomes socially marked, visible as a modern characteristic, it simultaneously comes to be prized and cultivated as a social value. That is, even though this fact is concealed by a constructed trope of normative ableism, it

follows that cognitive difference is in fact a core value and constitutive element of urban modernity. The chapters that follow this
one are attentive to this notion of internal contradiction, and thus
it is important to acknowledge the contradiction inherent in the
model of an obsessive social modernity that Davis establishes in
his work. The concept of "partial madness" becomes a vehicle for
this contradiction and its social embeddedness.

The emergence of partial madness in nineteenth-century Europe
is the key to understanding the through line of *Obsession: A History*. The term *partial madness* itself refers to a sea change in
diagnosis whereby the sharp division between those judged to be
mad and those who are not becomes blurred in the modern age.
Davis anchors his argument concerning the gradual emergence
of "partial insanity" by relying on two renowned scientific figures from nineteenth-century France: psychiatrists Jean-Étienne
Esquirol and Philippe Pinel (2008, 67). Esquirol and Pinel were
the two principal figures in modern Europe who led the scientific acceptance of the concept of partial states of mental distress.
These partial states also came to be referred to as "monomania"
or "obsession," and a modern culture of scientific expertise came
to distinguish them from those states of distress or madness that
were understood to be total in nature. These researchers of such
partial states such as monomania, neurasthenia, and obsession—
not solely from France, but also from the United States in the case
of George Beard—influenced medical and scientific thinking in
modern Iberia, a history mentioned briefly in Chapter 3.

It is deeply relevant that Davis provides readers with a compelling metaphor for understanding partial madness as spatial and
arguably even urban in character. He writes:

> it is apt that the earliest use of the word "obsession" has to do with
> war. In Latin, *obsessio* and *possessio* were two aspects of besieging a
> city. *Possideo, -ere* and *obsideo, -ere* are two phases in the assault. If
> you've obsessed a city, you've surrounded it, but the citadel remains

intact; while if you possess the city, the walls have been breached and you've conquered the citadel and its citizens. (31)

The broad argument made in *Obsession: A History* relies consistently on this distinction between obsession and possession, or phrased another way, between partial and total madness. The citadel metaphor, including its sub-element concerning the breach of the city walls, uses the social narrative of war to describe an individual cognitive state. By implication, a person whose citadel is merely surrounded is experiencing a partial state of besiegement. Their cognition would still be considered normal, the argument goes, even though it might demonstrate abnormal attributes. The person whose citadel is compromised, however, is thus fully besieged by madness and would be considered wholly abnormal. The power of such imagery, of course, is not limited to being a mere metaphor for cognition; it is at once a hallmark element of modern urbanism.

Planners who broke through medieval city walls in the name of urban modernity, as happened in the case of mid-nineteenth-century Barcelona, would by premodern standards have been opening up the city to danger. Yet in a modern age defined by circuits of urban cosmopolitanism, the destruction and removal of a given city's defining borders is indicative of urbanism's potentially infinite expansion. To remove a city wall was to blend its dense grouping of urban lives with surrounding areas, to acknowledge its connectedness with other cities, to facilitate trade, and to allow for its continued growth. Intriguingly, the expansiveness of the modern planning vision, the encroachment of urban upon rural space, and rural upon urban space, is paralleled in the encroachment of sanity upon madness and madness upon sanity. Modern spatial reproduction is aligned in this sense with the modern scientific account of cognition. In urban modernity, just as cities sprawled into connection with the countryside, with no clear division persisting between the two, similarly the sharp dividing wall between madness and sanity became blurred. This, argues Davis, is precisely what happens with the emergence of obsession.

The gradual emergence of the concept of partial madness made it possible to talk about a sort of democratization of illness. In Davis's words, "the diagnosis of monomania opened the doors to a wide-ranging application of the idea of insanity to the general population" (68). The idea was that anyone who was modern could, and perhaps should, also be seen as ill. The "normal state of being" in modernity arguably entailed being "somewhat mad" rather than completely sane. From the nineteenth century onward, a confluence of burgeoning literary culture and scientific discourse begins to reproduce this notion as modern society is continually refashioned. Strong links are forged between obsession, scientific method, and normative culture, such that "modernity may be seen as a period in which the normal state of being is defined as allied with being somewhat mad, and particularly with being obsessed. The form of this obsession is a singular attention to a particular thing or things, which in effect is the definition of specialization— itself an acknowledged feature of modernity" (81). Socially, Davis asserts, obsession is linked to specialist vocations, of which he gives three primary examples: "an artist, a writer, a scientist" (78). To be ill in this obsessive and modern way, Davis's text suggests, in line with his disability studies commitment, should be seen as a widespread cultural value of nineteenth-century European society.

Obsession: A History is quite clear about the fact that obsessive thinking becomes a prized aspect of social modernity. To the degree that obsession is understood to be partial madness, cognitive difference thus becomes a social value that is reflected in the behaviors, artistic products, and scientific works of successful moderns. As evidence of this social valuation, Davis cites the success and enduring impact of such artists as William Godwin (author of *Caleb Williams*), Samuel Johnson, Mary Shelley (author of *Frankenstein*), and Honoré de Balzac. In prizing intellectual and passionate devotion to a single idea, he writes, the scientific cultures that produced figures such as Darwin and Freud were also clearly obsessed (see Davis 2008, chap. 5). Moreover, literary culture was itself obsessed in a very scientific way. This trait is perhaps most notably revealed in the example of Emile Zola's explicit adherence to a scientific method of composition that became widely associated with a particular strain of naturalist literature (105–17). The dualism that structures the citadel metaphor for partial madness can be seen in Davis's account of a split between an observing and a performing consciousness in obsessive practices. Those who are obsessed—not possessed—by an idea are aware of their obsession at the same time that they engage in it. Thus, Davis writes of "the emergence of obsession as a known category involving doing or thinking one thing too much, being aware of that activity, but being unable to stop it" (32). The quintessentially modern figure of the writer who is working night and day, obsessed with their craft, finds in this time and place a fertile ground for self-realization. An exemplar of such a modern writer can be found in Fernando Pessoa, whose obsessive writing is discussed in Chapter 4.

It is crucial to understand that the democratization of illness that accompanied the emergence of obsessive activity was not unrelated to the industrialization of modern society. As Davis asserts, obsession became socially significant and intimately knowable only in the context of the machine age, which depended on and created new forms of repetitive physical and social behaviors. The prevalence of such behaviors was not merely limited to the physical labor of craft work—innovations in the textile industry that would lead to increased automation in the context of twentieth-century factory assembly lines, for instance. Repetitive behaviors were also more broadly relevant to planning and forms of intellectual labor. Modern cognition recapitulated the shifts observed in modern bodily work. Davis points out how the modern city over time becomes reproduced as an industrial and obsessive site: "we might consider the modernity of the city with its increasingly regularized space, regularized timetables for public transportation, standardization of

building practices, and so on as another instance of obsessive attention to detail" (83–84). Yet just as importantly, he also underscores
the ways those artists, writers, and scientists specializing in a single
activity or investigating a single branch of knowledge become the
most visible examples of this social wider trend toward obsession.
Though Davis does not explore the figure of the urban planner in
sufficient depth, he does imply its relevance to his argument—as
already signaled above—and it is here that there that the story of
modern obsession converges with the emergence of urbanism as
a form of specialized knowledge under modern capitalism.

Readers should keep in mind industrialization's role as a fore-
runner of urbanization.[6] If the close ties between industrialization and urbanization are acknowledged, Davis's own analyses
can serve as a prompt for a deeper consideration of urban theory.
The spatial and urban metaphor of the citadel that Davis selects
to explain the emergence of partial madness as a concept linked
with modernity serves as the inspiration for the present book's
reassessment of modern urban planning. Casting the modern
tradition of urban planning in a nontriumphant light—as does
a whole tradition of anti-urbanism supported by the theoretical
frameworks of Henri Lefebvre and Manuel Delgado Ruiz—allows
us to examine more closely its over-specialization, its obsessive
fixation, and its phobia of everyday spontaneity. In planning the
city's built environment, a new class of obsessed thinkers emerged
in the nineteenth century and forged a new branch of specialized
knowledge predicated on the notion that it was possible to structure, direct, influence, and even control urban life. This branch of
thinking was a modern project with clear aesthetic motivations.
It is thus not very difficult at all to widen the argument made in
Obsession: A History enough to include the figure of the urban
planner. The modern planner is thus equally an example of how
literary culture and "science, scientific medicine, and academic
specialization" become "aspects of the new problematics of obsession" in modern social life (Davis 2008, 23).

One of the twentieth century's most prolific and important urban thinkers, Henri Lefebvre (1901–1991) wrote more than sixty books and influenced subsequent generations of theorists.[7] Lefebvre detested the "specialization and compartmentalization" that arose with urban modernity (see, for example, Lefebvre 1982, 22–23, 59–88; 1991b, 249; 2003, 92). His characterization of nineteenth-century urban planning prioritizes notions of fragmented knowledge, urban alienation, and capitalist ideology. Planners were limited by a specialization that distorted their view of the urban phenomenon. Across two of his most pertinent and widely read works, *The Right to the City* and *The Urban Revolution*, he argued that even though "the complexity of the urban phenomenon is not that of an 'object'" (2003, 56), the bourgeois science of urban planning nonetheless imagined the city as a series of objects, external to one another and situated in a static space, instead of as an ensemble of relations (1996, 94). The fact that this reductive and reifying vision, one that saw things instead of relations, was so pervasive in nineteenth-century urban design was not unrelated, as Lefebvre himself explored extensively, to wider discourses that fragmented modern knowledge into specialized areas. The modern bourgeois city was then made up of a fragmented, spatialized set of objects that could be decomposed and recomposed on a whim by a specialist planning class (1996, 94–99; 2003, 49). Lefebvre understood that the conceptual space of the planner was thus entirely separated, in principle, from the lived space of the city as a use-value (1991a, 33). Decontextualized and instrumentalized to suit the needs of "capitalist speculators, builders and technicians," the design and production of city space instead became a way of normalizing the priority given to exchange-value (1996, 168). For Lefebvre and for other theorists he influenced—most of all Barcelona-based scholar Manuel Delgado Ruiz—the urban planner engaging in this activity ultimately failed to create "an urban reality for users" (1996, 168) and instead famously assisted capitalism throughout the twentieth century in its obsessive need to sustain itself "by producing space, by occupying a space" (1976, 21). Not only was this production of space itself obsessive, the creation of the modern city was also accompanied by the reactions by modern urbanites who were equally obsessed by the urban phenomenon.

Obsessed by the idea of the city as a pure geometrical form, modern planners indulged in the excesses of metaphorical thinking. The participation of late nineteenth-century planners in the construction of what Lefebvre has called a "triumphant and triumphalist" (1995, 3) urban modernity was based on excessively rationalized, rectilinear, and geometrical forms. The modern obsession with geometrical aesthetics thus belies, if not merely a practical erasure of, then an absolute disdain for, urban difference—a quality that in contemporary critical urban theory has come to be synonymous with the city itself (see Harvey 2005; Jacobs 1992; Young 1990). Lefebvre emphasizes the degree to which the fragmentary character of specialist thinking on the city is detrimental to modern urban life. Planners—demonstrating an error I would argue is an expression of obsessive thinking—understood the city as an object or set of objects rather than as a social relationship between people. They became fixated on one dimension of the urban experience. There was an obsessive, repetitive, and mechanical form of thinking at work in the cultural imaginary of planning. Lewis Mumford, a renowned scholar of the modern city, its historical legacy, and its geographical variations, notes that the mechanistic logic of industrialization had been carried over to the process of building cities, generally speaking (1970, ix, 149–50). Repetitive modern thought recapitulates the shifts observable in repetitive modern labor. It is here that scientific culture begins to overlap with artistic or literary culture. The obsessions of planning culture alternated between scientific, writerly, and even artistic forms. It might be most obvious to contemporary readers that city planning was a scientific culture, due to the perceived quantitative nature of the work. That is, even if one has not seen their visual designs, it is easy to accept that Cerdà and Soria y Mata sketched out plans for Barcelona and Madrid annotated with specific dimensions and distances. Neither should it surprise that Cerdà, for example, was characterized as having a mathematical and "algebraic" disposition (Soria y Puig 1996, 23–25). Yet there was also something of the obsessed author in these urban planners. Cerdà's two-volume *Teoría general de urbanización* (1867), which is full of intriguing metaphors of illness and health, is merely one demonstration among many of his obsession for writing. Likewise, Arturo Soria y Mata's scientific obsessions are on full display in his book *El origen poliédrico de las especies* (1894; The polyhedral origin of species), wherein he also tellingly includes a section explicitly devoted to the relative banality of madness. In delving into these figures and their writings, Chapters 2 and 3 provide evidence that modern urban planning drew from the three overlapping cultural pools of (scientific, artistic, and writerly) obsession that are so important to the through line of Davis's book.

The obsessions of modern planning were just as artistic as they were scientific. Unquestioningly, planners envisioned urban space as a blank canvas, or as an empty container that they could fill with so many streets and buildings. The planning of the Baixa area of Lisbon after the 1755 earthquake, discussed in Chapter 4, is a case in point. Urban thinker Richard Sennett describes the conceptual approach of modern planners in terms of "neutrality" and "detachment" (1992, 62) and he insists that "a visual technology of power alienated them, too, from their own work" (61).[8] Georges Haussmann may be the most recognized figure in modern urban planning, and his method provides ample evidence of the neutrality and detachment Sennett describes. In urban geographer David Harvey's words, Haussmann "bludgeoned the city [of Paris] into modernity" (2006, 3). His urban plan pushed working-class populations out of the central city and razed buildings in order to fashion the broad urban boulevards that still today are synonymous with the open aesthetics of the modern European city. The linear geometry of modern urban design was in this sense as much a destructive force as a creative one. The newly reimagined city's bold geometrical vectors were either underwritten by oppressive power structures or easily co-opted by such, sometimes despite their authors' better intentions (Choay 1969, 15). Yet whether they are understood as scientific or artistic thinkers, as both at once, or as writers of prose or inscribers of the city, there can be no doubt that modern urban planners were specialists in the obsessive manner described by Lennard Davis.

By urbanizing the argument from *Obsession: A History*, this book pursues a mode of criticism that diverges from but remains complementary to that valuable push by Rob Imrie and others to forge "environments free from physical and social barriers." By demonstrating that cognitive difference was, in fact, present in both modern planning culture and modern urban culture in the form of obsession—a form whose connection with disability was paradoxically privileged, if unacknowledged, rather than consistently stigmatized—we deconstruct the binary between normalcy and disability that sustains the ideology of ableism. As Imrie himself has written, "the basis for a non ableist theorization of disability can only occur if the dualisms of able/disabled, ability/disability, and normal/abnormal, are dissolved, that is for the fluidity of the concepts to be recognized and for the body to be situated and interpreted as a socio-cultural and biological construction" (1996, 46).[9] There is a value to showing that the ableism of urbanism's past was not neutral but rather a certain social construction that downplayed, and in fact benefitted from, its connections with forms of cognitive difference that privileged repetitive, cyclical, and endlessly obsessive thinking. That is, Imrie and others show how planning is ableist in its nature. I accept that planning is ableist in practice, but I want to show how that characterization is itself a form of constructed normalcy fashioned through social relationships that could equally qualify as being expressive of cognitive difference. In the present urbanization of Davis's argument one immediately encounters a paradox. As Imrie notes, "any sense of celebrating, even recognizing, the vitality of difference seems beyond the disablist nature of socio-institutional values and practices" (1996, 2). In line with Tobin Seibers's argument regarding modern art, I argue that in the case of modern urban planning, it is the presence of cognitive difference that lends perceived social value to the modern city, even though this has not been consistently recognized.[10]

Tanya Titchkosky and Rod Michalko have written that, for ableist society, "disability may participate in normalcy, but it can never be normal let alone be valuable, enjoyable, or necessary" (2017, 68). Thus, they write, it occurs that disabled people can at times and in certain contexts resemble non-disabled others.[11] But in order to dissolve the ability/disability binary, what is needed is a demonstration of how the social value of normalcy resembles or relies on tropes associated with the social construction of disability. Readers must consider the possibility that partial madness, cognitive difference, in the form of obsessive cognition, has a role in producing urban modernity. Does madness, or partial madness—its very constructed existence—suggest that cognitive difference is an ingredient present in normalcy but unrecognized as such due to ableist stigma? Because this may be a provocative argument, it is somewhat appropriate to compare it to the argument made by Lennard J. Davis in the title of his essay "Universalizing Marginality: How Europe Became Deaf in the Eighteenth Century" (1997). What Davis means by that title is not that Europe developed hearing impairment in the eighteenth century, but rather that Europe borrowed from the social relationships implied in deafness a certain understanding of human language. In the same vein, all of Europe does not become partially mad in urban modernity, but rather Europe borrows from the social relationships implied in partial madness a certain obsessive understanding of what the city is or could possibly be. It cannot be emphasized enough that the present book is taking on a very small corner of the interdisciplinary disability studies project, and that its aims are more theoretical than practical. Then again, even though it is focused on the Iberian city, its conclusions are in no way limited to a certain time period or a given geography.

The disability studies commitment outlined here finds its complement in an urban cultural studies method, grounded in the urban thinking of Henri Lefebvre and others. Lefebvre's notion of urban modernity as a "triumphant and triumphalist" discourse that develops from the nineteenth century onward can be explained in part as an expression of the partial madness whose origins Davis traces in cultural terms. While the tradition of modern urbanism has been critiqued over the course of the twentieth century and into the twenty-first by many scholars—among them Manuel Delgado Ruiz, David Harvey, Jane Jacobs, Lewis Mumford, Saskia Sassen, Richard Sennett, and Sharon Zukin, for example—its cognitive dimensions have rarely, if at all, been explored from the perspective of disability theory. My broader aim is thus to draw attention to a central paradox of modern urban planning: that it expresses ableist ideology through its normative regularization, a straight linearity or ordered geometry that pathologizes difference while at the same time it exhibits cognitive difference or "partial madness" through its own obsessive thinking. In the end, if we take to heart the idea that obsessive thinking has been, as Davis argues, a prized aspect of modernity, we may then begin to build a case for the modern city as the contradictory product of both normative ideology and cognitive difference. Affirming the modern city as the product of partial madness potentially destabilizes normative conceptions of urban modernity. This may also serve us in asserting the Lefebvrian narrative that the city belongs to all.

Chapter 2
Disfiguring Barcelona: Geometry and the Grid

The shape and design of the modern city is overwhelmingly ableist. As reflected in the sampling of disability studies scholarship mentioned in the first chapter of this book, contemporary planners and architects have more often than not failed in considering people with disabilities as an integral part of urban sociality. This remains true even despite the relative ease with which one can identify attempts to humanize the built and social environments of particular cities. These attempts, while they are in theory designed to make cities more inclusive and more livable, in practice are very seldom attentive to the ableist bias that drives their reproduction of cityspace. For this reason, the theoretical, practical, and radical political critiques offered by disability studies scholars such as by Imrie, Boys, Dolmage, Gleeson, Hamraie, and Serlin are welcome and must continue. Simultaneously it is crucial to think about urban aesthetics themselves through the notion of cognitive difference.

It is impossible to completely sever any notion of an urban aesthetics from the design and functioning of concrete urban places. Yet this aesthetic dimension of urban life is meaningful in its own way, and it thus merits a distinct approach. It must be understood on its own terms and simultaneously also in relation to broader social dynamics. The twenty-first-century disability critiques offered by Tobin Siebers in *Disability Aesthetics* (2010) and by Joseph Straus in *Broken Beauty* (2018) are important touchstones for this undertaking. These two books delve into visual art and music, respectively, evincing an understanding of how disability is present in modern aesthetics and how this presence is implicated in larger social matters. What both books achieve is a marked expansion of disability critique. This expansion understands the aesthetic realm as an integral part of social experience. For some, the exploration of aesthetic questions may appear as a sort of escape into what was once described as the superstructure of contemporary society. In this way of thinking, considering the arts may be far less important than fighting for access, for policy changes, and disability rights, which is to say human rights. Yet any hard distinction between the aesthetic sphere and a sociopolitical sphere represents a false choice, of course, as an entire legacy of postwar continental philosophy that recognizes culture as a primary economic motor of the production of social value has argued.[1] For it is the reciprocal influence of human thought and human action that have together created the modern world.

In the realm of disability critique, aesthetics are a primary battleground. Aesthetic questions are at the core of how social stigma and ableism operate and purport to normalize themselves whether within specialized artistic discourse or more broadly within social discourse. This chapter sorts through the critiques of Siebers and

Straus, whereby the seemingly separate area of artistic practice is restored to everyday life, and it applies them to urbanistic writing and architectural urbanism. This disability studies–adjacent journey begins with the highly metaphorical writing and privileged planning activities of Ildefons Cerdà in nineteenth-century Barcelona. It then works through the architecture of Antoni Gaudí, both in itself, as a nuanced disfiguring of urban aesthetics, and also as captured in a documentary film by Hiroshi Teshigahara, an avant-garde director whose formalist cinema aesthetics are just as estranging as Gaudí's creations. The chapter's focus on figuring and disfiguring the modern city wraps up with a documentary critique of Barcelona's more contemporary spectacular architecture and its exchange-value-obsessed neoliberal urbanism, directed by Mercedes Álvarez.

The Pathology of the Detail: Ildefons Cerdà's Urbanistic Writing and Planning

Tobin Siebers argued for the centrality of disability in modern art. The presence of disability he wrote, has not always been recognized as such in the history of art, but it is there, nonetheless. In fact, disability is quite frequently what lends prestige to a work, that which prompts an enduring understanding of the work as beautiful, even despite changing trends and standards (Siebers 2010, 4–5). For Siebers, disability is at the heart of "modern art's love affair with misshapen and twisted bodies, stunning variety of human forms, intense representation of traumatic injury and psychological alienation, and unyielding preoccupation with wounds and tormented flesh" (4). Siebers finds it useful to contrast two examples in the process of setting up his argument. The Nazis, he writes, preferred representations of what they took to be perfect bodies and famously rejected modern art as degenerate "because they viewed it as representing physical and mental disability" (5). The limbless Venus de Milo, on the other hand—along with a whole host of examples of more intentionally provocative visual art whose analyses Siebers offers in the rewarding chapters that follow—is beautiful in what might be called its imperfection.

Though *Disability Aesthetics* is framed as an analysis of visual culture, Siebers is aware that the implications of his study urge generalization. The book suggests something profound about modernity itself: "The more we enter into the modern age, the stronger the equation between art and disability—and to the point where it is difficult to recognize art in itself without summoning the notion of disability. Disability, disease, and injury have become the figures by which aesthetic beauty as such is now recognized, and more and more art critics are beginning to recognize it" (135). This recognition is all the more crucial because of the connections Siebers repeatedly establishes between aesthetics and the human. In remaking aesthetics we are remaking ourselves. In his affirmations that, for example, "art is the process by which human beings attempt to modify themselves" (136),[2] there is an insistence on the same figure of *homo faber* that drives urban thinker Richard Sennett's analysis in *The Craftsman*. The final sentence of Siebers's book is definitive: "Disability is now and will be in the future an aesthetic value in itself" (139). The implication is that as disability becomes "an aesthetic value it itself" it may also become a human value. Or rather, disability already is a human value. The point is that it is not routinely recognized as such either in aesthetics or in broader social discourse.

In *Broken Beauty*, Joseph Straus carries the premise of Siebers's book into analysis of an adjacent modern art form. He explores the relevance of disability to classical composers as well as the music they produced. While Straus defines disability as "any cultural stigmatized bodily difference" (2018, 9), he specifies further that by "bodily" he intends "the full range of physical and mental differences to which the human body is subject, whether congenital or acquired, including physical and mental illnesses or diseases, temporary or permanent injuries, and a variety of nonnormative bodily characteristics understood as disfiguring" (10). This is an emphasis that squares with the spirit, but not necessarily the practice, of much high-profile disability critique, which until relatively recently has tended to emphasize physical or sensory disability and not—not necessarily, that is, not fully—cognition, mental disability or the embodied mind per se.[3]

The distance between the arguments of Straus and Siebers is not as great as one might presume. Music may be nonrepresentational, as Straus affirms in his introduction (11)—and it is especially so by comparison with the (dis)figurative visual art Siebers explores. Yet Straus's notion of what he calls "disablist hearings" does not abandon the notion of figuration, but instead crafts an intriguing transposition of figurative representation from a visual modality to an aural modality. One would be right to ask the question: what is a figure? A term such as figurative representation implies that there must be a figure to represent, a figure that is presumed to be physical, tangible, or at the very least visible. To discuss the figurative would at times seem to depart from a literal world to enter a world of metaphor, metaphor that acquires its significance from the world of tangible or visual objects. This original—physical, tangible, or visible—encoding of the term *figure* hides its origin as a product of sighted culture. While *figurative* is commonly used to refer to a visual form or shape, there is no reason it cannot be applied to music. As musicians well know, in fact, a less-frequent usage of *figure* is employed in the realm of musical production and criticism. Stripped of sighted bias, the term evokes merely the replication of a set of expectations, the imposition of a norm, or an anticipation of coherence. Just such a habitual invocation of the normate is revealed in the usage of terms such as *disfigure, disfiguring,* or *disfigurement.* To the degree that disfigurement is not exclusively applied to the body, it can refer also to a mind, or for that matter to a nontangible creation of the mind such as music. Straus writes splendidly of modernist music's disfigurement, its "fractured forms, immobilized harmonies, conflicting textual layers, radical simplification of means in some cases, and radical complexity and hermeticism in others" (1). By calling into question the ableist notion of hearing, he emphasizes that disablist hearing "is not a pathology and it does not reside inside the individual body. Rather it is a mode of cognition [that] emerges among particular social groups, but it is not necessarily exclusively identified with them" (180–81). Both disablist hearing and what might be called disablist sight must be understood as modes of cognition, and this chapter regards them as crucial for the project of disabling urban aesthetics.

In astute analyses of selected classical compositions, Straus echoes Siebers's insistence that the "discovery of disability as a unique resource" (Siebers 2010, 5) was important to modern art as a widespread practice. In the same way, disability is also a unique resource for the modern invocations of architecture and urbanism. To the degree that both modern urban planning and architecture are—and have been understood as—art forms of a sort, careful readers of Siebers and Straus should not be surprised by this assertion. In today's increasingly urbanized world, the bromide that the "city is a work of art" continues to circulate.[4] Though perhaps self-evident, it is worthwhile to point out that the history of modern planning runs parallel to the history of modern art and the history of modern music. More important, disability has been present in all three histories even if hardly recognized as such. Siebers's notion of the pathology of detail can help readers to make the transition between modern visual/aural art and the aesthetics of modern urbanism. This notion can then be applied both to Ildefons Cerdà's urbanistic writing and his urban project.

Detail is a notion that brings with it a host of critical reflection surrounding the representation of reality. The title of the final chapter of Tobin Siebers's book, "Words Stare like a Glass Eye: Disability in Literary and Visual Studies," which takes its inspiration from a quote by William James, announces an intention to move beyond a simple consideration of the visible. Siebers wants to extend the disability critique elaborated throughout *Disability Aesthetics* beyond the visual realm to other forms of representation, and more pointedly to what might be called the mental image. His extension gains much from explicit discussion of *Mimesis* (1957), Erich Auerbach's classic text on narrative representation. Auerbach's intention was to distinguish two kinds of storytelling. In "Odysseus' Scar," the first chapter of *Mimesis*, Auerbach contrasted the relative absence of detail in the Hebrew Bible to the relative presence of detail in Homer's *Odysseus*. He explored this through commentary on the Homeric text's nineteenth episode where, despite returning home as a stranger, Odysseus is recognized. The character Euryclea sees, remembers, and identifies him. While washing his feet she is prompted to this recognition by the sight of a familiar scar located on his thigh. While the notable focus on scarring with which Auerbach's text opens signals right away its possibilities for disability analysis, it is not something he pursued. Siebers's referencing of *Mimesis*, however, serves the theorist's purposeful consideration of representation in tandem with disability.

In his own extended commentary on "Odysseus' Scar," Siebers pointedly states that "healthy bodies in art do not have details. They are unmarked" (2010, 125). Details mark bodies physically. Siebers understands this physical marking simultaneously as a social marking. Considered in relation to bodies, the notion of a detail, of its unhealthy or pathological nature, may first bring to consciousness the notion of a physical, tangible, or visible mark. In truth the scar is a concept that applies to both bodily and mental disfigurement. The scar's conceptual significance is irreducible to a single modality, thus it is relevant to the visible field and the realm of sound, to the written word and narrative, to the mental image, and ultimately the very realm of ideas, too—cognition itself. Siebers insists, based on a rereading of *Mimesis*, that in writing and in reading, the visible is always in play in this wider social sense.

Auerbach's text plays with notions of foreground and background in a meaningful way, and Siebers's analysis implicitly gains from this attention. For the detail to function as it does in the intended sense in writing, it must be distinguished from its background and disconnected from its surrounding context. Detail in writing is about close focus. I propose that it might be useful to think of detail in writing as a way of seeing that is opposed to the practice of deep focus in the cinema. In deep focus, the foreground, midground and background of a shot are all crisply represented, shown with equally high resolution. In the type of focus used in a standard close up, for example, the foreground is in crisp, high resolution, while the background is left in fuzzy, low resolution. Neither Siebers nor Auerbach uses the term *resolution*, or the cinematic comparison introduced here, for that matter, but the concepts are quite useful given that they are of exceedingly common usage. In writing, we might say that a detail is revealed and given its proper emphasis through various strategies of fixity and/ or precision. Auerbach's original text makes it clear that in such sufficiently granular resolution of a detail "no contour is blurred" (1957, 1). A detail is not the same thing as a physical object, as Auerbach is aware, stating, "there is also room and time for orderly, perfectly well-articulated, uniformly illuminated descriptions of implements, ministrations, and gestures" (1). The high resolution through which the written word can represent a detail applies equally well to both physical or visible and nontangible items, as he points out. "Clearly outlined, brightly and uniformly illuminated, men and things stand out in a realm where everything is visible; and not less clear—wholly expressed, orderly even in their ardor—are the feelings and thoughts of the persons involved" (2). Of course, this clear outlining is employed wholly in the service of a narrative that is by nature selective. Not all aspects of a written diegesis are related with equal precision.[5]

As can be seen in the usage of a visual vocabulary—clarity, contour, outline, and illumination—the concept or metaphor of vision assists Auerbach in crafting his more-than-visual argument. Vision serves precisely the same purpose for Siebers, who is seemingly interested—now, at the close of his book on visual art—in something altogether different, in a much broader mode of critique. He writes that "details appear as pathology in aesthetics because they discover the reliance of images on the difference of the disabled body. For ever since Odysseus's scar, wounds and images have been closely allied" (2010, 125). For Siebers, it is both the scar itself and the field in which it appears that deserve our attention. This approach implicates not only a field of vision but also the field of signification prompted by the written word. Constituted as a detail in narrative, the scar can exist as such only in the absence of a sort of cinematic deep focus. The scar relies on a narrative focalization that represents it crisply and clearly, at a much higher resolution than the representation of its surroundings. There is a disconnection evident in this kind of close focus. Encountering this selective high resolution in a text, Siebers suggests, is a prompt for further contemplation: "absorption in details, whether on the surface or not, is one signal that a reading has taken the unusual course from word to image and that the text calls for visual analysis" (125). Siebers advocates a way of refiguring disability critique metaphorically in visual terms, and at once signals a path to revealing ableism's own reliance on visual metaphor. Disability critique involves, it would seem, establishing a cinematic deeper focus, a higher resolution of mental image. To continue the visual metaphor, such critique restores the pathological detail from the foreground to the background against which it has been distinguished. Such an act of critical restoration, it would seem, should conceive of the scar—to use terms used by David Mitchell and Sharon Snyder in *Narrative Prosthesis*—not as a vehicle for dramatic action whose trajectory is linked with a form of narrative ableism, but as expression of a social fascination and stigmatization of difference. This approach should undermine the unexamined confidence in vision Auerbach had described in phrases suggesting the clarity of contour, or the hard light that illuminates an outline.

Considering briefly the preface to Ildefons Cerdà's *Teoría general de la urbanización* (1867) provides the opportunity to employ many of the concepts contained in Siebers's visual approach to writing, now in adapted toward understanding the mental image that drives modern planning. A visual analysis of Cerdà's preface reveals that disability has been as important to modern planning as it has been to modern art (Siebers) and modern music (Straus). It also casts Cerdà in the mold of the quintessentially modern and thus obsessed nineteenth-century scientist/artist (Davis). This characterization is further justified by the fact that, far from being merely a peripheral European figure, "Cerdà is a strong candidate for the title of the first modern urban planner" (Marshall 2004, 7; see also T. Hall 1997, 2; Choay 1969, 7). He is notable both for continuing and propagating a central visual or mental image of planning culture as surgical procedure.

Though Ildefons Cerdà (1815–1876) is increasingly common as a point of reference in Iberian urban cultural studies, a concise note can bring more general readers up to speed.[6] Described as an algebraic and mathematical personality, Cerdà was motivated as an urban planner by concern for the working class residents of Barcelona. He conducted an expansive study in the mid-1850s to document their living conditions, and drew from that experience in proposing an expansion plan for the Catalan capital. His Barcelona plan was accepted in 1859 and gradually implemented, slowly and only partially, over the following decades (see Soria y Puig 1996, 362; Miles and Miles 2004, 79). While his plan preserved the twisting, narrow streets and irregular blocks of the city's central medieval core, Cerdà's design of the newly surrounding Eixample area relied on broad boulevards that echoed Haussmann's redesign of Paris.[7] Like Haussmann, he similarly relied on equidistant blocks and the imposition of a large-scale grid pattern. As the author of numerous lengthy texts—including *Ensanche de la ciudad de Barcelona* (1855), *Teoría de la construcción de las ciudades aplicada al proyecto de reforma y ensanche de Barcelona*

(1859), *Pensamiento económico* (1860), and *Teoría de la viabilidad urbana y reforma de la de Madrid* (1861)—the planner was also a theoretician, and he was subsequently recognized for having coined the word *urbanización*.

In the expansive two-tome treatise titled *Teoría general de la urbanización* (1867), Cerdà offered the innovative idea that the modern city had evolved according to stages defined by the form of locomotion in use during each period.[8] In the implementation of Barcelona's Eixample, his use of the *xamfrà*, or truncated corner (Resina 2008, 22), was as much an aesthetic flourish of his geometrical planning vision as it was an acknowledgment that planning should ensure the proper circulation of urban traffic. Each of the four pointed corners of what would have been a standard intersection was blunted, cut back, so that the intersection's primary figure was not a square or traffic circle, but rather an octagonal shape. This geometrical flourish is a specific example of a much broader trend in modern urban planning, which drew insights from the science of anatomy, most of all regarding the circulation of blood, and conceived of the city as an organism.[9] The notion of circulatory motion was important for Cerdà's plan in a second way, too. His intention to integrate green spaces into each city block was a response to mid-century miasmic theories of health and suggested that breathing clean air was important for urbanites and, metaphorically too, that respiration itself was important for the city organism.

It is difficult to argue that urban plans are inherently good or bad, and readers should recognize that my intention is not to claim Cerdà is the omnipotent arm of power and the state. He sought to construct a city for all residents and to improve the quality of life for the city's working class in particular. The emancipatory aims of his planning practice were, in the end, betrayed by the state that implemented his vision. That said, what is of interest here is the discourse of planning itself—metaphorical invocations of illness and appeals to notions of perfectibility—with which he gave shape to his planning vision.

In some respects, Cerdà is arguably the most prominent representation of the broader trends of nineteenth-century European planning culture's obsessions.[10] Planners could also be specialist writers, displaying a singular passion and an obsessive devotion to their subject areas. Cerdà's preface to the *Teoría general de la urbanización* demonstrates the degree to which the nineteenth-century planning tradition was steeped in bodily metaphor. The city is repeatedly invoked there as a living body. As a consequence of this primary organic metaphor, the planner operated as an anatomist, one who sought to understand "el origen complexo y heterogéneo del organismo actual de nuestras ciudades" (1867, 1:3; The complex and heterogenous origin of the present organism of our cities). Not only was the city an organism, the urban planner was a surgeon. This specialist figure was tasked with distinguishing sick from healthy areas of the city before proceeding with "una verdadera disección anatómica de todas [las ciudades] y de cada una de sus partes constitutivas" (1:12; a true anatomical dissection of all [cities] and of all of their constituent parts).[11] Cerdà proves himself to be obsessed with details (remember Siebers: "absorption in details," "details appear as pathology in aesthetics," "where there are details [in a text], human difference is not far away"). His preface reveals his obsession with the idea that the city is a body, and perhaps even with the mental image of the city as a corpse prepared for dissection.[12] Cerdà's urbanistic appropriation of the organic or corporeal metaphor for the city reinforced normative understandings of illness, projecting them on urban space that became a sort of canvas for the planner's aesthetic figurative play.

What Siebers called modern art's "unyielding preoccupation with wounds" is also evident in the preface to this landmark modern planning text. Obsessed in the modern sense explored by Davis, Cerdà allowed himself to be carried away by the organic metaphor of planning. He was aware of this excess, yet simultaneously he was unable—it seems—to stop it. The surgical practice of the urban planner was obsessively depicted in his writing as a crusade against illness, a search for knowledge through vivisection. In one of his most obsessive digressions on the metaphor of planning, he wrote that: "introduciendo el escalpelo hasta lo más íntimo y recóndito del organismo urbano y social, se consigue sorprender viva y en acción la causa originaria, el germen fecundo de la grave enfermedad que corroe las entrañas de la humanidad" (1:16–17; introducing the scalpel into the most intimate and recondite area of the social and urban organism, one comes upon the original cause, alive and in the moment of acting, the fecund seed of the serious illness that corrodes the innards of humanity).

Given Cerdà's excessive indulgence in the primary metaphor of urbanism as surgery, the planner's mental image of the city is not so much city-as-fabric but rather city-as-skin. Siebers notes that critic Michael Fried demonstrates an understanding of "writing as cutting with the surgeon's scalpel" (2010, 126), and here we have Cerdà doing the same. As Siebers writes,

> The scar is exemplary precisely because it is a scar. It embodies Odysseus for readers—readers of every generation, past, present, and future—because while customs may change, technology evolve, and languages differ, human beings always have skin, and their deepest wounds always heal with a scar. Scars have the capacity to represent difference because the details necessary to individuation acquire their mimetic power by virtue of their connection to bodily wounds, cuts, defects, and deformities. To detail is in fact to cut, and many details preserve this primordial association with the slicing, abrading, or disturbance of a surface, whether the disruption involves flesh or nonorganic skin. (124–25)

It is in this sense outlined by Siebers that Cerdà operates on the skin of the city in his writing. He slices, cuts, sutures Barcelona's skin. The grid of the Eixample is the final outcome of a series of methodical surgical incisions. If readers are to accept the mental image of city-skin that Cerdà uses to organize and explain his approach to planning, the *xamfrà* itself becomes a surgical detail. It is a visible scar that will allow the proper functioning of the organic urban body, that will regulate the proper flow of urban traffic as bodily fluid.

All of this cutting—the writing as well as the urbanism—is carried out in the name of perfection. As a utopian socialist, Cerdà believed in the perfectability of the human being and—as a way to realize that human perfection—he advocated for "una urbanización perfecta" (1:17; a perfected urbanization (see also Cerdà 1867 1:47; Soria y Puig 1996, 74). This example from the annals of modern urban aesthetics confirms the more general point made by Siebers: "aesthetics is, implicitly, if not explicitly, about perfecting human beings" (2010, 134). The notion of perfecting the human being here is transposed, in urbanistic circles, to the perfection of the city. For Cerdà and for other modern planners following the mold configured during the nineteenth century, perfection is heralded as an aesthetic value of regularity, and not difference or variation. Perfection is the chief aim of the geometrical grid's aesthetic regularity. This gridded thinking prioritizes the straight line and not the curve (it is Antoni Gaudí who is the latter's most tireless advocate). The ornate decorative and nonetheless geometrical appeal of the *xamfrà* and the functional flow it regulates is in this sense merely the exception that confirms the rule of the grid. Of course, the importance of regularity in modern city design was not unconnected to the increasing role of regularization in mechanized and industrial production (see Stiker 1997; the work of Lewis Mumford). A modern system of production that valued and at once instrumentalized work, disrupting the holistic production of craft work to a series of concrete tasks, threatened to turn the modern laborer into a functional machine.[13] Urban planning followed suit.

A paradox emerged in modern planning between its artistic, metaphorical, aesthetic register of expression and the rationalized, regularized, geometrical language of its implementation. Cerdà's obsession with the organic metaphor of the city relied on the mental image of the human body, but the result of his plan was a surgical disfigurement of the city. Cerdà disfigured Barcelona by regularizing it. The twisting and turning streets that remain in Barcelona's medieval core are much more easily associated with an aesthetics of difference, variety, and the complexity of organic life, while the newly gridded Eixample area is far too symmetrical, far too geometrically harmonious, to in any way be compared to a human figure. To say that Cerdà "disfigured" Barcelona by excessively applying a geometrical and rational approach to planning is already a disablist way of seeing the city. This mode of thinking challenges the perception that expects the human body to adhere only to an ableist norm of symmetry and harmony. Here disfigurement is not a reference to a scarred body, but to the contrived nature of the normate.[14] The notion of the so-called healthy body itself is a harmful, constructed norm (remember Siebers's example of Nazi art). By contrast, it can be said that Antoni Gaudí's architecture, and Hiroshi Teshigahara's cinematic approach to that same architecture, figure or refigure the city. That is, rather than represent what the Nazis called degenerate art, this architecture and its cinematic representation value what might be understood as ambiguity, blurred contours, and lack of clarity. Rather than distinguish, privilege, and highlight the individual detail, Gaudí and Teshigahara restore the notion of detail to its wider context. The background, in the negative sense used by Auerbach, is in fact the key positive element of Gaudí's architecture and Teshigahara's cinema. As Siebers might have it, the detail does not appear in the foreground as pathological in these cases but is rather restored to the background as elemental, fundamental, constitutive of the whole. Both examples, architectural and cinematic, rely on disability aesthetics in the sense intended by Siebers—as a positive, productive, and defining value of modern art (2010, 133).

As explored next, the soundtrack of Teshigahara's film is just as important as its visual composition, and thus Straus's notion of disablist hearing is also relevant.

(Dis)figured Architecture and Disablist Hearing in Hiroshi Teshigahara's *Antonio Gaudí*

As part of chapter 3 of *Disability Aesthetics*, Siebers turns his attention, for a moment at least, to architectural aesthetics.[15] His analysis calls into question, in the realm of architecture, that same drive toward the notion of perfection that has just been shown to undergird Cerdà's urban planning. He writes that certain "aesthetic dictates represent architecture itself as providing a transcendental expression of human perfection" (2010, 72).[16] Siebers rightly insists that famed modernist architect Le Corbusier's conceptual diagram of what he called "the modular" is a case in point. For Siebers, it is an evocative example of normative corporeality applied to the built environment.[17] The modular was an "upright male—six feet tall, muscular, powerful, and showing no evidence of either physical or mental disability" (73). This concept was intended to promote what might be called ergonomic building practices in modernist architecture. At the same time, however, it tied those practices to a gendered and ableist constructed concept of the normate body. Based on this example, Siebers joins Rob Imrie in a broad critique of modernist architectural practices.[18] Yet even though he mentions the symbolism of disability, Siebers is intent on seeing the aesthetic component of attempts at or evasions of inclusive architecture. As a consequence, he attends most of all to the phobic, discriminatory motivation behind ableist architecture. He calls architecture, in this sense, hysterical "in its desire to ward off the signs of disability, for each attempt to make the building accessible produces another attempt either to block accessibility or to conceal the marker of disability tattooed by the accessible features on the skin of the building" (75). Despite this worthwhile focus on accessibility, however,

Siebers might have also applied the aesthetic critique central to his own analysis of visual art to the realm of modernist architecture in a distinct but complementary way. He might have been more willing to conceive of architecture as an aesthetic practice in the same way that he saw painting as an aesthetic practice.

That is, Antoni Gaudí's constructions, which are often subsumed within the broader category of Catalan Modernisme, provide strong reason to extend the main thesis of *Disability Aesthetics* at once to the notion of architecture as visual art, thus to the urban aesthetics of buildings, and not solely to architecture as a spatial practice. Located at the intersection of architectural discourse and global tourism, Gaudí's oeuvre has achieved what might be called an unparalleled cultural capital as an aesthetics in and of itself.[19] However, his works might just as easily be viewed—and in fact are indeed viewed by some, despite the prestige his constructions hold for urban boosterism and global tourist culture—as eyesores. They are works of art of a particularly strange nature. Some might consider them ugly. George Orwell, for one, certainly thought so; he once called Gaudí's Sagrada Família "hideous" (van Hensbergen 2001, xxxiii). This sort of aesthetic judgment, while it may take place at a remove from discriminatory social practices engrained into the ableist histories of so-called "ugly laws" is nonetheless connected to the broad social understanding of disability. Siebers himself makes this connection in *Disability Aesthetics*, for example when he writes that "works of art called ugly ignite public furor. Unaesthetic designs or dilapidated buildings are viewed as eyesores. Deformed bodies appear as public nuisances" (72). The fact that Gaudí's creations have largely been assimilated into a normative tourist economy as beautiful artworks—as one of the bases for Barcelona's reputation as a beautiful, European, and global city—seems to prove Siebers' point that disability is present but unacknowledged in modern art: present in architecture, just as in visual art, as in the mental images that bring meaning to writing, and as in modernist music.

To imply that disability may be present in Gaudí's architectural aesthetics may not be all that provocative. Siebers writes that
"while universal access must remain the ambition of the disability community, a broad understanding of disability aesthetics . . .
shows that aesthetic disgust with disability extends beyond individual disabled bodies to the symbolic presence of disability in
the built environment" (58). In order to approach the "symbolic
presence of disability" in the aesthetic sense outlined by Siebers
and Straus, it is useful to consider examples from the architect's
work. These three examples range from the general to the specific.

First, Gaudí's architecture—much of it built in or near the
Eixample district of Barcelona designed by Ildefons Cerdà—disfigures urban modernity in general terms by obsessively privileging
the curved line over the straight line.[20] Nothing will convince the
reader who is unfamiliar with Gaudí of this systematic preference
more than a visit to Casa Batlló (See Figure 2.1) or La Pedrera /
Casa Milà in Barcelona. Teshigahara's film footage is remarkably
helpful in immersing viewers in the spectacle of Gaudí's *modernisme*. The architect's preference for the curve is a counterphobic,
rather than a phobic response, in the sense discussed by Siebers.
Whereas Cerdà relied heavily on the purportedly superior, scientific, and geometrical logic prized by the nineteenth century's
specialist planning culture, breaking with the grid only through
a carefully calculated flourish of the *xamfrà*, Gaudí is obsessively
drawn to the irregular. The architect embraces a vastly different notion of urban aesthetics than does the planner. His is one
grounded in the unfamiliar, the spontaneous, and the unthought
or the seemingly unthinkable. He relies on distortion rather than
clarity. Embracing the curve was the most basic way of destabilizing the tyranny of gridded thinking that pervaded the Eixample
district. To wit, one critic writes of La Pedrera that "every house
in the *eixample* till then had employed symmetry, straight lines
and right angles. In the Casa Milà floor plan rectangularity had
been replaced with a very organic design that looked like a loose

FIGURE 2.1. Exterior of Casa Batlló, showing Gaudí's preference for curved lines in the design of windows and balconies, ornate use of color and excessive detail. Screen shot from *Hiroshi Teshigahara*, Antonio Gaudí (Criterion Collection, [1984] 2008).

cluster of bubbles, each signifying a room but attached haphazardly" (van Hensbergen 2001, 167–68).

At the same time, Gaudí "naturalizes" this preference for the irregular in architecture. This is true in more than one sense. Beyond normalizing a socially irregular invocation of architectural aesthetics, he wanted above all else to return urbanites to nature. His architectural forms found inspiration in the natural world, and they were at once a reminder of how much of the natural world had been pushed out of the staid urban environment of the nineteenth century. The structure of the attic floor of La Pedrera is said to have been modeled on the curves of a snake skeleton or other vertebrate animal. The sculptures on the building's roof are phallic images. The ornate balconies of Casa Batlló, known as the House of Bones, have been called "skull-shaped" and perhaps resemble the jaws of sharks.[21] Its fireplace is designed in the highly unlikely shape of a mushroom. Everything is organic. Even the window casings eschew simple geometrical shapes. At Casa Vicens one sees flowers, birds, insects, and a spider's web; at Casa Calvet, cornucopias of fruit and mushroom-shaped balcony railings (van Hensbergen 2001, 75, 116). This is not the cerebral organicism of Cerdà, who fled from the natural world to impose regularized order through the straight lines of the Eixample. Instead Gaudí's is a truer sensory organicism.[22] He intends to replicate in precise terms the irregularity, difference, and perplexing forms of nature. It is in this sense that Gaudí (dis)figures urban modernity. He underscores the figurative in his architecture, rather than banishing it to the world of medicalized metaphor. His products shun the regularized and therefore dehumanized monotony that is so paradoxically captured in Cerdà's "beautiful" imagining of the Eixample's grid.

Second, there is Gaudí's innovative preference for irregular mosaic patterns to consider. These patterns, known as *trencadís*, were made from cracked and discarded ceramic pieces. Perhaps most famously figuring into the long winding bench atop the elevated plaza of the Park Güell, *trencadís* was for Gaudí highly symbolic as an evocation of socially inclusive thinking. Josep Miquel Sobrer explains that "In symbolic terms, trencadís exalts the poor, the broken, the outcast; in artistic terms, it creates an illusion. . . . Trencadís is a perfect material metaphor: it elevates the lowly into the lofty, it makes one of the broken many" (2002, 212). Rather than prize the notion of a clean, uninterrupted, and therefore homogeneous surface or "blank slate," *trencadís* is a technique that lauds unevenness. It is a strong reflection of the architect's insistence, not on an unbroken and uniform whole, but on a totality made up by differences. These are differences that are not corrected, not smoothed out, not cut, extracted, and sutured, but instead preserved, allowed to exist as they are. Difference and diversity are the very building blocks of his work. Though of course Siebers does not mention Gaudí in his book, he does take time to praise aesthetics that represent "the fragmentary, broken and injured" (2010, 135; see also 62). It is all too easy to borrow this phrasing of the disability theorist's and apply it as a short-hand for the architect's own system of aesthetic values. There is very little evidence in Gaudí's eclectic oeuvre that he found value in simple harmonies or socially standardized notions of symmet-rical beauty. Nothing achieves center stage in the marked fore-ground. Everything is oddly shaped, contrasts are dulled, images are mixed, interpenetrating; all is coterminous in the spectacu-larly uneven background.[23]

Third is an architectural example that lends itself to precisely the same analysis of physical corporeality that threads through *Disability Aesthetics*. Siebers writes of a great number of works of art and artists whose hallmark aspect is "assaulting aesthet-ics that ally beauty to harmonious form, balance, hygiene, fluid-ity of expression and genius" (60). Combatting the social stigma through which a phobic disgust of disability operates in ableist culture, such artworks and artists directly foreground the object of that phobic attention—the body as site of difference or of dis-ease. It is this very same provocative acceptance of corporeality that finds its way into the Nativity façade—a prominent part of the Sagrada Família whose construction Gaudí lived to oversee. Late in his film, Teshigahara privileges the Nativity façade with close ups, zooms, a slow-moving camera movement that rises and falls in the form of an arch, and a dramatic, slow-moving sweep underneath. Figures abound. Robert Hughes writes of Gaudí that "when he needed infants for his scene of the 'Slaughter of the Inno-cents' on the Nativity façade he got permission from the nuns in the old Hospital de la Sant Creu to cast the corpses of stillborn babies in plaster" (2004, 134; see also van Hensbergen 2001, 256). Is there not something of the provocative visual artists that Sie-bers covers in his book in Gaudí's inclusion of such a death-casted figure in the arch of the Sagrada Familia? As Siebers writes, "state-ments that label cultural attitudes, minority groups, lifestyles, and works of art as 'healthy' or 'sick' are not metaphors but aesthetic judgments about the physical and mental condition of citizens" (2010, 57). Gaudí's oeuvre is markedly unhealthy in the sense that he consistently generates an architectural aesthetics of the margins, one intended to be provocatively accepting of the sick, the diseased, and those who are cast out of society.

Hiroshi Teshigahara's film *Antonio Gaudí* is unquestioningly attentive to these socially nonnormative aspects of Gaudí's architecture. His documentary pays homage not to the Gaudí whose legacy resurfaced toward the end of the Franco dictatorship, as Barcelona was implicated once again in global tourist flows; not to the star architect whose fame prompted recognition of 2002 as the Year of Gaudí; not to the storied designer whose still unfinished Sagrada Família is so popular that its role in attracting mass tourism to the city is seen as harming central Barcelona's urban communities; but instead to that strange and inimitable Gaudí whose aesthetics are tolerated and consumed as an oddity. Despite the prestige his name seems to carry today in certain circles, that fact is that Gaudí's work was quite quickly and thoroughly rejected by the elite of his day.[24] Teshigahara himself acknowledges the estranging quality of the architect's aesthetics. He has described his own visit inside the Casa Milà in visceral terms that evoke sea-sickness and seem to suggest a mild form of aesthetic disgust: "The moment I stepped inside that architectural space," the director once said, "I was overpowered by a sensation that, like vertigo, brought on a kind of queasiness. The motif of water was ubiquitous, as if the building were sculpted out of rock by water. All the fluid curves were connected by organic lines" (2008, 17). Here Siebers's comments on those visual and experimental artists who play with the social reaction of disgust should not be far from our minds. Not unsurprisingly, among more casual audiences who may not be accustomed to avant-garde cinema, discomforting music, or the aesthetic qualities of Gaudí's work, Teshigahara's film often provokes a familiar set of mild disgust reactions: it is likely to be described by such viewers as odd, weird, strange. The fascination of the director for the architect's work goes far beyond George Orwell's dismissal to find value in what might otherwise be called "hideous."

Teshigahara's film is credited with bringing about, in Japan, a surge of interest in Gaudí and his work (Caparrós Lera 2001, 108). Along with other "avant-garde documentary makers focusing on landscape," he was active in the late 1950s at a time when a small group of Japanese filmmakers were rejecting older forms of realism as authoritarian and fascist, and seeking out "new ways to capture reality" (Centeno Martín 2019).[25] He originally had the idea to document Gaudí's constructions when he traveled to Barcelona in 1959, prepared to take 16 mm footage and black-and-white photographs. Yet he completed the documentary only after returning to the Catalan capital once again in the early 1980s. Some of those earlier photographs are included in the completed film. Their inclusion is merely one of the strategies that Teshigahara uses to imbue his take on Gaudí's architecture with a sense of temporality and to put architecture in conversation with other forms of art. The film begins with a series of images of other art forms—such as medieval representations, modernist painting, and dance, here the sardana. This sequence expresses the director's understanding that all artistic production is interconnected—including documentary, of course.[26] He encourages a historical view of artistic production whose timeline he extends backward by centuries. Over the course of the film, Teshigahara employs an endlessly roaming, mobile frame to capture a great number of Gaudí's prominent sites: not only the Casa Batlló, the Casa Milà, and the Sagrada Família, but also the Park Güell, Colònia Güell, Palau Güell, the Casa Vicens, Casa Calvet, and more. Due to what is, with very few exceptions, an almost constant slow movement of the camera, viewers might themselves feel queasy, as if they are floating. In light of Teshigahara's desire to seek out a provocative and new form of artistic realism, this motion may be designed to effect a sort of momentary transcendence of the body into consciousness on the part of viewers. It also seems to be a reconstructed visual reference to the director's own bodily experience during his visit inside the Casa Milà.

Teshigahara has been described as one of a group of directors who "reveal something intimate that transcends the materiality of the filmed objects." Marcos P. Centeno Martín writes that the members of this select group "demonstrate how documentary cinema is only partially limited by the materiality of the external world. They interrogate details that evoke a human presence which makes documentary film expand beyond the physical appearance of its objects" (2019). Teshigahara's intention to push beyond the physical world, this seeking of transcendence, squares with Gaudí's own emphasis on architectural forms that evoke natural and spiritual thoughts and feelings. One must keep in mind the architect's attitude toward divine creation, concisely encapsulated in this statement: "Creation works ceaselessly through man. But man does not create, he discovers" (van Hensbergen 2001, 138). This focus on transcendence of the material world, an insistence shared by both Gaudí and Teshigahara, presents in the film *Antonio Gaudí* as a striking counterexample of what Siebers called the pathology of detail. Further consideration of this point prompts a return to the arguments of *Mimesis*.

If the pathology of detail in Cerdà's Barcelona comes from mimetic description (Auerbach) and relies on the visual analysis of writing (Siebers), in Teshigahara's filmic Barcelona, we have a text that, while undeniably visual, is akin to the biblical mode explored by Auerbach. To quote from *Mimesis*, Teshigahara "explains" nothing in his documentary film. "Everything remains unexpressed" (1957, 9) in the sense that Auerbach intends as a commentary on the Hebrew Bible. In the biblical text, he wrote, "the decisive points of the narrative alone are undefined and call for interpretation; thoughts and feeling remain unexpressed, are only suggested by the silence and the fragmentary speeches; the whole, permeated with the most unrelieved suspense and directed toward a single goal (and to that extent far more of a unity), remains mysterious and 'fraught with background'" (9). Similarly, Teshigahara's approach is to invite interpretation, rather than explain. He wants to sustain unrelieved suspense, and to preserve the mystery of his film as a path to preserving the mystery of Gaudí's architecture. Despite being constructed in a visual modality, the film's background is no less "fraught" than is the background of the Hebrew Bible as described by Auerbach.

Auerbach writes that the biblical stories do not seek to "bewitch the senses": "If nevertheless they produce lively sensory effects, it is only because the moral, religious, and psychological phenomena which are their sole concern are made concrete in the sensible matter of life" (11). In a similar way, to think that Teshigahara intends to bewitch the senses or privilege the sensory effects of image and sound in the sense that Auerbach intends is to misunderstand his film's accomplishment. The director seeks through his cinema what Gaudí sought through his architecture: the focus is on the transcendent qualia of the so-called "sensible matter of life." That which one sees and hears in the film pushes viewers toward not a denial but an acceptance and transcendence of materiality. The mysterious depths of what one might call psychology, morality, religion, or spiritual practice are undeniably present on film—as they are in Auerbach's characterization of biblical stories. The documentary is not coaxing viewers to "forget our own reality for a few hours" as Auerbach argues of the Homeric example *The Odyssey*, but rather pushing for individuals to interpret their own place in a deeper reality, a push that "seeks to overcome our reality: we are to fit our own life into its world, feel ourselves to be elements in its structure of universal history" (12).

Paradoxically, however, in terms of Auerbach's model of writing at least, the film achieves the same end as the Hebrew Bible not by eschewing but rather by immersing viewers completely within the myriad details of time and place. It is through the specificity of time and place that the at once cinematic and architectural mystery presents itself. The film's focus on Gaudí's architecture provides consistent reference to concrete anchors of place. Simultaneously, The director nurtures a sense of mystery with techniques that unfold along the axis of time. The duration of the shots, while not too extreme, is routinely lengthy. Teshigahara's clear preference for the long take allows an immersion in the present moment that allows spectators to think and feel their own way to the notion of transcendence at their own pace. The recurring use of the dissolve recreates Gaudí's blurred aesthetic in cinematic terms. The lack of narration, along with other aspects of the film, further requires the viewer's active engagement with the images. Among these other aspects one may count the floating sensation conveyed through the film's restlessly mobile frame.

The music only heightens the film's sense of mystery. Composed by Toru Takemitsu, with Kurodo Mori and Shinji Hori, it "plays a dominant role" in the film and "contains a hypnotic power aimed at projecting fascination as well as bewilderment on the screen" (Centeno Martín 2019, citing also Holden 1998, 23). The opening minutes of the film establish a number of musical tropes in quick succession. The music begins somewhat conventionally, with an orchestral interplay among flute and strings over shots of Barcelona's magic fountain. By the second minute, however, this orchestral interplay recedes and listeners are left with an airy and somewhat modernist aesthetic of faint and high-pitched notes played by a single instrument that proves hard to identify. In the fourth minute, over images of the painted medieval scenes of religious significance, a church organ gently intones a plodding and dour composition that nonetheless boasts a prominent melodic line. Images of sardana dancers appear and reappear, accompanied now by upbeat horn and reed instruments. At first it is unclear whether or not Teshigahara is using diegetic sound from an event recorded in Barcelona's public spaces. Despite the suggestion of a plausible diegetic connection between image and sound, however, in the eighth minute a punctuating close up of a man playing a flute is included as an afterthought, with no flute sound, and no music whatsoever. Next begins the sort of distorted music one might expect to hear after opening an antique music box that no longer plays at speed or in tune. It starts and stops frequently and abruptly, releasing a musical figure whose repetition proves disconcerting.

As Gaudí's buildings begin to appear on screen—both their exteriors and interiors—the music adopts a hauntingly minimalist approach. Individual notes reverberate as if produced by a finger circling the rims of partially filled glasses. Each dies out as the next begins. Their succession is hardly regular. Later on, cymbals are used to heighten the sensation of disorientation brought to consciousness by this technique. Over the course of the film, musical flourishes come and go. Once inside the Casa Batlló, the sound of winds and/or waves is layered over the haunting sonic landscape reminding listeners of the importance of nature for Gaudí's architecture. At times the faint minimalist music on the soundtrack seems to suggest a melody, but one that it is being played so slowly as to be unrecognizable. Soon the haunting music-box aesthetic returns. Introducing La Pedrera are the noise of quotidian traffic, a lone car horn, the rush of passing air, hints at the urban landscape to which we have no access. Once inside the building, the church organ music returns with its minor-key figures, phrasings, and resolutions. This time it is accompanied by a prominent flute and other instrumentation.

Musical forms change and shift continuously throughout the rest of the film. There are segments of orchestration approaching the aural grandeur of classical music, as well as attempts to signal the joy of simple pleasures through relatively sparse and simple yet playful flute interludes. No matter which moment of the soundtrack is considered, however, these attempts establish themselves in the foreground only for a mere moment before then dissipating. This creates a constant play between the presence and absence of musical figuration. The musical figures, such as they are, never stay present too long in the listener's consciousness. It is this type of interplay that pervades the rest of the film. At certain times, the classical music figures and the haunting minimalist tropes are layered over each other, inducing a novel form of blurred aural disorientation.

Straus writes at the end of his book that "the disablist hearing I am advocating here embodies resistance to the tyranny of the normal" (2018, 179). From the ableist perspective outlined and critiqued therein, the resulting soundtrack of *Antonio Gaudí* is defective twofold: first because it does not have a recurring melody, and second because it is a fragmented and unorganized mashup of unreconcilable musical themes. It does not reward, but instead consistently undermines, those listening strategies associated with what Straus calls normal hearing (165). The question is then whether this doubled defect makes the music hideous, estranging listeners from normative understandings of beauty in the aural, or whether it encourages listeners to hear the beauty in its very imperfection. In truth, this is the perfect (imperfect) aural complement to the architecture of Gaudí. It repeatedly constructs and, perhaps frustratingly, deconstructs the value of harmony. It eschews the aesthetic value of balance. This is music "perceived as a continuous flow, rather than a series of punctuated events" (175–76). It is a musical drift rather than a musical composition. There is no systematic juxtaposition made between a detailed musical foreground and a musical background.

Rather than adding a mood that is not already present in the film's images, the music is an effective complement and reinforcement of the persistently mild disorientation of both Gaudí's architecture and Teshigahara's camera work. Cinematic qualities such as the long take, the restlessly mobile frame, and the hypnotic music are employed deftly and subtly as mere extensions of Gaudí's extraordinary architectural vision itself. So much of the mystery is there in the original building façade, in the Park Güell bench, even before it is captured on film, and Teshigahara's film provides every indication that he knows it. It is through specifying time and place as pathways to mood, feeling and thought that the director achieves "the greater depth of time, fate and consciousness" that Auerbach attributes to the Elohistic text (1957, 9). In neither Gaudí's architecture nor its cinematic representation by Teshigahara does one become absorbed in details, in the sense that Siebers bemoaned—there are just too many of them. The spectator is not absorbed by detail but overwhelmed by it, immersed within it. The detail itself is what has been absorbed into the whole such that the proper way to view the film is a shift into the disablist cognitive mode. This section has argued that such a mode is pursued by both Gaudí's architecture and Teshigahara's film. In the next filmic example, however, architectural practice is a hindrance to inclusion of difference and may even rise to the level where it eschews the human.

The Obsessed Architectural Aesthetic:
Mercado de futuros by Mercedes Álvarez

Mercado de futuros (2011; Futures market), the second full-length film directed by Mercedes Álvarez (1966–), is many things. It is a stunning artistic product that engages the visual sense in order to explore the theme of the crisis in Spain. In this respect it is thus a complement to other post-15M works of visual art.[27] Understood as a critical text in its own right—thus irreducible to the medium through which this critique is carried out—the film also complements wider interest in thinking through the root causes and persisting consequences of the crisis in Spain. These root causes can themselves be taken as synonymous with an obsessed drive toward capital accumulation. That is, the film synthesizes and comments on economic, political, social, and aesthetic discourse, exploring the same issues brought to light in the 15M dossier organized by Bryan Cameron and published in the *Journal of Spanish Cultural*

FIGURE 2.2. Els Encants with view to highway and Torre Agbar, showing a sofa, chairs, and various other objects set on the ground outside of market stalls, as two pedestrians walk in the mid-ground of the image. Screen shot from Mercedes Álvarez, *Mercado de futuros* (IB Cinema, 2011).

Studies (2014), in Jon Snyder's *Poetics of Opposition in Contemporary Spain: Politics and the Work of Urban Culture* (2015), and in Luis Moreno-Caballud's *Cultures of Anyone* (2015), for example. In this sense, it also builds on a long tradition of cultural studies approaches to Barcelona's urban culture (Balibrea 2017; Bou and Subirana 2017; Degen 2008; Epps 2001, 2002; Illas 2012; Mercer 2013; Resina 2008; Vilaseca 2013). Finally, it is a visual, critical text that reflects deeply on the urban phenomenon. What arguably makes *Mercado de futuros* a masterpiece is the emphasis that Álvarez places on interconnected themes of space, architecture, and urban form. The result is a filmic challenge to the urbanistic ideology that continues to drive the production of space in the contemporary city. Most important, this filmic challenge hinges on questions central to urban aesthetics.

Mercado de futuros is concerned above all else with questions regarding the place and value of the human in the contemporary urban world. That this exploration unfolds with persistent reference to the city of Barcelona is important. Key sites used in the film direct the viewer's attention precisely to Cerdà's modern urbanist legacy. Most notably, the Torre Agbar, designed by French architect Jean Nouvel, and Els Encants, the market featured substantially during the film's second half, are both located at the border of the Eixample (see Figure 2.2). Álvarez uses these two locations in order to stage a confrontation between two competing visions of the city. These two visions have radically different understandings of human value.

For the city understood as the triumphalist site of neoliberal capital accumulation, the human figure is inconsequential. This is the networked urban realm wherein cities retain their historical role as command and control centers of economic and productive forces.[28] From this perspective, humanity is necessary merely to the degree that humans participate as laborers and consumers in an economy structured to benefit only the top 1 percent. Álvarez selects stock futures—for the title of her film as well as for select scenes within it that feature shots of the stock market and those working in stock trading offices—as a dimension of this predatory economy that best expresses the reduction of human beings to numbers. This vision of human beings is that of an exchange-value, valuable only insofar as they produce and consume. Such a bias toward the concept of productivity is precisely, as David T. Mitchell and Sharon Snyder argue convincingly in *The Biopolitics of Disability*, the ableist ideology that has been used to devalue and dehumanize those labeled as disabled in society.[29] They write, "non-productive bodies are those inhabitants of the planet who, largely by virtue of biological (in)capacity, aesthetic nonconformity, and/or nonnormative labor patterns, have gone invisible due to the inflexibility of traditional classifications of labor (both economic and political). They represent the nonlaboring populations—not merely excluded from, but also resistant to, standardized labor demands of productivity particular to neoliberalism" (2015, 211). In this obsessively neoliberal vision of human value, humanity is a mere residue, an irregularity, that is only conditionally relevant to the goals of capitalist accumulation.

Yet for the city understood as a place to be inhabited, lived in, and experienced, a place in which to dwell, the human figure is central. *Mercado de futuros* is ultimately about the devaluation of human emotion, human belonging, and connection to place in an urbanized market context that privileges exchange over use. Importantly, the film seems to make the case that both the object world and the urban built environment are similarly positioned in the market as commodities. In texts such as *Introduction to Modernity* (1995), *The Right to the City* (1996), and *The Urban Revolution* (2003), Henri Lefebvre charts the development of urban modernity from the nineteenth century as the period in which the city itself shifts from a use-value to being shaped as an exchange-value. In short, the city, place itself, becomes a commodity. Barcelona-based theorist Manuel Delgado Ruiz's own urban critique is explicitly indebted to Lefebvre's work as revealed in overt references in *El animal público* (1999), *Memoria y lugar* (2001), and *Sociedades movedizas* (2007). His *La ciudad mentirosa: Fraude y miseria del "modelo Barcelona"* (2007) in particular applies Lefebvrian insights on the capitalist production of space to the urban context of Barcelona. In the introduction, titled "La ciudad-negocio," Delgado Ruiz writes,

> quién ansía ocupar Barcelona y avasallarla es, hoy, un capitalismo financiero internacional que ha descubierto en el territorio una fuente de enriquecimiento y que aspira a convertir la capital catalana en un artículo de consumo con una sociedad humana dentro. Por supuesto, ése es un fenómeno que afecta a otras muchas ciudades del mundo, todas ellas objeto de recalificaciones masivas al servicio de los intereses de las grandes corporaciones multinacionales. (2007a, 11)

> *That which yearns to occupy and subjugate Barcelona is, today, an international finance capitalism that has discovered in space a source of enrichment and that aims to turn the Catalan capi-*

tal into an article of consumption containing a human society. Of course, this is a phenomenon that affects many other cities of the world, each of them the object of massive requalifications in the service of the interests of large multinational corporations.

Álvarez's cinematic critique effectively carries the insights offered by Lefebvre and Delgado to the screen. Her integration of speculative real estate projects and futures markets proves to be in line with Delgado's point that the Catalonian capital is immersed in a global system of exchange. The appearance of the Torre Agbar, which notably also appears on the dust jacket for Delgado's *La ciudad mentirosa*, anchors the film in the uneven geographical development of Barcelona. Yet also prominent are a range of other global spaces that appear indirectly—for example, through a preponderance of urban images and architectural models. Capitalist speculation is specifically urbanized through the on-screen representation of global real estate investments, including properties located in Dubai and Budapest. Álvarez complements the notion of place as a commodity by showcasing a variety of activities linking the city with business: not only real estate fairs (Barcelona Meeting Point and Salón Inmobiliario de Madrid) and a brokerage company (Bolsa de Ahorro Corporación), but also a convention dedicated to leadership (Expomanagement).

Mercado de futuros was awarded the Premio Miradas Nuevas del Festival de Nyon, Vissions du Réel, the Premio "Navaja de Buñuel" Película Revelación, TVE, the Premio Mejor Documental, Festival de Cine de Nantes, Francia, and the Mención Especial de Jurado, Festival Internacional de Cine de Buenos Aires—all in 2011. Beyond its own merits, the film is also important on account of its director's connection with the tradition of the *documental de creación* in Spain. Many point to Joaquim Jordà's disability-themed film *Mones com la Becky* (1999) as the origin of this form of cinematic expression, also emphasizing a debt owed to his work with the Escuela de Barcelona dating back to the second half of the 1960s.[30] At the end of 1998, the Universitat Autònoma de Barcelona inaugurated the Máster en Teoría y Práctica del Documental Creativo (Viveros and Català 2010, 123), and the Máster en Documental de Creación program began at the Universitat Pompeu Fabra (UPF).[31] Mercedes Álvarez was among the first students in the program, along with other notable figures such as Isaki Lacuesta and Ariadna Pujol (De Pozo and Oroz 2010, 68).

Like director Abel García Roure, whose disability-themed film *Una cierta verdad* was released in 2008, Álvarez had been a member of the team working with José Luis Guerín (Fraser 2016a; Balló 2010, 108–9). Specifically, she was the *montadora* (editor) on Guerín's film *En construcción* (Balló 2010, 113). Her first film project as director was *El cielo gira* (2004). Reduced to its barest content, this film explores the dwindling rural population of the small town Aldealseñor in Soria. Yet Álvarez uses this basic premise, along with paintings of Pello Azketa, an artist who is losing his sight, to forge a cinematic meditation on temporality, disappearance, and human landscape.[32] Themes of spatiality, time and memory were already interconnected in *El cielo gira* and they were implicated in its critical success. Yet, as noted by critic Javier Serrano (2012), in the director's sophomore effort these themes are notably and more directly urbanized.

With this, her second full-length film, Álvarez continues to question the border between documentary and fiction and to explore the way emotions are implicated in space/place. By effectively urbanizing *El cielo gira*'s cinematic insights regarding time, memory, and loss, *Mercado de futuros* contributes to an urban sub-tradition of the *documental de creación*. Two figures are obligatory references for understanding what she accomplishes with this effort. She has been inspired by her mentor Víctor Érice's *El sol del membrillo* (1991) and is following closely in the footsteps of José Luis Guerín's *En construcción* (2001).[33] These two films played with documentary approaches to urban themes, and both were in dialogue with a poetic mode of urban representation.[34]

Yet *Mercado de futuros* pushes both of these dimensions of the director's work to an extreme impossible in those earlier films. To explain: running through Érice's undoubtedly complex film there is also a more easily digestible biographical focus. The centrality of painter Antonio López García's artistic process to *El sol del membrillo* is a device that quite naturally supports the introduction of philosophical themes and subtly induces a poetic response in the spectator. Likewise, Guerín's challenging film centers on easily recognizable and iconic spaces that have long proven central to Barcelona's shifting identity as a global city. It is notable that *Mercado de futuros* does not rely on either of those advantages. Instead, the director has accepted the challenge of building a philosophical, poetic, and urban narrative from scratch.

Mercado de futuros showcases various elements of the poetic mode.[35] Perhaps most overtly is what documentary theorist Bill Nichols has called "the Voice of God commentator, whom we hear speaking in a voice-over but do not see" (2001, 13).[36] Yet simultaneously the film also provides evidence of a poetic mode variant that seeks to "hint and suggest rather than declare or explain," a tendency where "the point of view becomes implicit" (48). This mode characteristically "emphasizes visual associations, tonal or rhythmic qualities, descriptive passages, and formal organization," stressing "mood, tone, and affect much more than displays of knowledge or acts of persuasion" (103). The poetic mode, while it is quite often used without overt political intention—an example would be *Berlin: Symphony of a City* (Walter Ruttman, 1927)—at times can be effectively combined with an analytic directorial voice, as illustrated in the example of *Man with a Movie Camera* (Dziga Vertov, 1929).[37] Beyond the poetic mode, of course, *Mercado de futuros* also blends elements of expository, observational, and reflexive filmmaking, but stops short of demonstrating the director's need to "intervene and interact" (1991, 44). Thus what Nichols calls "the veil of illusory absence" is not "shorn away" (44)—as in the interactive mode of documentary film—but rather emphasized as a formal complement to Álvarez's interrogation of what has been lost in modern urban life. Her approach is poetic, mediated, but somewhat indirect; her style is thus more philosophical than interventionist. The effect is to preserve a visual sense of the seductiveness of urbanized power while nonetheless calling upon the mind to eviscerate its concomitant ideology.

It is worth asking why the poetic mode is seemingly incompatible with politics. Must that always have to be the case? And why is it a particularly apt mode for Álvarez in *Mercado de futuros*? What is perhaps most interesting in this regard is the posture of Álvarez's film concerning the figure of the worker or, by extension, a figure similarly contrasted with the class interests implicit in the capitalist city, the urbanite. Historically, the poetic and expository modes of documentary filmmaking represented such figures "within an ethics of social concern and charitable empathy" and thus "denied the worker a sense of equal status with the filmmaker" (Nichols 2001, 140). The film largely avoids depicting the worker or urbanite at all until its second half. Even here, the worker is presented as a nonproductive, nonconsuming, resistant laborer whose interest lies in day-to-day conversational pleasures rather than transactions.

The film is defined by and constructed through a series of tensions. It is both inaccessible and inviting, conceptual and topical. At the beginning of the film, after a section of animation that is worthy of critical attention in its own right, a voiceover by Álvarez outlines the contemplative agenda for the film:

> Una noche, hace más de dos mil años, el poeta griego Simonides de Ceos acudía a una casa con más de veinte invitados. Durante la cena, mientras Simonides se ausentaba unos momentos, se hundió el techo de la casa, sepultando a todos los habitantes. Los cadáveres quedaron tan destrozados que nadie podía identificarlos. Pero Simonides sí pudo hacerlo. Porque recordaba el lugar exacto donde estaba sentado cada uno de los invitados. Se dice que Simo-

nides inventó el arte de la memoria, y que fue utilizado durante siglos. Pero ese arte carece, desde hace mucho, de la más mínima importancia. (2011, 0:02:42–0:03:31)

One night, more than two thousand years ago, the Greek poet Simonides de Ceos arrived at a house with more than twenty guests. During dinner, while Simonides had stepped away for a few moments, the roof of the house came crashing down, burying all of those inside. The corpses were so damaged that no one was able to identify them. But Simonides managed to do so. Because he remembered the exact spot where each of those invited had been sitting. It is said that Simonides invented the art of memory, and it was used for centuries. But this art has, for some time, lacked any importance.

There is a coldness to this introductory voiceover, as the director cultivates the appropriate philosophical distance for conducting a clinical investigation of an obsessed contemporary urban society. The delivery of her words is decidedly dispassionate. Yet the subject matter is markedly familiar and even quotidian. The director's dispassionate tone and her verbal text's emphasis on the aporias of time—that is, notions of lack, forgetting, negligence— is reinforced by the still image of an empty white wall where a picture once hung. The scene that follows captures the clearing out of a house. It emphasizes common objects, wall-hangings, paintings, and furniture that, in the poetic mode of filmmaking, can be seen as repositories for the emotional connections that saturate our living environments. The belongings of the former inhabitants are thus revealed to be residue from the routine projection of human emotions onto architectural space. This is a primary tension established throughout the film—the coldness of a "pure" architecture versus the warmth of human relationships that imbue space with social meaning. We invest spaces, architectural forms, and objects with significance, humanizing and personalizing them, yet this significance is destined to fade, particularly if we are inattentive to it over time. *Mercado de futuros* has been carefully shot and structured to convey that this is very much the case. We do indeed forget what has come before.

Related to this theme, Mercedes Álvarez provides us with a somewhat routine cinematic memory exercise in *Mercado de futuros*. This exercise is all the more important given the way it foregrounds a representation of the human figure. Though subtle, and perhaps easily forgotten, a doll figurine from this opening sequence of a house being cleared reappears meaningfully toward the end of the final lengthy flea market sequence. This final sequence is filmed in the market Els Encants, located at the Plaça de les Glòries Catalanes, which is nestled near a highway exchange and not far from the shadow of the Torre Agbar (see Figure 2.2). As Delgado Ruiz writes, juxtaposing the flea market and the tower designed by French starchitect Jean Nouvel specifically, "cada mañana se reunían centenares de inmigrantes sin trabajo, de vagabundos y de otros miserables que compraban y vendían en un enorme bazar surgido espontáneamente, donde se podía encontrar todo tipo de objetos recogidos de los contenedores de basuras" (2007a, 51; there each morning gather hundreds of unemployed immigrants, homeless, and other pathetic people who buy and sell in an enormous market that has been spontaneously created, where one can find all manner of objects scavenged from garbage containers). Delgado Ruiz's prose scene acquires cinematic form in lengthy sequences from *Mercado de futuros* featuring Els Encants, with a view to both the highway and the Torre Agbar. The doll reappears in this context in the film's late sequences, and viewers may or may not remember it from the beginning of the film. Yet it is a reminder of our routine (in)attention to the emotional connections we forge with the object world. The doll symbolizes the human emotional connections to space, place, and other social objects, a use-value that is subjugated to the exchange economy. This prop's association with domestic family life and the use-value space of the home is important to its cinematic meaning. Its reappearance challenges viewers to confront their own levels of attentiveness or inattentiveness. Like those emotional connections symbolized and enacted by the doll, our emotional connections with place itself are similarly vulnerable to fading away, becoming less significant to us, and losing their sustained social import and use-value.

Architecture provides the primary imagery through which Mercedes Álvarez advances her critique of the reduction of the human figure to an exchange-value. The buildings, surfaces, and representations she catalogues throughout the film prove to be a sampling not of Gaudí's brand of counterphobic architecture, which celebrated difference and the diversity of figuration, but rather of the kind of thinking we now associate with Cerdà's urbanistic ideology. This is an extension, from urban planning into the adjacent realm of architectural practice, of a phobic architecture, anxious regarding human difference and profoundly ambivalent regarding human existence. Cerdà avoided the curve. He razed the urban imaginary to a flat surface, a blank canvas upon which the creative artistry of the privileged class of the modern planner could figure itself. Though his original motivation may have been a true concern for how the working class lived, the legacy of his project nonetheless established geometry and the grid as pathways to making the imperfect perfect, to imposing symmetry, and banishing difference from Barcelona. It is the planning of the nineteenth century, wrote Henri Lefebvre, that turned the city from a use-value into an exchange-value. In her careful selection, composition, and editing of everyday urban scenes, Álvarez undermines the notion of Barcelona as a spectacular city and at once questions what Lefebvre defined as the "triumphant and triumphalist" discourse of urban modernity. In doing so, she implicitly dialogues with a tradition of criticism that has critiqued Barcelona's reputation as a global city (Delgado Ruiz 2007a, 2007b; see also McNeill 1999, 2002; Degen 2001, 2004a, 2004b, 2008). In this case, the director advances trenchant critiques of neoliberal capitalism's colonization of urban space (Delgado Ruiz 1999, 2007a,

2007b, 2010; see also Lefebvre 1976, 1991, 1996, 2003). Her film poses the question of whether there is room for the human, for feelings, and for the everyday in the obsessive urbanistic rethinking of city form and its concomitant embrace of exchange-value.

It is interesting that some existing scholarship on the film has downplayed the relationship of architecture and the urban form to capitalist speculation, effectively ignoring the role of the city as a prioritized commodity since the nineteenth century (for an exception, see Castanon-Akrami 2014). For example, studies by Manuel de la Fuente (2017) and Isabel Estrada (2017) are valuable contributions noting the importance of *Mercado de futuros* that nonetheless fail to address architecture or the urban in sufficient depth. These accounts prefer to focus on the film's relevance to what comes across as essentially a political-economic crisis. While astute, these analyses tend to recapitulate broader trends in traditional economics in which the crucial role of urban environments in strategies of capital accumulation is overlooked. Even Marxian traditions are not immune from this tendency to take the city as the mere setting for contemporary capitalism rather than a key commodity in and of itself (see Harvey 2012, who explicitly follows the Lefebvrian tradition). That is, in addition to being the backdrop for the continuing exploitation of labor by capital, the urban landscape is both a product of capitalism (the result of speculative activity) and also its key generative component (a producer of value).

Some of the film's most striking poetic-analytic scenes occur in the first half of the film and either neglect the human figure, limit its significance, or poetically acknowledge its subjugation to—dehumanization by—the engine of capitalist-urbanistic production. There are still-camera images that capture ruins of the built environment that lack any human forms whatsoever (see figure 1 in Picornell 2017, 186). Or else the human figures that do appear are immobilized, seated in outdoor chairs, and—their faces hidden from viewers—stripped of their human attributes (see the image in Serrano 2012). Such urbanites are somehow anaesthetized to the ideological nature of the urban form and have effectively been turned into just another object in the built environment. The shot of businessmen immobilized in individual massage chairs is similarly evocative (see figure 4 in Picornell 2017, 189). This is one of the most absurdly powerful images in *Mercado de futuros* precisely because it illustrates, with no need for voiceover, how human beings are anaesthetized, via consumption, into a cognitive slumber.

Similar in this regard are the upper-middle-class functionaries who in practice sustain the capitalistic-urbanistic machine. That is, the day-to-day business work of these professionals contributes fundamentally to the accumulation of capital in a small number of hands. Because of the nature of the work in which they engage, even if they are not themselves capitalists, these workers thus become indistinguishable from capitalist accumulation in practice. One memorable shot of such a white-collar professional shows a man in jacket and tie working on a laptop against the background of what might seem an idealized urbanized coastline (see figure 2 in Picornell 2017, 186).[38] The physical distance of this figure from the spectacularized urban image making up the background recapitulates a social distancing. Symbolically, he represents the disproportionate (and disproportionately patriarchal) social power enjoyed by the European planning class. Cinematically, he embodies the idea advanced by Richard Sennett that the "visual technology of power" employed by modern urban planners "alienated them, too, from their own work" (1992, 61). Poetically and critically, he becomes in the viewer's imagination a servant to the capitalist production of space.

Overall, there is a poetic if grotesque beauty to the image of the city in *Mercado de futuros*. There is no question that this is a beautiful film. The generalized emphasis of the poetic mode on concerns such as mood, tone, rhythm, and affect can be observed continually. As De la Fuente reflects, "all the characters move like automatons in a beautiful but empty environment" (2017, 189). At least initially, in what might be called the first half of the film, the director's artful choices of compositional framing and the lingering gaze of the camera seem to intentionally treat the urban form as an aesthetic object. Yet there are nonetheless wonderful moments when the superficial, slick, bird's-eye view, or two-dimensional image of the modern city is undermined to showcase the role of human labor in its production.

One such scene presents an entire indoor wall in what could be in a conference center or shopping mall that bears the image of a triumphantly urban scene.[39] After the still camera lingers a moment on the wall's urban scene, suddenly a door opens in the wallpapered image. An employee steps out of a hidden office, walking the length of the wall. This moment reveals, in symbolic terms, that behind the aesthetic splendor of the modern urban form there is human activity shaping the landscape as the result of social work. The architectural surface—of the wall, and of urbanism by extension— is only an illusion constructed in the interests of those who would profit from the image of the city as an exchange-value. The slick architectural façade thus comes to symbolize a negation of the very human difference and vitality in diversity that theorists such as Jane Jacobs posited as the core of urbanity.

As this example in particular drives home, Álvarez's film demonstrates a tendency to aestheticize urban form and then politically undermine this aestheticization in subtle ways. As Picornell has argued, the use of the cinematographic trompe-l'oeil encourages spectators to question what they see, to look beyond surface appearance (2017, 185, 189).[40] Tying this back to the classifications made by Bill Nichols, the hybrid poetic-analytic documentary mode becomes for Álvarez an apt method for creating a conflict in her film's viewers. As cinematic spectators appreciating the beauty of the film's composition and architectural images, we become complicit in the spectacularization of urban form and somewhat anesthetized to urban conflict. Simply put, the splendor of photographic composition and cinematic montage in *Mercado de futuros* is entrancing. It mimics the way obsessed planners have crafted the modern city as a beautiful aesthetic object. Yet at the same time, Álvarez challenges us to do the work of peering under the shining architectural surface and returning space to time. In the process, she vindicates a form of urban memory that our wider society has neglected and that we may collectively choose to recapture at any moment whatsoever.

As the film moves through its second half, the figure of the worker/urbanite comes more clearly into view. Álvarez spends more time with Jesús, a junk collector who works in the flea market known as Els Encants. In light of comments made by Nichols, this can be seen as a correction of the poetic mode's historical marginalization of the worker. It is the nonproductive laborer that Álvarez foregrounds. The director allows Jesús significant on-screen time, with no voiceover. He progressively acquires a privileged position in the film and in the viewer's consciousness. This gradual shift needs to be understood in relationship to the film's development of the trope of surface and depth as it relates to the urban phenomenon. Here Mercedes Álvarez shifts from the architectural aspects of the built environment to the immersive urban social context inhabited by the individual.

Jesús, while he is not presented in any way as disabled, nonetheless becomes a cinematic symbol of nonproductive labor. This concept itself—that is, the distinction between so-called productive and nonproductive individuals—it must be recognized, is a result of the social meaning disability acquires during the nineteenth century as a labor designation prompted by increased industrialization. In the words of Mitchell and Snyder, "*disability* was first coined in the mid-1800s to designate those incapable of work due to injury" (2015, 211) and that over time "disabled people [were] thrown out of the labor system on the basis of their lack of normative productivity in a competitive labor market" (205).[41] It is useful to ponder the questions they raise in the afterword to *The Biopolitics of*

Disability while viewing the film's increased focus on Jesús in its second half. That is, "Who are the inhabitants of 'nonproductive bodies?' What do they have to do with disabled people?" (Mitchell and Snyder 2015, 211).

Jesús sits at a market stall that is in reality a large container. The container is overflowing with used, discarded objects—to such a degree that he must sit out in front of it. As Jesús speaks with one flea-market visitor after the next, it becomes immediately clear that he has little-to-no desire to sell any of his wares. At times, he mentions that he probably has the item that is being requested, but is unable (or unwilling) to retrieve it. In this, he becomes a cinematic portrayal of the resistant subject (Mitchell and Snyder 2015, 211–14), one who embraces his nonproductive position relative to the labor market. Thematically, these sequences effectively function as a cinematic return of the commodity from exchange-value to use-value. The goods in Jesús's container are useful to him not because he makes money off of them, but rather because they serve him as prompts for social interaction. The fact that Els Encants is shown in physical proximity to the Torre Agbar and the highway interchange of the Plaça de les Glòries Catalanes keeps viewers cognizant of the spectacular architectural image of Barcelona even as they spend time with one of the city's most forgotten urbanites.

These scenes centering on Jesús are also important in terms of their mise-en-scène. Here the items with potential exchange-value are hidden from view, and it is the human figure that is instead prioritized visually. Jesús is positioned in front of the goods and not behind them. The juxtaposition of this scene with the one discussed above—where a man exits from the hidden office door— could not be more clear. Whereas in that scene, the slick image hides the real human work, here by contrast use-value triumphs over exchange-value. As this juxtaposition illustrates, the film has shifted from surface to depth. Whereas before it foregrounded the surfaces of buildings and the exchange economy, now it highlights the individual urban dweller and the use-value of time. This is simultaneously a shift in scale, from the architecture and built environment of the monumental city toward the personal scale of those who inhabit and dwell within place. The camera and editing allow viewers to dwell with Jesús, and in doing so they shift from the presentation of the passive, immobilized human figure as part of a commodified urban world toward a form of human sociality that has been systematically neglected by urbanistic modernity.

These final scenes of *Mercado de futuros* contrast with the cold, if contemplative, voiceover of the film's beginning and return viewers to the association between human warmth and what the modern city should be. The doll from the beginning of the film also reappears, a subtle but poignant figure reminding viewers of our emotional human connections with the object world, and ideally also with the architectural form of the city. Mercedes Álvarez arguably employs both Jesús and the doll figure to hammer home the central idea of the film, which is this: it is only our memory—of human connections, of an urban form of life not yet completely colonized by exchange-value—that can stem the tide of the dehumanizing consequences of capitalist-urbanistic ideology. The film's juxtaposition of the Torre Agbar and Els Encants both renders concrete and also symbolizes more broadly the continuing effects of the nineteenth-century urbanistic practice. Álvarez's documentary work proves distrustful of the sleek architectural surface, and thus simultaneously of its concomitant values of obsessive profit-seeking and productivity. She establishes, through quite poetic and contemplative means, that contemporary neoliberalism is so obsessed with profit making that there is no room for the human figure in the aesthetics of architectural modernism and urbanism.

Chapter 3
Madrid Mania: Linearity and the Zig-Zag

Approaching the Iberian city as the outcome of urbanism's obsessive thinking and partial madness allows us to account for the modern struggle that emerges between two distinguishable social groups.

On one side of this struggle are the urbanists themselves, a special class of modern planner empowered to treat the fabric of the city as their personal canvas. Through his specialized and urbanized thinking Arturo Soria y Mata (1844–1920) emerges as a paradigmatic case study in obsessive modernity. Fixated on the nineteenth-century technology that Wolfgang Schivelbusch has called the railway ensemble, Soria y Mata famously imagined the Linear City (1892) in Madrid—a city to be built along a single line that would cover vast distances and in theory extend almost infinitely, over the surface of the earth. After forming the Compañía Madrileña de Urbanización (Urbanization Company of Madrid) in 1894, he was able to begin a short stretch of his plan in the Spanish capital, where it still can be visited today. Recalling Davis's analyses in *Obsession: A History*, Soria y Mata demonstrates the monomaniacal thinking typical of modernity through his fixation on the straight line. The conceptual violence of his resulting plan banishes urban spontaneity to the margins.

On the other side are those modern figures who might be considered more typically obsessive in the sense outlined by Lennard J. Davis—artists, writers, and scientists. Standing in as Iberian exemplars of such figures are long-standing canonical author of realist and naturalist-inflected fiction Emilia Pardo Bazán (1851–1921), and Nobel-prize winning neuroscientist, photographic pioneer, and sometimes writer Santiago Ramón y Cajal (1852–1934). These artists are obsessed, not with imposing a strict plan, but rather with recovering a kind of urban spontaneity and rejuvenation that modern city planning in practice eschews. Their short fictions analyzed here, Pardo Bazán's "La gota de sangre" (The drop of blood) (1911) and Ramón y Cajal's "El pesimista corregido" (The corrected pessimist) (1905), end in implicit affirmations of a modern city whose streets have a spontaneous use-value for its inhabitants. The urban environment is invoked as a site receptive to the imagination of these prose protagonists, who wander to and fro in captivated and single-minded attention.

From an urban perspective, both of these literary works can be seen as a Baudelairean zig-zag, one whose affirmation of the use-value of the city streets contrasts with and challenges the linear excesses of urban modernity. These stories laud the spontaneity of urban experience that persists in the modern planned city. While Pardo Bazán's writings can also be meaningfully explored in the context of her native Galicia,[1] the main character in this mysterious tale lives in Madrid and becomes obsessed by a possible murder.

Believing he is the only one who can solve it, his obsessive investigation turns the city streets into the stage for an imaginative flight of fancy. The transformative moment for the pessimist of Cajal's story involves a visual distortion rooted in scientific obsession and it takes place in Madrid's central green lung, the Retiro Park. While urban planners are complicit with the phobia of the everyday (see van Zuylen 2005, 2)—as exemplified by the stifling linearity of Soria y Mata's plan—these literary texts demonstrate the persistence and use-value of spontaneity as their protagonists zig, zag, and forge an urban experience that suits their own whims.

Infinite Extension: Arturo Soria y Mata's Linear City

The Linear City was a major urban project of the late nineteenth and early twentieth centuries that has itself been the object of substantial, one could also say obsessive, academic interest (see, for example, Collins and Flores 1968; De Terán 1968). A proper contextualization of the project would more broadly acknowledge Madrid's urban cultural history before and since—Edward Baker and Malcolm Compitello's collection *Madrid: De Fortunata a la M–40: Un siglo de cultura urbana* (2003) was a pathbreaking volume in this respect, forging a tradition that can be traced through to more contemporary texts such as *Cartographies of Madrid: Contesting Urban Space at the Crossroads of the Global South and Global North* (2019), edited by Silvia Bermúdez and Anthony Geist (see in particular Larson 2011; Ramos 2010; Resina 2001a, 2001b). Instead, however, this section seeks only to present a concise introduction to the planner's project and its resonance, before highlighting those dimensions of his work and thought that prove to be obsessive, in line with the argument established by Davis.

Soria y Mata's project allows a consideration of the urban aesthetics inherent in the expression of a normative spatial imaginary. On one hand, the planner's obsession with geometrical, Euclidean forms is classically ableist. In Soria y Mata's thinking—just as in the work of Ildefons Cerdà, Haussmann, and others—the straight line, the broad avenue, the city linked by a string of monuments, all these reflect a certain conceptual violence done to the human body. In practice, Modern urban planning negated the human body by producing the city in the interests of capital and consumption, thus creating a built environment for exchange-value rather than use-value. It also systematically ignored the diversity of human bodies. The planner's urban project in Madrid is a synecdoche for the rational, rectilinear, and geometric obsessions of modern urban planning as a whole. Yet Soria y Mata is not only producing a modern built environment for Madrid, he is also reproducing a markedly obsessive form of thinking. This is also rendered visible in a brief consideration of a tangential work he authored, *El origen poliédrico de las especies* (1894; The polyhedral origin of species), its title a clear reference to Darwin's *On the Origin of Species*.

Arturo Soria y Mata first introduces his project for a linear city in a brief essay published in *El Progreso* in 1882 (Collins and Flores 1968, 38; De Terán 1968, 5).[2] Therein he puts forth his theoretical proposition and suggests it can be universally applied, with considerations made for local conditions (De Terán 1999, 107). Though the specific plan is situated seven kilometers from the center of Madrid, other linear cities might be constructed "from Cadiz to St. Petersburg, from Peking to Brussels," by its indefinite extension (Chueca Goitia 2011, 205; Collins and Flores 1968, 38). He republishes ideas from 1882–83 in appendix A of *Ferrocarriltranvía de circunvalación* (1892) as his plan assumed the form of a horseshoe shape on the periphery of the Spanish capital. The completed project was to be five hundred meters wide and fifty-two kilometers in length.[3] By contrast with Cerdà's approach to Barcelona, Soria y Mata was arguably more intent on preserving the status quo of urban class relationships in Madrid (see Velez 1983, 131–32). The Linear City was constructed along both sides of a central railway artery.[4] Soria y Mata forms the Compañía Madrileña de Urbanización (CMU, Urbanization Company of

Madrid) on March 5, 1894, "to promote linear development near Madrid upon the basis of his plan of 1892, and to construct and operate the associated tramways" (Boileau 1959, 232). The first section of the Linear City is mostly developed by 1931—the first year of the Second Spanish Republic and the year in which the CMU put out a guide to the area—but the project languishes under the dictatorship of Francisco Franco.[5]

Even given its limited execution, the Linear City plan had a wide impact on twentieth-century planning cultures. It served as a precursor for other projects and stimulated multiple reflections and subsequent re-elaborations (De Terán 1999, 105). Susan Larson writes that Arturo Soria's Ciudad Lineal is a "notable exception" to the fact that "the most influential concepts of urban planning in the first part of the century are undeniably Anglo-Saxon" (2011, 41; see also Mercer 2013, 179; Ramos 2010, 184). C. A. Doxiadis, the Greek architect and planner of Pakistan's modern capital, Islamabad, lists other ideas that were "inspired probably by Soria" such as Tony Garnier's Cité Industrielle and N. A. Milyutin's Stalingrad plan (Doxiadis 1967, 35; see also Collins and Flores 1968, 38; Sambricio 2004, 21–23). Though the Linear City is not explored in any of the numerous contributions to *The City Reader*, still it appears as an illustration in the brief introduction to that book's section five, with a pair of sentences touting Soria y Mata's fame (LeGates and Stout 2005, plate 34, 408–9).[6]

Not unsurprisingly, the planner's extensive writings on the Linear City project obsessively praise the straight line, mixing geometric with economic, moral, and democratic nuance (Collins and Flores 1968, 40).[7] Soria y Mata's rhetoric exalts the linear city as a seed idea for positive change in elemental terms.[8] The line has a generative and (re)productive power: "Geometry offers also in this case its valuable cooperation. The point engenders the line; and this, the plane" (1892, 49).[9] "The straight line is the most characteristic element of the physiognomy of modern cities," he states unequivocally (57). Even in this basic principle there is an explicit connection with the organic metaphor of the city that pervaded modern urban planning culture—George Collins writes that Soria saw the linear city as a vertebrate animal, a fact also confirmed by the planner's own statement that the principal organs of some animals are linear.[10] While Le Corbusier and others had reimagined the city on a concentrated vertical axis exemplified by the skyscraper, Soria y Mata instead conquered space along an infinite horizontal extension (61).

While the planner's clear obsession with the straight line can be seen from the vantage point of urban planning as an ordering and regularizing force, a disability studies perspective might simultaneously see it in terms of a normative ideology and reproductive biology. Published at a time when Soria y Mata's Linear City project was taking off and the CMU had just been formed, *El origen poliédrico de las especies* gives voice to a most curious desire of the planner: "I am impatient to leave my obscure corner and be something in the world; and complete and perfect the work of Darwin, and see the unity and sexuality of regular polyhedrons" (1894, 5). Whether he is or is not obsessed, either in the modern usage of the term or that particular to the nineteenth-century sphere explored by Davis, it is sufficient to note that Soria y Mata grounds his perspective within the discourse of specialized scientific obsession: "During my entire life I have had the constant longing to dedicate myself solely and exclusively to the study of the exact and natural sciences" (6). This scientific obsession can be seen throughout his work, in which Soria y Mata blends "indisputable elemental principles of Arithmetic and Geometry" (9) with ideas of biological evolution. He argues that "Darwin has not had the good fortune to see with clarity that the origin of species stems from the origin of forms; which is the regular tetrahedron, derived from the sphere; and that the laws of production and of propagation of forms are applicable to the entire universe" (9).[11]

Given the comments made by Davis in *Obsession*, it is also quite pertinent to the present argument that *El origen poliédrico de las especies* contains a section titled "Genius and Madness" (81–82). In line with modern notions of partial madness prevalent at the time, Soria y Mata insists explicitly that "my theory makes it possible to establish a perfectly clear dividing line between genius and madness" (81). In line with the way modern notions of obsession democratized madness to the wider population, he paradoxically hints at the relative banality of madness, writing that "madness is nothing other than an illness like any other" (81). The book's inclusion of a folded insert revealing an obsessive chart is a testament to Soria y Mata's own partial madness. A distilled visual reflection of the arguments he makes in the book, the chart depicts polyhedral forms such as the closed dodecahedron along the x-axis, while the y-axis matches each form with mathematical equations, colors, musical notes, and a strict male or female sex typology classification. More important, in ideological terms, Soria y Mata tends to reproduce the same sort of normative biological arguments that have historically been used to stigmatize disability and perform violence on the disabled body. Here one encounters the notion of perfection that was so productively critiqued by Tobin Siebers. The planner writes that "all that is imperfect dies and dies soon because it is born already condemned to infecundity and to death due to the incontrovertible judgments of Arithmetic and Geometry" (42–43; this appears on an illustration between numbered pages). It is not out of line to say that— for the casual contemporary reader—*El origen poliédrico de las especies* reads as if an obsessive fever dream written by a partially mad specialist. This book provides a compelling counterpoint to the planner's more widely known work on the Linear City and as such prompts some brief reflections on connections between disability studies and urban studies.

The example of Soria y Mata and the discourse of modern urban obsession in general invite insights grounded in a potentially crip/queer form of urban thinking. They reveal the fixation with normality and suggest the notion of normality itself as a socio-cultural construction subject to temporal context. As crip studies forges intersectional linkages with queer studies and seeks greater global coverage (see, for example, Kafer 2013; McRuer 2006, 2010; McRuer and Mollow 2012; Puar 2007), forays into urban cultural studies thus need to be seen as deeply relevant to the disability studies project. Normative ideology is present not merely in the material experience of urban life, not merely in the very structure of the built environment, but moreover in the legacy of large-scale planning trends that emerged in the nineteenth century. The planner's obsessions with straight linearity and the transcendent aims of its pathologization of difference resonate with ableist ideology. Yet paradoxically, the partial madness of the planner's obsessions implicate cognitive difference in the construction of the modern city. Soria y Mata's legacy thus expresses a more general paradox of modern urban planning, one that is deserving of further cultural, metaphorical, and even literary investigation by disability studies scholars.

The Art of Neurasthenic Detection in Emilia Pardo Bazán's "La gota de sangre"

At fifty-seven pages, "La gota de sangre" ([1911] 2001) is the longest story in the *Cuentos policíacos* collection of Pardo Bazán's selected fiction. Discrete sections bearing roman numerals break it up into eight parts. This internal division into an episodic structure, along with the story's relaxed narrative pacing, suggests that Pardo Bazán's extended piece is more of a short novella. A concise account of the main plot events is necessary in order to understand the story's relation to the obsessive fixation and urban wandering that became hallmark traits of modernity.

The principal character is named Selva. Launching the story is a first-person account summarizing his visit to a doctor for psychological consultation: "Para combatir una neurastenia profunda que me tenía agobiado—diré neurastenia, no sabiendo qué

decir—, consulté al doctor Luz, hombre tan artista como científico" (25; In order to combat a profound neurasthenia that had me
overwhelmed—I will say neurasthenia, not knowing what to call
it—, I consulted with Doctor Luz, a man just as artistic as he was
scientific). Selva exhibits a detachment from life and a generalized lack of interest. After seeing the doctor, he initially remains
unchanged. He has a relatively boring day, wanders the streets of
Madrid, and later decides to go to the Teatro Apolo theater. It is
here that he observes a minor detail whose continued and obsessive rumination brings him back to life. At the theater, he sees
someone he knows named Andrés Ariza: "Era—en la pechera de
la camisa de Andrés, y casi cubierta por el chaleco—una diminuta
manchita roja, viva como labio encendido por el amor; una reciente
gotica de sangre" (28; There was—on the front of Andrés's shirt,
and almost covered up by his vest—a small red speck, as vibrant
as lips lit up by love; a recent tiny drop of blood). Selva—who is
quite puzzled both by the speck of blood and by Andrés's behavior
at the Apolo—becomes instantly certain that there is a mystery
underneath it all begging for an explanation.

On the way back home, he finds further evidence to support
that suspicion. Selva encounters the dead body of a twenty-five-
year-old with a mustache in a *solar* adjacent to his residence ("¡Un
cadáver!," 30). Over the next ten pages, readers learn that the
cadaver is Francisco Grijalba, a man whose business brought him
frequently from Málaga to Madrid, who had been staying at the
Hotel de Londres, and whose death—at approximately 11:30, coinciding with the period of Selva's aimless urban wandering, thus
prior to his entering the Teatro Apolo at 11:45—was prompted by
two puncture wounds, one straight into his heart (30–39). Murder
seems self-evident. Though Selva promptly contacts the police, he
is not ruled out as a suspect—not cleanly at least, and this blurring of lines is crucial. A subsequent search of his home turns up a
package containing the murder victim's possessions. Curiously, the
package is found in the area of an open window directly adjacent

to the *solar*. Nevertheless, a judge and the officer overseeing the investigation allow Selva to attempt to prove his innocence by identifying the real killers. This he does over the course of several days. His obsessive detection ultimately proves successful. He is cleared of having murdered Grijalba, but retains a sense of guilt nonetheless due to the way the investigation is concluded. The story's elevating dramatic tension is conveyed carefully in sequence by Pardo Bazán, all through Selva's first-person narrative focalization. In the end, the obsessed amateur detective uncovers that both Andrés Ariza and Julia Fernandina, a neighbor with ties to Málaga, carried out the crime together. They were motivated by the promise of the businessman's money. In retrospect, what Selva judged to be Ariza's strange behavior at the Apolo that first night had been carefully calculated to establish his presence at the theater as a possible alibi.

Emilia Pardo Bazán's choice of the detective story format is not casual. It has been well established and often rehearsed in literary criticism that she played a role in importing and modifying the detective form to Spain as part of a broader importation and modification of realism and naturalism from France.[12] The literary figure of the modern detective was itself the product of an urbanizing society. The increased population density, social complexity, and role of property value in city life led to the creation of the modern police force in early nineteenth-century Europe, as exemplified by the French Sûreté in 1812, Robert Peel's metropolitan police in 1829 London, and later the formation of Scotland Yard in 1842. Perhaps the most important author to play a role in popularizing the modern detective story was Edgar Allan Poe (1809–1849). Poe's influence in Europe was substantial, aided by translations carried out by Baudelaire in France, which led in due course to translations published in Spain. Contemporaries of Poe were simultaneously crafting the urban mystery tale during the 1840s: in France, for example, *Les Mystères de Paris* by Eugène Sue (1842–1843), and in Spain, *Los misterios de Madrid* by Juan Martínez Villergas (1844) and *Los misterios de Barcelona* by José Nicasio Milà de la Roca (1845). Poe's own definitive contribution to the genre included in equal parts romantic and realist literary sensibilities. He explored the darker sides of modern social life through themes of mystery, crime, and the supernatural, but also introduced the amateur detective of superior intellect, known as Dupin, who was not affiliated with a police agency. Such a superior detective figure used science, observation, reasoning, and deduction to unravel urban mysteries, yet he also had a darker side in that he was able to think like the criminal. The historical ground for this dualistic model of the detective figure—reflected to a degree also in the Sherlock Holmes stories of Arthur Conan Doyle—had its historical complement in the fact that a former criminal, Eugène François Vidocq, led the founding of the Parisian Sûreté.

In light of this legacy, Selva embodies the almost canonical ambiguity of the darker and more marginal detective figure. He is at once the product and symbol of literary realism and of literary romanticism. He is a careful observer of reality and quite attentive to the psychological motivations of individuals who operate within a defined social context. Simultaneously he is driven by feeling and intuitions, immersed in sensation and flights of imagination, and pushed forward by individual desires. This tension is fundamental throughout Pardo Bazán's telling, appearing in Selva's own self-aware thoughts and his amorous leanings toward Julia, as well as being reflected in the use of various literary strategies and symbols, from description of the urban context to careful wordings that reflect his partially mad, obsessive, state of mind. These aspects of Pardo Bazán's story can also be explained through reference to the late nineteenth- and early twentieth-century discourse on neurasthenia in Spain. Throughout, the implication is not merely that Selva is obsessed, but that he lives in a modern urban society where obsession is a defining element.

In the first pages of the story, after leaving the visit with Doctor Luz, Selva ostensibly rejects the logical thinking that is pertinent to science: "me fui convencido de que la ciencia, ante mi caso, se declaraba impotente" (26; I left convinced that science, with respect to my case, was impotent). Yet just a mere page later, he expresses a central tenet of scientific psychologism as he thinks through Ariza's behavior at the Teatro Apolo, "Los actos humanos siempre reconocen algún móvil, alguna causa" (27; Human actions always recognize a motivation, a cause). The oscillation of these two perspectives in Selva's mind is once again established almost immediately. He observes carefully Ariza's behavior, engaging in "el estudio de su alterada fisonomía" (27–28; the study of his altered physiognomy, but once out the door, his observations of reality cede ground to the fantasy of imagination. His thoughts are racing, mercurial, mutable: "mi fantasía volaba, y no acertando ya a sujetarla, iba arrastrado por ella" (28; my fantastic imagination flew, and not being able to restrain it, I was carried away); "cuando, media hora después salí del teatro para recogerme pacíficamente a mi domicilio, cambiaron de giro mis ideas" (28; When half an hour later I left the theater to return peacefully to my home, my ideas changed their direction). From this flight of fancy, his mind abruptly returns to a guiding scientific principle: "Desgraciadamente la mayor parte de las cosas tienen siempre explicación vulgar y prosaica, y la vida es un tejido de mallas flojas, mecánico, previsto: nada romanesco lo borda" (29; Unfortunately the greater part of things always has a vulgar and prosaic explanation, and life is a weave of loose, mechanical, predictable mesh: nothing Romanesque embroiders it).

As the story progresses, his faith in rationality, logic and scientific method never fully disappears. Selva continues to observe the facial expressions of those involved in the tale—not only Andrés but also the judge, the officer, and Julia, for example[13]—searching for clues of a psychological sort and considering the socially contextualized motivations behind statements he hears. Yet just as often, his mode of detection is that of the literary romantic rather than the literary realist. In these moments he does not use deductive reasoning so much as call on feeling, emotion, and intuition.

One such moment occurs when he intuits the victim was dressed by his assailants after he was killed—while talking to the judge, Selva even exclaims "¡Adivino!" (35; I guessed it!). Having guessed and now confirmed this fact, he is then able to reason and rule out the possibility the man was killed by common street assailants (35–36). Later he asserts the body was dropped at the *solar* by two people, perhaps a logical conclusion, and yet he goes further out on a limb with no evidence to assert with confidence that the crime was committed by a man and a woman (46). This guess once again turns out to be correct. On two other occasions, the narrative describes Selva's dreams, as if these were to provide him with the information he needs to resolve the case.[14] That the truth of a murder case would be accessible in the irrational world of dreams is at once an affirmation of the late nineteenth-century psychological investigation of the unconscious and of the social understanding of the value of blending of art and science (e.g., the description of Doctor Luz as both an artist and a scientist). Continuing his amateur investigation at the Hotel de Londres, Selva has another intuition: "Era como si la intuición confusa y vaga cristalizase de repente. . . . La inspiración debe de revelarse en tal manera, por una especie de dolor exaltado, al impulsar a los actos que no tienen que ver con la razón, con sus cálculos lentos y sus vuelos cortos" (51; It was as if a confused and vague intuition suddenly came into focus. . . . Inspiration reveals itself in this way, as a kind of exalted pain, prompting actions that have nothing to do with reason, with its slow calculations and its short flights). He then prompts the owner for confirmation of his intuition that Andrés Ariza was a friend of Grijalba's, an intuition "lanzada al azar, desde lo desconocido" (51; coming from out of nowhere, from the unknown). As it turns out, Ariza did, in fact, know the victim. The investigative method Selva follows is much different than the deductive reasoning preferred by a Holmes-type detective or even Poe's Dupin. For Selva—a character whose name denotes the tangled, twisted growth of the *selva* (jungle)—first comes the guess, the dream, the intuition, and only afterward comes the rational understanding contemporary readers traditionally associate with the literary detective form.

If the psychology of crime investigation is simultaneously both an art and a science, Selva's emphasis ultimately trends toward the art. Later in the story, art—specifically music—becomes the primary metaphor for his intuitive brainwork. As Selva considers Julia Fernandina's character and past, he narrates, "mi memoria se tendía como una cuerda de guitarra, cuando aprietan la clavija" (57–58; my memory stretched out like a guitar string, when they tighten the tuning peg), stating soon after, "en los rincones de la subsconsciencia seguía trabajando el recuerdo. El fonógrafo en que archivamos las impresiones pugnaba por emitir una; ansiaba hablar" (58; in the corners of my subconscious memory contin-ued to operate. The phonograph in which we archive our impres-sions fought to release one; it yearned to speak). Fittingly, given the investigative method that has guided Selva throughout, he solves the crime in a final act of imagination. He reflects, "¡Y todo lo había yo descubierto sólo con la fuerza de mi instinto, con el romanticismo de mi fantasía, combinando los sucesos reales, visi-bles, para encontrar la clave de los recónditos!" (61; And I had dis-covered everything only through the force of my instinct, by the romanticism of my imagination, combining real, visible, events in order to discover the key of those that were hidden!). He decides to act the detective, to put on a literal performance. He dons a dis-guise and assumes the character of someone from Málaga raised in London to gain Julia's confidence. His obsessive devotion to this role prompts her to reveal the hidden truth of her role in the events leading to Grijalba's murder (64, 69). Just before she reveals the entire story over the course of six pages, Selva triumphantly declares for readers, "mi adivinación había ido derecha a la ver-dad" (69; My guess had led straight to the truth).[15]

That the Teatro Apolo is introduced at the beginning of the story is part of Pardo Bazán's realistic approach to representing the life and habits of the accommodated class of Madrid. Her story notes for readers its location on "la calle de Alcalá," referencing Madrid and the Spanish capital's Ateneo explicitly.[16] Though these references might suffice to paint Selva's class status in broad strokes, the narrative also includes his own assessment that he considers himself an "hombre de inteligencia y cultura" (40: man of intelligence and culture) who "ocupa posición desahogada y tiene gustos de arte y literatura" (42–43; holds a leisurely social position and has artistic and literary tastes). As discussed below, this is an important part of the story's design, given the turn-of-the-century association between class and neurasthenia diagnoses.[17] The site of the Apolo is nonetheless also carefully chosen to emphasize for the reader the power of the artistic side of a modern binary. This theater is the urban anchor for the story because it is a world in which the power of imagination—of representation, disguise, sensation, emotion, trickery, flights of fancy, and aesthetics—holds more sway than scientific rationality.[18] Selva's obsession with the crime is, of course, really an obsession with his own imaginative faculties. Using religious allusion, he suggests that there are greater powers guiding his observations, thoughts and actions: "desde el primer momento, como guió a los Magos una estrella, me había guiado a mí la gota de sangre" (53; from the first moment, as the Wise Men were guided by a star, I have been guided by the drop of blood). Even beyond his self-aware forays into acting the theatrical part of the detective, he also recognizes the power that fictional prose has to spark the imaginations of others.[19]

Even if Selva leans toward art rather than science, the story is an exercise in duality or blurred categories. This quality manifests itself directly, as the protagonist-narrator is quite aware that he is playing two roles simultaneously: the detective and the possible culprit. When the package that contains the victims belongings is found in his home, Selva himself suggests taking fingerprints off the metal and leather facets of the contents inside. At this suggestion, he notes for readers that "el policía me miraba con expresión mixta de triunfo y de asombro" (44; the officer looked at me with a mixed expression of triumph and shock)—triumph because the suggestion is consistent with the logical reasoning driving his own side of the investigation, and shock because the package would seem to incriminate Selva. At one moment, Selva notes that the police officer "entreveía un mundo de ciencia policíaca y una escuela de arte a la europea, que le avergonzaba por no conocerlas" (47; was catching a glimpse of a world of police science and of a European-style art school, that he was ashamed to be unfamiliar with). The statement both reflects Selva's own superior self-image as a detective in development compared with the less-capable officer and asserts that art and science can each inform the other. Later, in the protagonist's interactions with Julia, he plays both the objective investigator and the enthralled love interest. Struggling with himself over which role to embrace, he encourages her to leave town, or else allows her to leave town, so that the blame for the murder may rest solely on Ariza's shoulders.[20] And because Andrés Ariza, confronted with the crime, steals Selva's pistol and apparently commits suicide, Selva is both detective and, in a certain sense at least, also complicit in this second death.[21] Certain matters are left unresolved, such as what happens to Julia at the end of the story, whether Selva continues with his romantic pursuit of her, and thus also—since he is the one narrating the story— just how complicit in Ariza's death he might in fact have been.

The notions of internal duality and moral ambiguity are central to Pardo Bazán's telling. She threads these staples of the modern detective story through the pages of "La gota de sangre" beyond the protagonist's own statements and characterization. The package thrown through the window of Selva's home takes on a symbolic quality. As the amateur detective explains, with recourse to testimony of his servants, it must have been thrown in to distract police from the real killers. The window itself is the architectural representation of the porous boundary between inner and outer, just as it is the symbolic representation of the thin line between vulnerability and safety, guilt and innocence, or Selva's presumed objectivity and his actual complicity. In cognitive metaphor, this is the very porosity that has allowed Selva to be so easily led to boredom and abulia in the first place, and subsequently to be so easily led, once again, back to spontaneous life through his obsessive concern with the murder case. It is a question of the willing transgression of boundaries. Once he is on the case, the role of obsessed detective has seemingly cured his boredom. Early on he states definitively, "solo el crimen podría conseguir interesarme" (40; only the crime could manage to interest me), and as the case evolves he reflects that "el caso es que desde ayer no me aburro . . ." (40; the thing is that since yesterday I haven't been bored . . .).[22]

That Pardo Bazán has Selva tentatively diagnose himself with neurasthenia on the first page of the story is not inconsequential. Physicians in Spain began writing about the condition in the 1890s, directly influenced by the work of French researchers working at Salpêtrière, writes Violeta Ruiz Cuenca (2020).[23] The term was introduced by American George Miller Beard as early as 1869, but popularized in his 1881 book *American Nervousness*, which was well received in European scientific circles (see Davis 2008, 26). The condition was said to be a widespread health issue, with some authors referring to neurasthenia as a pandemic or plague. Some thought it was "la enfermedad del siglo o la enfermedad de moda" (Bernabeu-Mestre et al. 2008, 91; the illness of the century or the fashionable illness).[24] In their study of neurasthenia in Spanish medicine from 1877–1936, Josep Bernabeu-Mestre and his scientific co-authors call it "una enfermedad de los tiempos modernos" (2008, 91; an illness of modern times). As A. Díaz de la Quintana y Sánchez Remón wrote in 1893, "todos somos neurasténicos en potencia, llevamos en nosotros mismos las predisposiciones nerviosas más temibles, y como la paja seca favorece el incendio, así una sola chispa, suelta al menor descuido, permite la descomunal hoguera que destruye en un instante la labor de muchos años" (qtd. in Bernabeu-Mestre et al. 2008, 92n34; we are all potential neurasthenics, we carry within us the most fearsome nervous predispositions, and as dry straw favors the fire, thus a tiny spark, released at the slightest carelessness, incites the bonfire that will in an instant destroy the work of many years).

The changing conditions of modern life were in fact themselves thought to be causing neurasthenia's prevalence (Bernabeu-Mestre et al. 2008, 91).[25] Spanish medical writings dating to the general period in which Pardo Bázan's 1911 story was published supposed a direct link between rising literacy levels and overstimulation of the nerves.[26] While even the working class was seen as vulnerable to the condition, it was often considered an illness of the aristocracy.[27] Presumedly, neurasthenia would have been a topic of conversation at the Ateneo that Emila Pardo Bazán herself attended in Madrid as a member of its most learned and accommodated classes. Nonetheless it was a vaguely delineated condition. Neurasthenia could present in widely divergent ways (Bernabeu-Mestre et al. 2008, 93). It is fitting that in the story, Selva expresses doubt about its applicability, and doctor Luz suggests his condition presents in "atonía" (atonia), in indifference, in the absence of amorous and vital passion (Pardo Bázan [1911] 2001, 25).

In *Obsession: A History*, Lennard Davis lists neurasthenia among "nineteenth-century mental disabilities" (2008, 90). A key premise of late nineteenth-century medicine was the idea that the nerve was a pathway for energy and emotions. As Davis writes, "If your nerves were overly excited you were nervous; if your nerves were weak or exhausted (as in nervous exhaustion) you were neurasthenic. This model of medicine, in turn, was a product of a new way of seeing the body based on a model of balance in which too much or too little of something caused a disease, while the mean or norm was considered good health" (26). Modern, nineteenth-century Europe was increasingly regularized, industrialized, mechanized, and urbanized. Neurasthenia was said to be caused by monotonous work, and yet its diagnosis and treatment also envisioned the human body as a machine that should be balanced, calibrated, tuned-up from time to time. Machines could break down and require repair, and now the human mind was conceived metaphorically as a machine that could also suffer a breakdown.

A standard prescription for neurasthenic breakdown would have been "ceasing mental activities and increasing exercise and fresh air" (Davis 2008, 89). In this respect, it is key to Pardo Bazán's story that Selva is only able to embark on the road toward recovery after he spends some time wandering the streets of Madrid. At one point, "como en todo el día no había hecho ejercicio y me sentía muy aburrido y de muy mal humor, paseé sin objeto por las calles, desentumeciéndome" (Pardo Bazán [1911] 2001, 39; since I had not exercised all day and I was feeling very bored and in a bad mood, I wandered aimlessly through the streets, loosening up). By his own admission, Selva belongs to a modern leisure class. His ability to enjoy the city streets in a leisurely fashion—as a use-value— connotes a certain class privilege, as does the description of his residential location: "vivía yo en una de esas calles nuevas, no urbanizadas ni edificadas enteramente" (29; I lived on one of those new streets, which had not been urbanized nor built-up fully). Readers of the story might more or less easily accept that the aimless wandering of Madrid's streets could conceivably induce a more restful mood for such a person. Yet Doctor Luz specifically recommends that Selva get more, rather than less, stimulation. After experiencing the fresh air of the city, the protagonist's mental activities increase abruptly and significantly.

The specific diagnosis of the fictional Selva character is of less interest than the ambiguous way his existence speaks to the role of the nerves in turn-of-the-century medicine and to the presence of obsession in modern urban life. One might view conditions like neurasthenia and monomania as points of entry into understanding the partial madness of modernity. Davis explores the two-forked role of obsession in modern life throughout his study. The neurasthenic, beaten down by modern life's regularity, craves unpredictability and spontaneity. It is unpredictability and spontaneity that the monomaniac fears and attempts to avoid or eliminate. In visualizing this distinction it helps to oppose the straight line (Linear City) to the zig-zag (aimless urban wandering). The routinized obsessive behaviors encouraged by industrialized modernity's emphasis on constant production cause a form of mental imbalance, but obsessive thinking and fixation are also the hallmark driver of scientific inquiry. A singular attention to detail becomes a strong value of modern society and comes to be reflected in the specialization of disciplinary knowledge in general as well as the regularization of city life (see Davis 2008, 83). A continual circuit is established, as Davis writes, such that

> the stress deriving from living this kind of increasingly specialized and regulated existence creates and necessitates a life of obsessive activity. This latter kind of obsession is seen both as fitting into modernity and paying the price for modernity. The nervous exhaustion that is the metaphor behind neurasthenia, the repetitive activity of the mind in mental breakdown, the fixed notions that characterize the "shattered" nerves and enervated brain of the nineteenth century are the products and results of modernity as a lived experience. (84)

It is a quintessentially modern problem: Selva's original malady is an imbalance that is corrected by indulging in another form of imbalance. Imbalance is both cause and remedy. Obsession is revealed as the ground that explains all of his circumstances and activity. From this perspective, it is Selva's protean conception of self, his ability to adopt different mindsets, that reveals what Davis has described as "the kind of obsessive disorder that we have seen as characterized by being partial" (89).

While in the end it may not be a convincing presentation of a specifically neurasthenic diagnosis—considered as diagnostically separate from what have come to be recognized as a slate of other mood disorders—Pardo Bazán's story succeeds masterfully at presenting Selva's disorder as "being partial." He both is and is not ruled out as a suspect. He is a singularly focused investigator, seeking for the facts of the case to line up cleanly, yet he is bored by too much predictability. His method is spontaneity itself. He is driven forward by whim, coincidence, dreams, intuitions. The partial state of the story's protagonist is reflected in marked vocabulary choices toward the end of the story that employ "semi-" as a prefix. As an amateur detective he has "la extraña facultad de semiadivinación" (77; the strange faculty of semidivination), and the city at night is defined by "la semioscuridad de la calle" (79; the semidarkness of the street).[28]

Selva's distaste for that which is "vulgar and prosaic" (read: predictable) in modern life is at once a rejection of the subjugated role to which the passions have been relegated in an overly regularized and planned urban life. If logical thinking, such as that embodied by Doctor Luz, has eliminated the thrill of enigma from daily life, then it is the duty of the individual to rekindle the spark of imagination. It is here where Pardo Bazán's unrelenting literary romanticism—that is, the fact that she "peca al mezclar el puro azar con las reglas de la lógica" (Manera 2001, 18; sins by mixing pure chance with the rules of logic) in her invocation of the detective form—expresses the partial state of the modern urbanite.[29] Selva's rejection of logic is partial, just as Pardo Bazán's rejection of the literary values of realism is partial. In the same way, the modern obsessive urbanite is driven to partial madness, to use Davis's terms, aware of the mind's drift but unable or unwilling to stop it.

Visual Distortions of Science in Santiago Ramón y Cajal's "El pesimista corregido"

Nerves are also at the center of "El pesimista corregido" (1905), by Santiago Ramón y Cajal (1852–1934), yet this story's connection with science is more robust. In the figure of Cajal the neurohistologist, Spain has not merely a scientist of the first order, but also a literary visionary. A practicing scientist, Cajal worked at the University of Valencia in 1883 as an anatomist, at the University of Barcelona in 1887 as a histologist, and at the University of Madrid in 1892 as both histologist and anatomical pathologist. His fame led to his role as president of the Junta para Ampliación de Estudios e Investigaciones Científicas (Board for the Expansion of Scientific Studies and Research), which had been inspired by the famed Institución Libre de Enseñanza (Fernández Santarén, García Barreno, and Sánchez Ron 2006, 76–80; Fraser 2008, 9). In addition to being recognized with multiple awards—he received the Moscow Prize in 1900 and the Helmholtz Gold Medal in 1904—he was appointed to the Spanish Royal Academy in 1905, and in 1906 was awarded the Nobel Prize in Physiology or Medicine, which he shared with the Italian anatomist Camillo Golgi. Against the generally accepted notion that neurons had reticular connections, by around 1888 Ramón y Cajal had managed to establish that each neuron was independent from the others.

Relegated to the status of synecdoche for the nation and symbol of the potential triumph of the scientific spirit, Ramón y Cajal, the investigator, has always attracted more attention than Ramón y Cajal, the artist. Nevertheless, Helene Tzitsikas asserts that "Cajal tiene el doble honor de ser un precursor científico y literario de la Generación del 98" (1988, 9; Cajal has the double honor of being a scientific and literary precursor of the Generation of 98), concluding that "no es Cajal solamente un maestro de generaciones científicas, es un maestro de generaciones humanistas" (9; Cajal is not only a teacher of generations of scientists, he is a teacher of generations of humanists). The histologist possessed a well-developed extra-scientific creative capacity that, during the course of his lifetime, pushed him to excel in various artistic fields. It is well known that painting was his first love as a child, and that his father nonetheless wanted him to become a doctor. He was also a photographer and an author of fiction—the latter interest yielding several short stories and even a novel that is presumed lost.

The publication of the volume *Cuentos de vacaciones* (Vacation stories)—a collection of five of the twelve stories he wrote during 1885 and 1886 during a stay in Turia—in particular exemplifies Ramón y Cajal's literary spirit (Ramón y Cajal [1905] 1999, 15; Durán Muñoz and Burón 1960, 142; O'Connor 1985, 100). These stories infuse the world of science with his unique imagination and simultaneously advance a scientific vision of everyday life by, for example, describing a kiss at the molecular scale and depicting in detail the microbes that inhabit the city of Madrid.[30]

Cajal's simultaneous interest in both science and art is rooted in his fundamentally visual personality—this being his own description (see Laín Entralgo 1957, 296; Otis 1999, 83–84). Moreover, critics such as García Durán Muñoz and Francisco Alonso Burón have emphasized the histological author's visual sensibility and commented in their critical biography *Ramón y Cajal* that, "sin lugar a dudas, puede clasificársele como un visual en su manifestación artística. Captaba con facilidad y sentía fuertemente aquello que llegaba a sus sentidos por medio de la visión; en cambio, no apreciaba ni le emocionaba lo que a él llegase por el oído. No fue, por tanto, aficionado a la música, y mucho menos a la oratoria" (1960, 349; Without a doubt, he can be classified as a visual person in his artistic manifestation. He grasped easily and felt strongly that which arrived to his senses through vision; by contrast, he neither appreciated nor was he emotionally impacted by that which might have arrived to him via hearing. He was not, thus, drawn to music, and much less to oratory). Clearly this obsession with vision is what made it possible for him to spend so many intense hours seated in front of a microscope in a laboratory and, likewise, working on the numerous lithographic prints that he created specifically to accompany the scientific articles he published between 1880 and 1890 (Durán Muñoz and Burón 1960, 120). From this perspective, his decision to specialize in histology was not made casually, "for histology probably makes greater use of and depends more on illustration than any other branch of medicine" (Hellman 2001,

98–99). Given the present emphasis on his visual sensibility, it is also appropriate to highlight that one of his notable scientific contributions involved the retinas of various animals (*La rétine des vertébrés*, The retina of vertebrates, originally published in the Belgian *La Cellule* in 1892). His book *Fotografía de los colores* (1912, Color photography) remains as testament to the passion he had felt for photographic representation since his childhood.

If his interest in all things visual influenced his decision to become a histologist and to accompany his professional publications with his own images, the visual world of his profession also influenced his literary prose. Ramón y Cajal worked extensively with microscopes under the tutelage of the famous Aureliano Maestre de San Juan in Madrid around 1877 and had constructed a laboratory of his own in his residence (Durán Muñoz and Burón 1960, 99). Seen in light of what was undoubtedly a transformative experience for him, it is not surprising that one of the *Cuentos de vacaciones* takes place in Madrid and even describes a scientific researcher who undergoes a radical change in his way of seeing things—in both the literal and figurative senses. In "El pesimista corregido," we are introduced to Juan Fernández, "doctor joven, de veintiocho años, serio, estudioso, no exento de talento, pero harto pesimista y con ribetes de misántropo" (165; young doctor, twenty-eight years of age, studious, not lacking talent, but fully pessimistic and with a misanthropic streak). After experiencing an ocular distortion of long duration that obliges him to see as if through a microscope, in the end, his normal vision is restored and his pessimism remains noticeably attenuated.

To read "El pesimista corregido" from an urban perspective suggests a way of reconciling scientific discourse with the great changes affecting nineteenth-century Spanish society. Cajal's story not only marks a transitional moment in the development of modern science, it also memorializes a key moment in the formation of a decidedly urbanized Spanish consciousness. To emphasize the author's visual sensibility in this context permits a synthesis

of scientific, literary, and urban discourses with the goal of less-
ening the distance between modern urbanites who more than
ever lived alienated from one another. In fact, Laura Otis points
out that upon moving to Madrid in 1892, Ramón y Cajal elected
to install himself in the working-class neighborhood of Cuatro
Caminos, one of the concrete references that figure in his story
titled "El pesimista corregido" (2001, xvii). As Antonio Lafuente
and Tiago Saraiva document in their article "The Urban Scale of
Science and the Enlargement of Madrid (1851–1936)," during the
second half of the nineteenth century, new attitudes on modern
science reshaped both the infrastructure and the architectonic
surface of the city. In effect, the expansion of Madrid was carried
out in parallel to the expansion of science (2004, 533, 539). As
Lafuente and Saraiva point out—and as can be verified upon reading Cerdà's *Teoría general de la urbanización* (1867)—nineteenth-
century miasmic theories that sustained the idea of the city as
a sick being invited a technical approach to the city based on a
predominantly clinical view.

Given that both are described as misanthropes, the fictional
protagonist Juan Fernández is a possible literary representation
of Cajal himself.[31] Fernández, readers are informed, is a pessimistic doctor who reads the works of Schopenhauer, Hartmann,
Nietzsche, and Gracián (165). Having neither father nor mother,
and in the process of recovering from typhoid, he has recently lost
his girlfriend, Elvira, and has failed to obtain a professorship at
the University of Madrid (166–67). Regarding the depressed and
alienated state in which Juan finds himself, the narrator writes
that "hacia la época en que le enfocamos se habían recrudecido
en nuestro héroe el asco de la vida y el despego a la sociedad" (165;
around the time with which we are concerned a disgust with life
and detachment from society had intensified in our hero). Even
more depressing for our protagonist is his understanding of the
human body as a poor vehicle through which to truly understand
the rigors of science.[32] Part of the problem, the narration suggests,

has to do with his deterministic scientific view of the world: "La humanidad," he says, "surgida de la muerte, en la muerte ha de parar. Nos lo prueban con sus férreas fórmulas la mecánica del cosmos y las ineluctables leyes de la entropía" (171; Humanity, having arisen from death, must return to death. With their ironclad formulas, the mechanics of the cosmos and the ineluctable laws of entropy prove it). Facing a world replete with "insidiosas y crueles bacterias patógenas" (172; insidious and cruel bacterial pathogens), Juan pleads with the "motor del universo" (172; motor of the universe): "¡Si al menos, a guisa de compensión, nos hubieras otorgado sentidos e inteligencia poderosos a evitar tamaños peligrosos! . . . ¡Si para preservarlos de tales riesgos contáramos con acuidad visual suficiente a percibir los gérmenes virulentos" (173; If at least, by way of compensation, you had given us senses and intelligence powerful enough to avoid dangerous specks! . . . If as a way of protecting against such risks we possessed visual acuity sufficient to perceive the virulent germs). His wish is soon granted.

One night the so-called "numen de la ciencia" (175; spirit of science) comes to visit Juan in his residence. As the narration explains, holding true to the dualistic Cajalian emphasis on both art and science, the "numen" has various names: "llámame el filósofo, *intuición*; el científico, *casualidad feliz*; el artista, *inspiración*; el mercader y el político, *fortuna*" (175; by the philosopher I am called *intuition*; by the scientist, *happy coincidence*; by the artist, *inspiration*; by the merchant and the politician, *fortune*). This apparition induces in Juan a "prodigiosa transformación" (184; prodigious transformation) programmed to last a full year: "desde mañana, y en cuanto tus ojos se abran a la luz, contemplarás los objetos, a la distancia de la visión distinta, como si estuvieran dos mil veces amplificados" (184; starting tomorrow, as soon as your eyes open to the light, you will see objects at the distance of a distinct vision, as if they were magnified two thousand times). Upon waking, "sus ojos se habían convertido en microscopios" (185; his eyes had been converted into microscopes)—and Ramón y Cajal strives to give the reader a sense of Juan's experiences by way of extensive detailed descriptions regarding, for example, "corpúsculas variables de dimensión y color" (184; corpuscles of variable size and color). Throughout the process, Ramón y Cajal's narrator necessarily relies on the precise terminology of the scientist. Page after page, the narration distorts Juan's daily experience of the world, harnessing a microscopic view to describe his hands, his bed, the light of his bedroom, and even "el torbellino de la calle de Alcalá" (185; the whirlwind of Alcalá street) and "las aceras, los edificios, los árboles y las personas" (188; the sidewalks, the buildings, the trees and the people). "En vez de colores uniformes, jugosos, fundidos por suaves transiciones; en lugar de superficies tersas y unidas, mostraban doquier los objetos mosaicos o conglomerados de partículas coloreadas y agregados de filamentos y células. Masas grises, y aun blancas, a la vista ordinaria, exhibían granizadas de motas y manchas de color chillón que nadie hubiera sospechado (188–89; Instead of stark, uniform colors, blendings of smooth transitions; in place of undifferentiated and coherent surfaces, the objects all around him displayed mosaics or conglomerates of colored particles and aggregates of filaments and cells. Masses that were grey, or even white, to the ordinary eye, exhibited densely concentrated specks and stains of shocking color that no one would have suspected).

As Ramón y Cajal himself had done, Juan constructs "un laboratorio micrográfico y bacteriológico" (210; a micrographic and bacteriological laboratory) in his house where his amplified vision aids him in making all kinds of discoveries. He also spends much time outside of the house traversing the spaces of the city. Among other emblematic places of Madrid, our urban stroller visits not only the street of Alcalá but also the neighborhood of Cuatro Caminos, la Puerta del Sol, el Prado, the Neptune fountain, el Teatro Real, and the Observatorio Astronómico (192, 194, 202, 210). Upon reaching Puerta del Sol, Juan voices the miasmic theory, declaring that the area is a "respiradero de todos los vahos humanos y cloaca máxima de los detritus aéreos de la villa y corte" (192; filter for all the human vapors and great sewer for the aerial detritus of the city). Although he is similarly out of place in the city's outskirts, it is in "el tráfago y el estrépito de la ciudad" (the hustle and bustle of the city) where he experiences greater torture, "a causa de la extrema impureza del ambiente" (208; due to the extreme impurity of the environment).

For this reason, it is in Madrid's central green lung, the Retiro Park, that he feels more at home. Harnessing a tradition that has imagined the park as a recreational green space promising escape from worldly noise,[33] the Retiro serves him as a calm oasis where Juan can study the bacteriological life of the city, which he can now perceive in great visual detail. The distortion of his microscopic vision evokes not only the paradigmatic rupture wrought of scientific potential but also the continuous flow of urban life itself. Georg Simmel would soon characterize the life of the city in chaotic terms in a classic early twentieth-century essay titled "The Metropolis and Mental Life," and in Juan we have an archetypical representation of the figure of the modern urbanite. The basis of modern urban existence, according to Simmel, consists precisely of "the *intensification of nervous stimulation* which results from the swift and uninterrupted change of outer and inner stimuli" (2000, 149, emphasis in original). He emphasizes "the rapid crowding of changing images, the sharp discontinuity in the grasp of a single glance, and the unexpectedness of onrushing impressions," saying that "these are the psychological conditions which the metropolis creates" (150). In "El pesimista corregido," although Juan's fictional ocular change may have been induced by a spirit, the result of his visual nervous intensification is easily compared to Simmel's description of the effects brought on by urban changes. It should come as no surprise that the Retiro Park offers Juan a unique place in which to relax and separate himself from these shifts in nineteenth-century urban consciousness. The Retiro is invoked precisely in this sense as a site separated from the characteristic overstimulation of the city, a place reserved for tranquil and serene contemplation. One must keep in mind the advice that circulated at the time for mood disorders: "entre las medidas higiénicas y profilácticas se recomendaban el reposo combinado con un ejercicio moderado, alejar a los pacientes de actividades que comportasen una actividad intelectual importante, y enviar a los enfermos urbanos a 'rusticar'" (Bernabeu-Mestre et al. 2008, 99; hygienic and prophylactic measures recommended rest combined with moderate exercise, keeping patients away from activities that involved significant intellectual activity, and sending ill urban dwellers to the countryside). Parks famously promised that integration of nature in the city that would be beneficial for those needing a release from the stressors of urban life.[34]

As emphasized by the "numen de la ciencia" who visits Juan, setting the story's narrative action in motion, the visual perspective offered by the microscope has its limitations: "Mal haríais, sin embargo, en vanagloriaros de tan grosero instrumento. Juguete harto imperfecto todavía, a su capacidad resolutiva escapan millones de vidas infinitesimales, ultramicroscópicas: las bacterias de las bacterias" (182; You would not be wise, however, to boast of such a crude instrument. It is still but a quite imperfect toy, and from its capacity for magnification there escape millions of infinitesimal ultramicroscopic lives: the bacteria of bacteria). In Juan's experience, just as in Cajal's experience as a practicing histologist, it is sensibility that leads one toward the discovery of a world that is much wider that the one we normally perceive, whether visually or conceptually. In her own analysis of the story, Otis writes that Juan's "tour of the city reveals that most boundaries and hence identities are created by society, forcibly imposed on a richer and more complex biological reality" (1999, 83). Ramón y Cajal's real triumph should be seen as the cultivation of this very attitude. The histologist of flesh and bone possesses something that his protagonist lacks—the sensibility of the artist.

The title of the story itself points toward the risk of accepting a scientific doctrine unquestioningly, and its moral—if the story can be said to have one—is that one should not put all one's faith in science alone. The consequences of the exclusive mania for all things scientific are that Juan has become someone who Durán Muñoz and Burón describe, characterizing not Juan but rather Ramón y Cajal himself, as "algo misántropo y nada aficionado al trato social" (1960, 79; somewhat of a misanthrope and not at all fond of social interaction). Juan's lesson hinges on finding an equilibrium in affirming the border of his own organism while at the same time seeking out and establishing connections with others. Ramón y Cajal's Nobel-worthy scientific discovery—which he would divulge around 1888, only a few years after having originally written "El pesimista corregido"—speaks to this very same question.

On one hand, Ramón y Cajal would prove that neurons are independent entities and not part of a neuron net as asserted by the reticular theory: "for Cajal, the fundamental characteristic of every cell and every human being was its individuality, made possible by the membrane that separated one living unit from the next" (Otis 1999, 71). Juan's pessimistic state at the beginning of the story represents the triumph of an alienated individuality to the exclusion of other influences and by extension the myopia of a strictly scientific perspective. On the other hand, as Otis also points out, individualism was not the only thing that captured Ramón y Cajal's attention in the laboratory:

> Even though the identity of the cell depended on the distinction between inside and outside, the very function and existence of neurons depended on outside influences: on inputs from other cells and from the environment. . . . Cajal conceived of life and mental activity as interactions among autonomous units. Neurons and individuals influenced one another yet retained their identities as distinct beings. (73)

Cajal knew very well that the existence of a hard border between cells did not in any way preclude the interconnection of neurons.

In hindsight, informed by the discovery that won Ramón y Cajal the Nobel Prize, "El pesimista corregido" demonstrates a similar focus on the need to reconcile the individual with his or her urban environment. Juan's struggle is precisely to find another mode of appreciating life that might constitute a complement to rational, logical, scientific thought, as represented in the story by microscopic observation.

Cajal is still regarded as a great figure in Spanish science today not only because he was awarded the Nobel Prize but also because his work suggested a number of new directions in scientific research (Andres Barquin 2001, 13; Delgado García 2006; Lafuente and Saraiva 2004, 561; López-Muñoz, Boya, and Alamo 2006, 391). For example, Hamburger has noted, "Many of Cajal's original ideas have been confirmed by modern developmental neurobiology" (1991, ix), and other critics detail his influence on studies regarding the structure and function of the brain, neural plasticity, and even the use of what are called random dot stereograms (see Bergua and Skrandies 2000, 69; DeFelipe 2002, 481; Ramón y Cajal 1901, 41; Stahnisch and Nitsch 2002, 589). The impressive visual image prints of microscopic views produced by the neurohistologist remain as another part of his gift to the world of contemporary science, and his name has been memorialized in the Escala de Control de los Impulsos Ramos y Cajal, a scale used for categorizing the control of impulses—notably established by a group of three investigators, two of whom work for the Ramón y Cajal Hospital in Madrid (Boyde 1992, 246; Ramos Brieva, Gutiérrez-Zotes, and Sáiz Ruiz 2002, 160; Sotelo 2003, 74).

In Cajal's story, a singular and transformative escape from the monotony of "regulated" urban life only becomes possible due to the fortuitous convergence of two conditions. One is spatial, or environmental, and the other is cognitive, or perceptual. The visual distortion visited upon Juan by the spirit of science lasts an entire year, but it is the moment he experiences in Retiro Park that serves as a catalyst for his true transformation.

Acknowledging the link between obsession and urban aesthetics suggests a different interpretation of "El pesimista corregido" than might be produced by, let us call it a "standard" disability reading. Such a reading would emphasize, correctly of course, that the notion of narrative prosthesis theorized by David T. Mitchell and Sharon L. Snyder is undoubtedly in play throughout. The ocular disability of the story is here conceived in prose as an extended period of visual distortion. The narrative arc corresponds with the model put forth by Mitchell and Snyder in their canonical and valuable text; disability is represented "as a problem in need of a solution" (2000, 47). The character returns from his liminal experience of debility to fully appreciate his life circumstances. Disability has been a vehicle designed to affirm, rather than contest, the normative ableism of society. In terms of the turn-of-the-century scientific understanding in Spain of vaguely defined mood disorders such as neurasthenia, the story follows a medical model. Juan is given a diagnosis in the very title of the story itself, he receives a treatment, and he recovers from the malady, coming to take on a much more normative role in society. In mood, he is rejuvenated and no longer pessimistic. In terms of social norms, he is now married, and no longer bears the social stigma of the aloof bachelor. From this perspective of narrative emplotment there is very little to say. Yet from a perspective interested in urban aesthetics, the story confirms without a doubt the social, literary, scientific, and artistic ambiguity surrounding disability that Tobin Siebers signaled in visual art. These perspectives of course can, do, and must coexist. Their dissonance is evidence of the very friction caused by the social construction, stigmatization, and aestheticization of disability.

It is essential to attend to the role of scientific obsession in the construction of the story. Readers must remember that it is written by a scientist obsessed with the visual field, someone who was—according to the typology established by Davis—obsessed with the new forms of vision rendered possible with the microscope.

Thus while there is a sense in which Juan's microscopic visual distortion is a metaphor for disability, it is not solely a literary metaphor to stoke the imagination of the reader. It is simultaneously a rendering of a specific scientific reality understood by Cajal to have enormous social value. While one might say it is fictionalized, it is not entirely fictional. Cajal's use of scientific vocabulary for describing what he has seen under the microscope in his own laboratory serves to bridge the diegesis with the embodied social reality of the reader. Though the visual experience indeed ultimately comes to an end, it has provided him not with a mere momentary escape but rather with an ongoing awareness and a significantly greater knowledge of the natural world and a greater respect for its diversity of forms. The visual distortion is not a problem to be solved as much as an experience that shifts the protagonist's own consciousness and enriches his understanding. Due to the scientific encoding of the experience and its overlap with the author's own scientific obsessions, as well as the nature of the transformed state and the impossibility of returning to it, Juan is not in any real sense restored, but rather he is pushed to recognize the limitations of his normative vision. This is true both literally in terms of what the naked eye can perceive, and metaphorically in terms of what might be called the arbitrariness of social expectation.

Mitchell and Snyder appropriately take to task those stories that "rely on the potency of disability as a symbolic figure" but that "rarely take up disability as an experience of social or political dimensions" (2000, 48). While considering disability as a construction in the realm of urban aesthetics—thus not solely as an attribute of what the authors of *Narrative Prosthesis* call "characters constructed as disabled" (Mitchell and Snyder 2000, 50)—might seem to move us away from corporeal difference, in this case it moves us closer to understanding how obsession, understood within a wider realm of cognitive difference, demonstrates social value. Harnessed by scientists like Cajal, fixation and obsessive rumination have led to new knowledge of the natural world.

Keeping in mind the notion of disablist hearing developed by Joseph Straus, one might entertain the connection of Juan's experience with disablist seeing. Such a nonnormative sight is valuable because it defies, challenges, and undermines the clean lines and precision of an overregularized, monotonous, mechanized, and urbanized modern society. As an aesthetic, Siebers theorized, disability does precisely this: it disrupts and restores, it provides meaning and lends significance to normative society, in the process of becoming a modern aesthetic value, albeit one unrecognized and unacknowledged as such. Modern society makes use of the aesthetic of disability without attribution or awareness at the same time that it ignores the social reality of disability. But the construction of disability is there, nonetheless, present in the city, present in literature, in art, in science, made manifest as obsession.

In her book *Monomania: The Flight from Everyday Life in Literature and Art* (2005), Marina van Zuylen looks at obsession and its influence on nineteenth and twentieth-century creative production. As Lennard Davis does later in *Obsession* (2008), she turns to the work of pioneers like Esquirol and Etienne-Jean Georget. Her definition of the monomaniac, a term that Lennard Davis also invokes frequently in his own study, is quite relevant:

These "neurotic" characters have such a deep fear of intimacy, of reciprocity, that they compulsively resort to the impersonal, as though it will purge them of their selfhood, evacuating whatever might place them in dialogue with others. The weight of a life lived "on its own," that is, following its own course rather than a pre-structured pattern, is intolerable to the monomaniac. Flaubert's obsessive return to the imagery of the straight line, the anti-arabesque, is symptomatic of this. So is the intensely structured quality of Mondrian's paintings, designed, in Bonnefoy's words, "to break with the existential content of visual perceptions." Whatever appears on the surface of the painting must have nothing to do with the individual's connection to experience. Art must defeat personal relationships and help "time to settle, like an impurity that has been contained, in the alembic of transparence." (2005, 6)

Van Zuylen writes that Piet Mondrian found nature to be disgusting, that he was aesthetically "allergic" to it, and that he "he chose to strike out against the real with the absolutism of his vertical and horizontal lines" (1). The abstract painter is a fitting reference on the first page of a monograph devoted to "the obsessive strategies people use to keep the arbitrary out of their lives; . . . the fanaticism and intolerance linked to their ideas of perfection and permanence" (1). These are people who "do everything in their power to stabilize their universes and expel indeterminacy from their worlds" (1). It is impossible to read her book and not think of urban planners as monomaniacs in this very same sense.

From such a point of view, Arturo Soria y Mata's linear city becomes a paradigmatic representation of the straight line's triumph over urban indeterminacy. Ildefons Cerdà's drive to perfect the modern city is an attempt to bring stability to an urban realm where spontaneity and the arbitrary have long prospered—even, for example, in the very structure of the tangled web of streets in the city's medieval core. While the modern European city was planned—in part and ostensibly—to regulate movement, maximize trade, and even control unrest, at the same time it was a reaction against those values—the unpredictable, arbitrary, and spontaneous elements of life—that persisted even despite the rise of industrialization, or rather, those values that acquired a new significance as the world of leisure and the world of production began to pull apart from one another in modern times (see Lefebvre 1991). Van Zuylen herself is attentive to the work of Lefebvre when she writes of Pierre Janet (1859–1947) that "Janet is one of the great forerunners of our contemporary fascination with the poetics of the everyday; he would have been the first to agree with Henri Lefebvre who urged his readers to seek 'a philosophical inventory

and analysis of everyday life that will expose its ambiguities—
its baseness and exuberance, its poverty and fruitfulness—and
by these unorthodox means release the creative energies that are
an integral part of it'" (2005, 1).[35] Janet's work shows how modern urbanites respond with obsession and mania to the fact that
"habit is so deadening" (22). As van Zuylen explains, an "allergy
to the unpredictable" is what drives people toward "a cruel and
codified life" (34).

Modern urban planning as a social activity can thus be understood as a collective project of building the normate. The regularization of streets and blocks is at once an aesthetic and practical regularization of human activity, the subordination of human activity
to the crude contours of industrialized production, the reduction
of human expression to a strict linearity. Monomaniacs are driven
by the repetition of a single idea, a repeated form, or a reduced set
of variables. They ignore context and with it nuance, competing
understandings, and differing sets of variables, and seek to min-
imize, plan, shape, or regulate spontaneous expressions, alternative uses, and the unpredictable in social life. It is worthwhile to
ask why urban planners of the nineteenth century—or those of
our own, for that matter—who impose an infrastructure, a grid, a
system, with insufficient regard for the perspectives of those living in the city, are not themselves considered obsessed thinkers?

The truth is, as van Zuylen's arguments show, there are two
forms of obsession in play in the modern era. They are both related
to the same set of social circumstances. The values underlying the
rigidity and certainty of modern urban planning can be seen as
a response to the fear of ambiguity, of wandering, of the unpredictable. Dreading uncertainty, the urban plan provides a crushing order. Reciprocally, the urbanite—faced with this crushing
order and unambiguous certainty—then responds with play and
ambiguity, the freedom of use-value. There is an obsession that
restricts and an obsession that opens up. One form of obsession

is a closed, hard shell imposed from above, while the other is a shifting and changing thing, lived below as a form of resistance.[36] On one side is the obsession of Arturo Soria y Mata, whose linear city is so easily dismissed as the geometrical whim of a privileged bourgeois planning class Lefebvre despised, or that of Piet Mondrian, whose linear aesthetics reveal his inability to confront the natural world. On the other is the creative zig-zag of Baudelaire's flâneur, of Selva's vitalist and meandering investigation, and the wonder of Cajal's scientist protagonist upon perceiving the infinite variety and diversity of natural forms.

There are fundamental similarities between Emilia Pardo Bazán's "La gota de sangre" and Santiago Ramón y Cajal's "El pesimista corregido." Both feature someone whose senses have been dulled by drudgery, by boredom, by a depressive episode that is imprecisely defined. In Pardo Bazán's story, the condition of neurasthenia—itself a confused category during the time in which she was writing—is corrected via a life-restorative experience that involves an intense and exploratory journey through Madrid's streets. In Cajal's, the urban is coded as a drab and uninspiring environment defined by drudgery in opposition to the freedom of thought that is associated with the countryside and green spaces in the modern city. Visual observation is a key component of both stories. They each dramatize fixity as a hallmark element of modern urban life, and spontaneity as its hallmark solution. Both stories present the opposite of someone like Mondrian who flees from spontaneity. They each show, in their own way, how spontaneity, change, the fleeting, the ephemeral, rather than the predictable and solid, the linear, the unchanging, are valued in urban modernity. In each case, the protagonist's obsession is viewed through a clinical lens and presented as a form of cognitive or perceptual difference, yet at the same time it is a catalyst for positive change. Disability is present as an aesthetic element, but not necessarily as a prosthesis in the way Mitchell and Synder had considered it. In each case,

the urban environment is reclaimed as a site of spontaneous play—
whether that is the role-play of the amateur detective or the ser-
endipitous experimentation of a visionary scientist—and thus as
a use-value rather than a restrictive, regularized plan determined
by a privileged planning class.

Chapter 4
Shattering Lisbon: Destabilization and Drudgery

In 1755, Lisbon suffered an earthquake that devastated the Baixa, its central lower-city area, and left an imprint on the city's collective imaginary. From an urban planning perspective, this event is crucial. The earthquake is estimated to have been equivalent to a magnitude of 9.0 on the Richter scale. Along with the tsunami and fires that followed it, the quake caused massive destruction. This event prompted a complete redesign and reconstruction of the central Baixa area, which was led by Sebastião José de Carvalho e Melo (1699–1782). Commonly known as the Marquês de

Pombal, Carvalho e Melo served under José I of Portugal and was a statesman with a reputation for being strict, but not a trained architect or planner. The architects he recruited to rebuild the Baixa Pombalina de Lisboa used a novel wooden-cage design intended to make the area's foundational structures more flexible and thus resilient to future recurrence of earthquakes. The rebuilt Baixa area also stood out for being a rectilinear grid. This strict form was imposed on what had previously been a more organic street pattern, thus anticipating the hallmark aesthetic geometricality of modern planning's contemporary legacy.

The Marquês de Pombal's response to the earthquake reshaped Lisbon through its monumental design, open urban spaces, and a regularized street pattern. By the nineteenth century, the so-called Pombaline street had emerged as a key element of the area's modernizing, bourgeois urban lifestyle. While Fernando Pessoa (1888–1935) captured the city's enduring tributes to the earth-quake in an English-language travel guide titled *Lisbon: What the Tourist Should See* (2008), he is most remembered for his complex collection of prose fragments published posthumously as *Livro do Desassossego* (1982; *The Book of Disquiet* [2017]). Therein, the thoughts of the author's narrators turn obsessively toward the hall-mark urban and architectural aesthetics of Lisbon's Baixa. With this port-adjacent area now increasingly dedicated to commerce and luxury, it becomes almost a self-contained segment of the city for Pessoa's fictional bookkeeper-narrator. Public and private spheres of urban life overlap for the bourgeois resident of the new Baixa. The regularization and drudgery of modern urban living is insistently referenced in the book in a variety of ways: repetitive accounting work that relies on obsessive attention to numerical tabulation as well as excessively repetitive walks, to work and back home again, along a single Pombaline block. The urban environ-ment itself becomes intertwined with details from what might seem to be the author's autobiography and ultimately comes to reflect, resonate with, and substitute for his interior mood and conflicts.

Pessoa himself was a compulsive writer, and the narrators he employs in this work share this trait. Their observations on everyday urban life prove to be obsessively repetitive; they are aware of their compulsion to write endlessly and yet unable to stop. Their cognition is a flight of imagination that never aims for a conclusion, but instead remains fixated on the sights, sounds, and movements of life in the Baixa. While the repetitive urban movements of Pessoa's narrators do not quite fit the aimless wandering of the flâneur, this figure is a clear point of reference. Pessoa's mention of fellow Portuguese poet Cesário Verde (1855–1886) prompts a comparison in thematic and narrative terms. Verde, who was considered to be a Portuguese Baudelaire, also lived in and wrote about Lisbon. Each in their own way, Pessoa and Verde dedicate themselves to a poetic re-creation of Lisbon's obsessive urban modernity.

Rebuilding the Baixa after the 1755 Earthquake: The Pombaline Street

One of the places readers can look for Pessoa's thoughts on the city he called home is a slim volume titled *Lisbon: What the Tourist Should See*. Discovered posthumously, its contents were originally written in English during the 1920s. This is precisely the period of time that separates the found pages that would become the first and second parts of Pessoa's *Book of Disquiet*, which were written in the 1910s and the 1930s, respectively.

Although the author begins his tourist guide with a prose flourish, by noting the "seven hills [over which] the vast irregular and many-coloured mass of houses that constitute Lisbon is scattered" (2008, 11), this slim volume is hardly a literary endeavor. Travel guides arguably became a mass genre in the nineteenth century—as they became associated with the Baedeker rail-guide tradition—and Pessoa competently delivers on the genre's promise. He anticipates the imagined traveler's practical concerns—for instance, how traffic flows, how to access the train, or where one might go after disembarking at the city's port. At one point he mentions that a certain building has an elevator—the Baixa has become modern, indeed! All is imagined as a trip taken in a motor-car. Many paragraphs begin with a phrase intended to buttress the arc of this ongoing narrative: "Our motor car now comes back again through the Avenida da Republica . . ." (27), "We get back into our car . . ." (32), "Our car now crosses . . ." (36), "Our car now goes on . . ." (42), "Our car speeds on . . ." (60), "Our car now carries us swiftly on . . ." (65), Pessoa insists. Quite far from injecting the project with any sort of literary voice, the author is most concerned with objective reporting, with the specific measurements of buildings and sculptures, tabulations of the numbers of books housed in the city's libraries, all while heaping on no shortage of praise for the city's splendor. The tourist will thus find that there are "remarkable works" (54) of architecture to be admired, "luxuriously furnished rooms" (63) to be visited, and views that are "not easily forgotten" (61). Modern Lisbon is a destination city.

Pessoa keeps his observations circumscribed so as to approximate the objectivity of a list, and he eschews embellishment. He offers intentionally rote descriptions of specific buildings, sculptures, and paintings. These could be read—and are indeed perhaps intended, given the expectations of the travel guide genre—as a prosaic form of historical aggrandizement. He notes which buildings are "worth seeing" (26), and where one might find a pleasing atmosphere—or entertainment, food, rest, and relaxation for that matter. He peppers his observations with references to a slew of literary and historical figures and events. It is crucial to know precisely where the Republic was proclaimed, for example, and his prose implicitly encourages visitors to seek out that hallowed ground. Lisbon is a city rich in history, made up of important architecture and dotted with grandiose churches. If there is a literary or even journalistic voice at all in this unembellished prose list of landmarks it is subtle—even more so when compared with the audacity of such a sprawling work such as *The Book of Disquiet*.

Though Pessoa's guide hews so closely to fact, still, one of its most interesting aspects for the reader unacquainted with Lisbon is surely to be found in its insistent references to the city's earthquake. Early on, Pessoa offers an obligatory, if passing, reference to "the Marquis de Pombal and the reconstruction of Lisbon effected by him after the great earthquake" (14). The aftershocks of this reference continue to resonate later on in the text. One of Pessoa's concise tourist snapshots in prose focuses on the Praça do Comércio. Of the plaza's statue of King José I, made by Joaquim Machado de Castro, he notes that "the pedestal is adorned with magnificent figures depicting the rebuilding of Lisbon after the great earthquake in 1755" (16). Later, he visits the Praça Marqués de Pombal, another monumental tribute, and takes the opportunity to list the statesman's many collaborators (22). The earthquake's continual referencing provides a crucial historical anchor for discussing the buildings destroyed, partially destroyed, and rebuilt in its wake (see, for instance, 32, 35, 35, 41, 42, 67). It is, for the tourist, as for the resident of Lisbon, a constant presence. This persistent referencing is not so much a quirk of Pessoa's narration but rather an indication that the event remains vivid in Lisbon's cultural history.

Lisbon's experience of the earthquake is not merely an intangible memory; it is structured into the city's very streets in the Baixa area that Pombal's team rebuilt. John Mullin's article "The Reconstruction of Lisbon Following the Earthquake of 1755: A Study in Despotic Planning," published in the *Journal of the International History of City Planning*, introduces readers to details culled from the historical record. On the morning of November 1, 1755, the earthquake reduced central areas of the city "to rubble." As Mullin sees it, "This tremor was so devastating that the entire city centre, the Baixa, ceased to exist" (1992, n.p.). He describes the damage as a consequence of three aftershocks, a tidal wave that flooded the city's core, and fires, looting, and disease. While Mullin estimated the death count to be between ten thousand and thirty thousand people out of a population of some 250,000, others have suggested the number of dead to be far greater.[1] Many churches, palaces and homes were destroyed.

> The greatest damage occurred in the Baixa. Authentically reminiscent of the Middle Ages with its narrow streets, winding alleys and densely packed wooden housing, the Baixa (literally translated as "Lower Town") was built on alluvial soft soils and Miocente fine sands and surrounded by steep hills on three sides. This combination of structural, spatial and soil characteristics created a set of conditions that, once the tremor struck, caused the Baixa to collapse inward upon itself. (Mullin 1992, n.p.)

This area, as Mullin documents, was not merely the urban center of Lisbon but the central "commercial, financial, judicial, bureaucratic and royal centre of the Portuguese nation and empire." The need to rebuild the Baixa was indeed an urgent one given these overlapping areas of symbolic significance.

The plan accepted by Pombal was carried out with relatively little hesitation and is thus often referred to as an example of swift and efficient large-scale urban reconstruction in early modern Europe. Mullin describes it as a controlled exercise in military precision: quite quickly following the quake, multiple ideas were drafted. These varied in their approach and ranged from restoring the pre-quake city more or less as it was, to making minimal or modest improvements to its previous pattern, to what Mullin calls the "'clean slate' option." Pombal selected the latter. There were some dynamic aspects included in the selected plan, such as the realignment of squares to allow for more sunlight and prioritization of open area by the river access. Anticipating the concerns regarding health and commerce that Ildefons Cerdà would later build into his Barcelona plan, members of Pombal's team were motivated by ideas of "comfort and hygiene" and they "rationalized fluid traffic" (Barreiros 2008, 218).[2] Yet the plan's general coordinates were staid and geometrical. Linking the Rossio square toward the north and the Terreiro do Paço and the Praça do Comércio to the south were straight arteries that erased what had formerly been curved streets and narrow winding alleys (218).[3] In Mullin's assessment, "the grid-iron pattern was a foreign concept that was brought to Lisbon as an expression of the will of the state. There was nothing natural about it. To impose such a design on a city that was so organically patterned before the earthquake was to announce that a new order was at work" (1992, n.p.).

Along with the military efficiency driving the plan's implementation and the abstracted design of its result, urban social life in Lisbon was going through an upheaval as well. In "Urban Landscapes: Houses, Streets and Squares of 18th-Century Lisbon," Maria Helena Barreiros notes just how striking and sharp the distinction between pre- and post-1755 urban life was for the city's inhabitants. She asserts that the reconstruction efforts "gave birth to an almost entirely new city, both in architecture and in social structure" (2008, 206). The changes she describes are hardly inconsequential for understanding the modern-era Baixa in which Pessoa would later live, work, and write: "Pombal, Manuel da Maia and the team of military engineers and architects who designed and built modern Lisbon after 1755 set the architectural and urban framework of the city's development for the century to come" (232). The social changes of late eighteenth-century Lisbon were reflected in and prompted by the city's architectural and urban design (206).[4]

> The Pombaline street effectively ceased to be the street in which one also lived; it announced the modern channel-street that guaranteed flows and nourished the complementarity between the private domain of the bourgeois apartment and the public sphere of professional and social life. This was how the *Baixa* district was meant to be. Its later transformation into a shopping and production centre was slow (1760 to 1840), as it was only then that it became animated by the everyday movement of clients and sup-

pliers among whom the residents went almost unnoticed—and joined the world of commerce, services, and small-luxury industry that settled there. (223)

In this way, the Baixa became a test site for what Barreiros calls "the first systematic Portuguese—or perhaps European—use of modern multi-family residential building" (218). Public and private spheres became differentiated along both horizontal and vertical axes. Yet while commercial buyers and sellers met in the city center to conduct their business, the accommodated bourgeois was also a resident.[5] Offices and residences coexisted in close proximity in the Baixa, yet each could be distinguished by an architecturally distinct entrance or a location on an upper floor of the building (215).[6] The close proximity and even overlap of the private and public spheres in modern Lisbon proves to be a source of anxiety and endless rumination in *The Book of Disquiet*.

Pessoa himself, just as the heteronyms who serve as the book's narrators, is easily situated in both the rebuilt urban streets and structures discussed by Mullin and in the modern social milieu of the Baixa analyzed by Barreiros. The Bernardo Soares narrator of the second part of the book, in particular, obsessively recounts his movements through the Pombaline streets.[7] He hardly leaves the Baixa. When he does, it is more frequently via a mental, rather than a physical, movement, one carried out through acts of imagination and obsessive flights of fancy. Within a very circumscribed modern area of the city, he repeatedly shifts back and forth between two distinguishable roles. Soares is at varying times the professional bookkeeper embodying the "public sphere of professional and social life" and also the quintessential bourgeois fourth-floor apartment dweller in his private space. His office and his apartment are both located on the very same street. His daily movements are thus brief, monotonous, and endlessly recurring drifts up and down a single, modern channel street constructed after the 1755 quake—the Rua dos Douradores. Whether arriving to his office or his home, Soares often sits motionless staring and, especially, listening to noises emanating from the modern streets below.

While unsurprisingly *The Book of Disquiet* is less specific in its urban references than was Pessoa's travel guide for the city, it is no less concerned with the urban modernity of early twentieth-century Lisbon. This urban modernity needs to be understood at once in both social and visual—that is, aesthetic—terms. Barreiros notes that "Old Lisbon had a cluttered look" (2008, 208), but that the new Baixa was beautiful by comparison:

> After 1760, the newly rebuilt downtown (*Baixa*) emerged as an island of modernity—and of "beauty," as conceived by 18th century (French) architectural culture—amidst a dense, over-crowded, violent, unhygienic city deprived of water, a sewer system, paving, and public lighting, where stray dogs, chickens, and pigs roamed freely, insects and beggars swarmed, apartments dumped rubbish straight onto the street, and mayhem, robbery, and murder abounded. (213)

As Barreiros notes, the urban differentiation between new and old Lisbon after the 1755 quake corresponds also to the social differentiation of the developing Baixa as a new center for bourgeois socialization, for trade, and even as a residential area for privileged classes. Yet the language she uses to characterize the class distinction between new and old is as much about the socially marginal and the unsightly as it is about material progress.

It is pertinent to remember the state and nature of the social associations and stigmas in eighteenth-century Europe concerning beggars and disability. In *A History of Disability*, Henri-Jacques Stiker explores a pertinent shift regarding the social visibility of the disabled, which is in evidence from the late Medieval period through the end of the seventeenth and early eighteenth centuries.

This shift saw the emergence of disability as a stigmatized social categorization of its own, and a gradual distinction between the disabled and a generalized mass consisting of the poor and the marginal ([1982] 1997, 67–72). Despite this, there is sustained a certain ambiguity whereby those understood to be disabled were included among the poor but also distinguished from them. With this in mind, it becomes difficult to disentangle the economic and the aesthetic aspects of urban modernity. To construct a space cleansed of poverty is not to address a social problem but to push an existing matter aside in spatial and geographic terms, to push existing populations aside. Against the poverty, the social marginality, the unsightliness, and the clutter of the old city, the Baixa was touted as a quintessentially ordered modern space. Against disorder, clutter, social inequality, and poverty, the normative modern project asserts an ordered and regularized aesthetic. Yet it so happens that the aesthetics of modern literary production are not wholly comfortable with this modern urban aesthetic. They are out of joint, off-kilter, cluttered, jumbled, and sprawling. What *The Book of Disquiet* does, then, is convey this disordered sense, this cluttered sense of modernity, through narrative's capacity to reflect endless and obsessive thinking.

At the level of content, Pessoa's pages affirm the urban bourgeois social values embedded in Lisbon's rebuilt central city. Guedes and Soares—and the heteronyms' author, through them of course—embody the conditions of the Portuguese capital's own urban modernity. Their life circumstances, their situated-ness in the central city, the nature of their daily activities, and their time spent sitting, chatting, daydreaming, are all quintessentially bourgeois. Yet Guedes, Soares and Pessoa are markedly modern, also, in the way that Lennard Davis claims: they are writers, they are obsessed, their cognition is not at all at ease. The singular focus of these narrators, their obsessive thinking, is expressed in an iterative narrative form that celebrates the boundless creative energy of thought while blurring any notion of its goal or resolution. The paratextual elements of the book, the incessant starting and stopping of the string of narrative entries, allow the obsessive qualities of thought to emerge in a form that is quite easily identified as repetitive. In this way the assembled fragments assert cognitive clutter and continual recursion as a hallmark value of modern literature.

Monotonous Urban Modernity in *Livro do Desassossego* by Fernando Pessoa

Lennard Davis begins chapter 4 of *Obsession: A History*, which is titled "Never Done: Compulsive Writing, Graphomania, Bibliomania," by acknowledging the impressive output of earlier writers such as Shakespeare, Milton, Defoe, Addison, and Steele. Quite quickly, he asserts how and why the nature of writerly output soon changed. Great nineteenth-century writers, he states, by contrast with their predecessors, "were engaged in a single-minded work project that had to precedent—the continuous, cumulative production of words. . . . These writers wrote not only novels but journalism, criticism, and letters—they were in effect writing all the time. They had become obsessives in the cause of letters" (2008, 105). This shift, of course, cannot be reduced to being a mere consequence of the individual will or writerly temperament of Dickens, Balzac, Trollope, Zola, Goncourt, for example, although personal traits are also crucial in these cases, as he explains. Instead, Davis makes clear that any explanation must at once go beyond mere contemplation of the individual to also include reference to social conditions, material and technological advances, and newly established norms. For instance, the time period in question saw an increase in the mass production of books, the popularization of long-form prose, and the cultivation of an obsessive consumerist readership. The social prestige given to specialization and specialized thinking institutionalized new forms of compulsive scholarship that flourished in universities. Accommodated populations enjoyed unregulated access to drugs that had the effect of regulating and modulating cognition—stimulants among them (2008, 105). And the repetitive habits progressively instilled in a modern population through the adoption of serialized or even mechanized factory production were becoming prevalent also in forms of intellectual labor such as writing (106). Zola, as Davis reminds readers, had the Latin phrase for "no day without a sentence" displayed prominently on his mantel (106).[8]

Though he is not discussed in Davis's study, Fernando Pessoa nonetheless fits quite well into the repeated pattern of concise obsessed writer portraits that comprise its fourth chapter. Like the single-minded authors profiled there, Pessoa was obsessively engaged in multiple avenues of written production: "poetry, prose, drama, philosophy, criticism, political theory, . . . occultism, theosophy, and astrology" (Jull Costa 2017, ix). He published a book of poems in Portuguese titled *Mensagem*, four chapbooks of English poetry, articles in journals and newspapers, and translations of works by authors such as Hawthorne, O. Henry and Poe (viii). Other works and letters were published posthumously. Educated in the English-language schools of Durban, South Africa, due to his stepfather's employment there as Portuguese Consul, he returned to Lisbon in 1905. After Pessoa died in 1935, in his mid- to late forties, a vast archive of writing was discovered. Estimates suggest some twenty-five thousand to thirty thousand pieces of paper were found in at least two trunks among his possessions (Morris 2014, 127; Jull Costa 2017, viii–ix).

As Margaret Jull Costa notes, Pessoa "appeared to spend all his spare time reading or writing" from an early age (viii). A childhood classmate later reflected that Pessoa was "brilliantly clever but quite mad" in his youth (vii). Already he had "begun creating the fictional alter egos, or as he later described them, heteronyms, for which he is now so famous, writing stories and poems under such names as Chevalier de Pas, David Merrick, Charles Robert Anon, Horace James Faber, Alexander Search, and more" (vii). As the posthumous excavation and publication of Pessoa's written works has continued, the count of his heteronyms has risen. Recent estimates range from eighty to one-hundred thirty-six (Morris 2014, 127; Jull Costa 2017, viii; see also Aslanov 2012, Sarfati 2012). Importantly, Pessoa's own remarks frame his heteronyms in terms that recall Davis's exploration of partial madness: "They are beings with a sort-of-life-of-their-own, with feelings I do not have, and opinions I do not accept. While their writings are not mine, they do also happen to be mine" (Jull Costa 2017, viii).[9] What is essential is their partial status. They are creations betwixt and between the fictional representation and the author's own writerly self. This very distinction is blurred. Pessoa explicitly negates the possibility of their autonomous existence. These are beings who despite having been written into the world as a creation are denied even the fictive suggestion of a separate selfhood. One might consider as a contemporaneous Iberian counterexample Miguel de Unamuno's agonist in *Niebla* (1914), Augusto Pérez. That fictional character's dramatic search for the author of flesh and blood who created him is what imbues the novel with tragic tone. The entire conceit of Unamuno's text thus rests on assuming—even if for a moment—a hard border between the notions of a fictional self and an authorial self. Yet for Pessoa, such a clean break proves even more elusive. The Portuguese author both is and is not identified with his narrators.[10] Thus while the narration in *Niebla* can be taken as a space of encounter, a somewhat neutral meeting ground for two opposing creative forces, no such neutral space can be discerned in Pessoa's work. The Vicente Guedes and Bernardo Soares heteronyms of *The Book of Disquiet* are elevated from the narratorial to the authorial without a clean distinction between those levels of the text.

What, then, are readers of to make of passages like this one, in part two of *The Book of Disquiet*:

A minha mania de crear um mundo falso acompanha-me ainda, e só na minha morte me abandonará. Não alinho hoje nas minhas gavetas carros de retroz e peões de xadrez—com um bispo ou um cavallo accaso sobressahindo—mas tenho pena de o não fazer . . . e alinho na minha imaginação, confortavelmente, como quem no inverno se aquece a uma lareira, figuras que habitam, e são constantes e vivas, na minha vida interior. Tenho um mundo de amigos dentro de mim, com vidas proprias, reaes, definidas e imperfeitas. (Pessoa [1982] 2017, entry 83, ellipses in original)

My mania with creating a false world is still with me, and will leave me only when I die. I no longer line up in my desk drawers cotton reels and pawns—with the occasional bishop and knight thrown in—but I regret not doing so . . . and instead, like someone in winter, cozily warming himself by the fire, I line up in my imagination the ranks of constant, living characters who inhabit my inner world. For I have a whole world of friends inside me, each with his or her own real, definite, imperfect life.[11]

It is significant that the original Portuguese of this passage begins with the words "A minha mania" (my mania). As quoted above, Jull Costa's English translation "mania" is just as faithful to the medical and psychological discourse that shaped the Iberian and more broadly European context in which Pessoa lived and wrote. This choice reflects the widespread European impact of American George Beard's work that Davis chronicles and that can help readers seeking to understand, for example Emilia Pardo Bazan's mystery tale "La gota de sangre" (1911). Yet neither would it be incorrect to render the Portuguese word *mania*, through what risks being understood as a form of translational presentism, as the English word *obsession*.[12] The quotation from *The Book of Disquiet* all too easily lends itself to the sort of analysis Davis pursues through case studies of obsessive French and English writers and their works. Bernardo Soares (and simultaneously Pessoa?) is aware of his repetitive behaviors but unable to stop them. The trope of "lining up" physical objects suggests a repetitive ordering impulse that emerges during adolescence. Its repeated presence in the above fragment swiftly achieves, in the realm of the heteronym's imagination, a transposition of that ordering impulse to the cognitive realm.

While he may not be a bookseller, it is deeply relevant that Soares is a bookkeeper. Davis's discussion of "bibliomania" is focused on the obsessive nature of the modern practice of collecting, storing, reading, selling, and writing books. Yet there is in bookkeeping, too, no shortage of connection with his book-length history of obsession (see, for example, Davis 2008, 86, 92, 121). One must consider the repetitive nature of bookkeeping, the single-minded focus on numbers, counting, and mathematics required by the profession. There is the solitary and mechanical nature of the work. There is also the social position of the bookkeeper within an entire trade industry supported by the social value placed on precise tabulation and the written record. This profession, this position, and this larger industry are the very social coordinates that one identifies with Lisbon's modern bourgeois urban milieu.

In his editor's note to the most recent translation of Pessoa's work by Jull Costa, Jerónimo Pizarro calls *The Book of Disquiet* "a portrait of Lisbon and of its portraitist," noting that "the portrait of an assistant bookkeeper in Lisbon . . . is impossible to separate from the description of the city" (2017, xvii). He writes that the book's landscape is one constituted more by Pessoa's malaise more than it is by the urban landscape of Lisbon (xviii).[13] But in a certain sense, at least, this statement underplays the book's fundamental interconnection between city and mood. Of course Pizarro's comment can be taken as an affirmation that *The Book of Disquiet* lacks sustained urbanistic specificity. The overall effect of Pessoa's book is not even remotely comparable to *Lisbon: What the Tourist Should See*. By comparison, the number of sites mentioned is quite reduced, and these take the form of brief toponyms lacking the descriptive text that appears in that travel guide of the city. Yet despite this difference, the urban context is supremely important to the *Livro do desassossego*. Lisbon, its streets, and its landmarks are mentioned explicitly, yet their context remains somewhat imprecise. One might say that the central malaise of the book, too, receives a similarly vague treatment. Both the urban environment and the urban context are only vaguely defined. Yet they are obsessively present nonetheless. The form that the city takes in the book might be considered atmospheric, were it not for the coevality of both urban and obsessive modernity. Considering the book's organizing principle, along with the cyclical moods, obsessive thoughts, and the compulsion to write shared by the heteronyms, is crucial for understanding the book's portrayal of urban modernity. The Baixa and the Rua dos Douradores, beyond enjoying a form of obsessive referencing in the text, become key landmarks for assessing the obsessed nature of the heteronym's urban social life in the book's second part.

While in 1913 *The Book of Disquiet* already existed as a concept named by Pessoa, it appeared in book form in Portuguese only in 1982—thus well after the author's death and the discovery of his many thousands of dated but unorganized manuscript pages (Jull Costa 2017, ix–x). Pessoa conceived but never completed the "rigorous process of selection and adaptation" (x) he envisioned for the volume. But he did indeed put his plan for it to paper. His notes lay out that "there needs to be a general revision of style, without it losing the personal tone or the drifting disconnected logic that characterizes it" (x). In Jerónimo Pizarro's 2013 Portuguese edition, which forms the basis for Jull Costa's 2017 translation, this drifting and disconnected logic is preserved in the style but also of course in the structure of the text. A preface is followed by 438 fragments whose lengths range from a few lines to a few pages each.[14] These are sequentially numbered without restarting once the Guedes heteronym cedes narrative control to Soares in the second part or "phase." Authored mainly in the late 1910s and early

1930s, these hundreds of fragments tend to be provided along with a specific year of composition. Even these dates are many times followed by a question mark to indicate uncertainty.

Both heteronyms are relatively close in temperament, and they share a penchant for personal introspection and drifting, cycling thoughts. They are alienated and estranged from life, from others, and from themselves. They each deny, suppress, or evade their own desires and passions. The volume's loose, drifting logic allows very similar thoughts to emerge first as fleeting or philosophical, and later as recurring, intrusive, and obsessive. Both Guedes and Soares seem to be more or less equally obsessive thinkers. They are plagued by recurring thoughts of ships and shipwrecks; of the sea, nature, and the countryside; of death, suffering, and suicide; of pain and of pleasure or its absence; and especially by anxiety, illness, and madness. They ruminate on artistic production, painting, literature, music, poetry, metaphor, and most of all, writing. More than a logic of drift, it is obsessive thinking that ties the fragments together and lends the volume a poetic coherence.

Returning to the through line of *Obsession: A History*, the central paradox of *The Book of Disquiet*'s drifting and disordered logic is very similar to the one that Davis identifies as a value of social modernity, that is, "that the open-mindedness is actually a form of activity geared to create single-mindedness" (2008, 129). As their creator Pessoa also has, the heteronyms engage in what Davis describes as the "endless process of giving up and then trying again" (120). This is a single-minded starting and stopping, one whose iterative nature, along with the particularly concise results of the activity, suggests an obsessive stripe. Some of this obsessive thinking concerns socially normative behavior, with which Guedes and Soares are unable or unwilling to comply. Both heteronyms explicitly define themselves in opposition to those they consider normal.[15] Their attention locks on tightly to seemingly insignificant things, and the very act of thinking proves exhausting. Even without the supposedly divine intervention experienced by the protagonist of Cajal's story "El pesimista corregido," Guedes is driven to delight by "a mera existencia insignificante dum alfinete pregado numa fita" (frag. 59; "the mere insignificant existence of a pin stuck in a piece of ribbon"). He also is flooded with amazement and wonder "deante da contemplação duma pequena pedra parada numa estrada" (when contemplating one small stone in the road), which suggests to him "o desassocego do mysterio (frag. 59; "the disquiet aroused by the mystery of life").[16] For Soares, thinking itself is explicitly and repeatedly invoked as a burden. This appears as a sort of refrain: "É uma vontade de não querer ter pensamento" (frag. 229; "It is a wish not to think" [frag. 224]); "O homem vulgar, por mais dura que lhe seja a vida, tem ao menos a felicidade de a não pensar" (frag. 271; "However hard his life may be, the ordinary man does at least have the pleasure of not thinking" [frag. 265]); "Feliz, pois, o que não pensa" (frag. 419; "Happy the man, then, who does not think" [frag. 412]). What appear as aspects of personality—seemingly ordinary minutia viewed with transcendent zeal, and ongoing, uncontrolled thoughts—acquire significance when considered within the framework of obsession.

Plagued by nonspecific anxieties, the heteronyms usually connect these with general observations about everyday life, the constant weariness, the monotony or the tedium with which they view their ordinary movements and their daily thoughts.[17] Whether the specific word used is monotony, boredom, anxiety, sadness, illness, disease, or emptiness, this undercurrent of generalized malaise is central to the *Livro do Desassossego*. References to "o tedio" are consistent throughout the first and second parts of the book.[18] In the passage that Pessoa himself specifically designated as the preface to part one of the book, readers are informed that "V G supportava aquella vida nulla com uma indifferença de mestre. Um stoicismo de fraco alicerçava toda a sua attitude mental" (n.p.; "Vicente Guedes endured his empty life with masterly indifference, the foundations of his mental attitude being built on the stoicism of the weak. He was constitutionally condemned to suffer all kinds of anxieties, but fated to abandon them all" [Jull Costa 2017, 5]).[19] Guedes later writes of how "os dois grandes tedios que me cingem — o tedio de poder viver só o Real, e o tedio de poder conceber só o Possivel" (frag. 43; "the two great tediums encircle me—the tedium of being able to live only the Real, and the tedium of being able to imagine only the Possible").[20] For his part, Soares writes that tedium can only be understood by those who have experienced it (frag. 394). The disquiet continually and reiteratively experienced by the heteronyms is both cause and effect. At one point, Soares replicates quite well the cyclical cognitive process of an obsessive thinker unable to stop. There exists, he writes, "um tedio que inclue a anticipação só de mais tedio; a pena, já, de amanhã ter pena de ter tido pena hoje—grandes emmaranhamentos sem utilidade nem verdade, grandes emaranhamentos . . ." (frag. 203; "a tedium that contains only the prospect of more tedium; the anticipated sadness of feeling sad about having felt sad today—great tangles of feelings that lack utility or truth, great tangles . . ." [frag. 198]). The punctuating ellipsis in this example ends both the sentence and the self-contained paragraph of which it is the only component, indicating the self-perpetuating nature of this thinking. These thoughts and feelings are not of use to the heteronym. Unwanted, they are continuously presented to his consciousness nonetheless. They are far too ordinary to be madness, yet they approach it and suggest a lesser or partial variety of madness.

Indeed, toward the end of the book, Soares writes about "um tedio que parece ser loucura" (frag. 421; "a tedium that verges on madness" [frag. 414]). He mockingly suggests madness as a modern value, and he pauses to reflect on the apparent strengths of epileptics, paranoiacs, and religious maniacs.[21] Tedium is most of all a nonspecific malaise, one that tends to erupt as if an earthquake—without warning and without an apparent cause. Waking one morning, Soares is overcome by a wave of this nonspecific tedium: "Uma inquietação enorme fazia-me estremecer os gestos minimos. Tive receio de endoidecer, não de loucura, mas de alli mesmo. O meu corpo era um grito latente. O meu coração batia como se soluçasse" (frag. 222; "A terrible anxiety gripped and shook my smallest gesture. I felt afraid I might go mad, not from madness, but just from being there. My whole body was a suppressed scream. My heart was beating as if it were sobbing" [frag. 215]). Many times he reflects on natural disasters, sometimes using the word *earthquake*, in fact, as a way of reflecting on the threat posed by such sudden changes in consciousness or mood.[22] There are also sudden moments of full clarity, wherein Soares understands that "tudo quanto tenho feito, tudo quanto tenho pensado, tudo quanto tenho sido, é uma especie de engano e de loucura . . . os meus propositos mais logicos, não foram, afinal, mais que bebedeira nata, loucura natural, grande desconhecimento. Nem sequer representei. Representaram-me. Fui, não o actor, mas os gestos d'elle" (frag. 226; "everything I have done, everything I have thought, everything I have been, is a sort of delusion and madness. . . . My most logical aims were, after all, nothing but an innate drunkenness, a natural madness, an immense ignorance. I did not act the part. It acted me. I was merely the gestures, never the actor" [frag. 221]). As these lines reveal, Soares is haunted by his obsessive thoughts but never fully given over to them. While this madness does not define him, neither can he be separated from it. It is a partial madness. He is a careful observer of it, if not also an unwilling participant in its drama. It is significant as well that this notion echoes throughout the book in a slew of poetic wordings indicating partiality, such as "half-light," "half-shade," "half-open," "half-cleaned," "half asleep," "half nothing," "semi-reflections" and "penumbra."[23]

It is writing, obsessive writing, that makes it possible for the Bernardo Soares heteronym to deal with the generalized malaise of which he is aware but unable to dispatch. Through writing, he is able to exorcise what he calls a "terrible weariness with life" (frag. 345). Here the sudden nature and the sharp peaks of experience are dulled and his consciousness is able to relax.

E, assim, muitas vezes, escrevo sem querer pensar, num devaneio externo, deixando que as palavras me façam festas, criança menina ao colo delas. São frases sem sentido, decorrendo mórbidas, numa fluidez de água sentida, esquecer-se de ribeiro em que as ondas se misturam e indefinem, tornando-se sempre outras, sucedendo a si mesmas. Assim as ideas, as imagens, trémulas de expressão, passam por mim em cortejos sonoros de sêdas esbatidas, onde um luar de idea bruxuleia, malhado e confuso. (frag. 333)

And that's why I often write without even wanting to think, in an externalized daydream, letting the words caress me as if I were a little girl sitting on their lap. They're just meaningless sentences, flowing languidly with the fluidity of water that forgets itself as a stream does in the waves that mingle and fade, constantly reborn, following endlessly one on the other. That's how ideas and images, tremulous with expression, pass through me like a rustling procession of faded silks amongst which a sliver of an idea flickers, mottled and indistinct in the moonlight. (frag. 326)[24]

While philosophical meditations on topics ranging from love to art to beauty are not hard to find in *The Book of Disquiet*, the obsessive writing returns again and again to the city. Urbanized life is implicit in recurring examples of *beatus ille*, the praise heaped by both heteronyms on the countryside, on gardens, on nature. Yet the urban environment itself is also the explicit subject of a great many reflections.

For all of its attention paid to inner worlds and mercurial moods, *The Book of Disquiet* is a remarkably urban text. Lisbon is explicitly named in the very first sentence of the preface, and it is invoked increasingly throughout the book's second part.[25] Vicente Guedes captures well the city's symbolic stamp when he links "o amontoado irregular e montanhoso da cidade" (frag. 38; "the irregular, hilly heap of the city" [38]) and its cold, mist, and fog to his dreary feelings. With melancholic apostrophe Bernardo Soares later exclaims "Oh, Lisboa, meu lar!" (frag. 258; "Oh Lisbon, my home!" [252]).[26] These continued references are not functional, at least in terms of a traditional plot, character movements, or any sort of dramatic arc. Since very little actually "happens" in the text, it cannot be concluded that they appear in order to keep the reader oriented to changes in setting. Neither are they ornamental or merely poetic. The heteronyms are certainly given to poetic description and flights of visual imagery, as this characteristic passage conveys:

> Alastra ante meus olhos saudosos a cidade incerta e silente. As casas desegualam-se num aglomerado retido, e o luar, com manchas de incerteza, estagna de madreperola os solavancos mortos da confusão. Ha telhados e noite, janellas e edade media. Não ha de que haver arredores. Paira no que se vê um vislumbre de longinquo. Por sobre de onde vejo ha ramos negros de arvores, e eu tenho o somno da cidade inteira no meu coração dissuadido. Lisboa ao luar e o meu cansaço de amanhã! (frag. 270)

> *The uncertain, silent city lies spread out beneath my nostalgic gaze. The houses, all different, stand together in a tightly packed crowd, and the equally uncertain moonlight puddles this dumb, jostling confusion with mother-of-pearl. Nothing but rooftops and night, windows and a faint medieval air. Nothing else. A breath of the far-away hovers over everything. From where I stand, what I see lies cradled in the dark branches of trees. I hold the whole sleeping city in my poor, dispirited heart. Lisbon in the moonlight and my weariness at the prospect of another day! (frag. 264)*

Yet for all its poetic description, the urban in *The Book of Disquiet* cannot be truly considered an object of contemplation. The city is intimately wrapped up in the heteronym's mood and is, in a sense, inseparable from his consciousness. The heteronyms imagine themselves to be, and write themselves into the text as marginal people, using spatial and decidedly urban metaphor: "Tenho quintas nos arredores da Vida" (frag. 71; "I own country estates on the outskirts of Life")—Guedes; "Sou os arredores de uma villa que não ha, o commentario prolixo a um livro que se não escreveu. Não sou ninguem, ninguem (frag. 344; "I am the outskirts of some nonexistent town, the long-winded prologue to an unwritten book. I am nobody, nobody" [frag. 337])—Soares. Houses appear as a depthless spectacle, their haphazard distribution across the landscape a seeming reminder of the imperfection of the world. They are also a metaphor for the boundaries that separate the inner from the social or spiritual self. Vicente Guedes writes, "em torno a nós poderão as outras almas erguerem-se os seus bairros sujos e pobres; marquemos nitidamente onde o nosso acaba e começa, e que desde a frontaria dos nossos /sentimentos/ até ás alcovas das nossas timidezes, tudo seja fidalgo e sereno, esculpido n'uma elegancia ou surdina de exhibição" (frag. 28; "Let other souls build their poor, shabby dwellings around us, but let us clearly mark where ours begin and end, and sure that from the façades of our houses to the inner sanctums of our timidities, everything is noble and serene, elegantly and discreetly sculpted").[27] In their recurring and obsessive invocation, the city's rooftops thus become an architectural symbol of the heteronyms' restricted access to other souls, of contemporary alienation, of their feelings of isolation. Here too there is disarray, irregularity and imperfection in a blurred visual form. What Soares calls "o agglomerado diffuso dos telhados" (frag 238; "the diffuse jumble of rooftops" [232]) and "os telhados da cidade interrompida" (frag. 287; "the rooftops of the uninterrupted city" [282]) are a clear metaphor for his state of mind, isolation and obsessive ideation, a metaphor that is stated explicitly: "De repente estou só no mundo. Vejo tudo isto do alto de um telhado mental" (frag. 246; "Suddenly, I am alone in the world. I see all this while looking down from a mental rooftop" [240]).[28]

The Bernardo Soares heteronym in particular is quite aware of how profoundly the urban social life of Lisbon has affected him.

It is "os arruamentos" (the arrangement of the streets) or "o facto de que existem arruamentos" (the very existence of streets) that "Mais que uma vez, ao passear lentamente pelas ruas da tarde, me tem batido na alma, com uma violencia subita e estonteante" (frag. 272; "more than once, while out strolling in the evening ... has often struck my soul with sudden, surprising violence" [266]), he writes.[29] Soares, as mentioned above, both lives and works in the Baixa, the rebuilt modern area of the city where the very existence and ordered arrangement of the streets is most notable.

Constructed after the mid-eighteenth-century earthquake, the Rua dos Douradores is a straight avenue that is home to both the office in which Bernardo Soares works and the apartment in which he lives. The written name of this street saturates the fragments of the book's second half. It is explicitly referenced in at least fifteen distinct fragments and is implicated indirectly in a great number of others. Frequently, when sitting in his apartment or office, Soares writes of staring out the window, noting the rooftops, the arrangement of the houses, and most of all listening to the indirect sound of the streets emanating from below and around his building. His descriptions of the urban street life seem to be tied into his obsessed mood. When he is unable to write, in those prolonged periods of time when he is caught "entre o escriptorio e a physiologia, numa estagnação intima de pensar e de sentir" (frag. 309; "between the office and physiology, marooned in an inner stagnation of thinking and feeling" [303]), he states that the streets hold no allure for him: "as ruas são ruas para mim" (frag. 309; "the streets are just streets to me" [303])." His obsessive writing about the streets thus can be understood as taking the pulse of his mania, revealing Soares's (Pessoa's) state of mind indirectly. His written descriptions of urban street life are a chronicle of his rising and falling moods. When obsessed, he writes, and the streets come to life on the page. In those moments he puts what he hears to paper, for example, indistinct chatter, whistling, laughter, or the clatter of a tram, of a cart driven over cobblestones, of street vendors selling their wares.

The Rua dos Douradores is, for Soares, an entire and seemingly self-enclosed world. The heteronym sets up a revealing, if ultimately unsatisfying analogy. After defining A Vida [Life], with a capital letter, as "monotona e necessaria" (frag. 350; "monotonous and necessary" [343]), he differentiates between Life and Art and maps these concepts to his office and his home, as two sets of coordinates on the straight line that is his street:

> E, se o escriptorio da Rua dos Douradores representa para mim a vida, este meu segundo andar, onde moro, na mesma Rua dos Douradores, representa para mim a Arte. Sim, a Arte, que mora na mesma rua que a Vida, porém num logar differente, a Arte que allivia da vida sem alliviar de viver, que é tam monotona como a mesma vida, mas só em logar differente. Sim, esta Rua dos Douradores comprehende para mim todo o sentido das coisas, a solução de todos os enigmas, salvo o existirem enigmas, que é o que não pode ter solução. (frag. 350)

> *As if the office in the Rua dos Douradores represents Life for me, the fourth-floor room I live in on that same street represents Art. Yes Art, living on the same street as Life but in a different room. Art, which offers relief from life without actually relieving one of living, and which is as monotonous as life itself, but in a different way. Yes, for me Rua dos Douradores embraces the meaning of all things, the resolution of all mysteries, except the existence of mysteries themselves, which is something beyond resolution. (frag. 343)*

This spatialized urban analogy ultimately proves unsatisfying because, as the heteronym himself acknowledges, monotony is present in both Life and Art. The heteronym is just as conscious as the reader of its aggravating presence. Despite later acknowledging that he will never leave the Rua dos Douradores, he longs for escape—"Partir da Rua dos Douradores para o Impossivel . . . (frag. 295; "to leave Rua dos Douradores for the Impossible . . ." [295])—

and bemoans the baseness of this "Rua dos Douradores que me é a vida inteira—este escriptorio sordido até á sua medulla de gente, este quarto mensalmente alugado onde nada acontece senão viver um morto" (frag. 206; "Rua dos Douradores that makes up my entire life: the squalid office whose squalor seeps into the very marrow of its inhabitants' bones, the room, rented by the month, in which nothing happens except the living death of its occupant" [206, 207]). Monotony is a fundamental attribute of his existence whether at the office or at home. Moreover, this monotony is quintessentially urban in origin.

It is significant that the very preface of *The Book of Disquiet* includes the statement that "No quarto á moderna o tedio torna-se desconforto, magoa physica" (frag. 122; "In a modern-style room, tedium becomes a discomfort, a physical pain" [Pessoa's unnumbered preface in Jull Costa's translation]." With the context provided by Davis in mind, one can read here the idea that tedium comes into being in a certain space at a certain time—an urban space and a modern time. The book as a whole suggests the rebuilt Baixa in modern Lisbon as one such space and time. It is a modern urban life in the Baixa that has turned Soares into a machine. He is a person of habit, an automaton who inscribes the same trajectories onto the city's streets day after day. No surprise that he notes it is "a pobreza das ruas intermedias da Baixa usual, tantas vezes por mim percorridas que já me parecem ter usurpado a fixidez da irreparabilidade, que formam no meu espirito a nausea, que nelle é frequente, da quotidianidade enxovalhante da vida" (frag. 225; "the poverty of the usual Baixa streets separating room and office [and which I've walked so often they already seem to have achieved a fixity beyond that of mere irreparability] that provoke in me my frequent feelings of disgust for the grubby everydayness of life" [220]). This situation is in one sense out of joint with what are often touted as the hallmark aspects of modern urban life: the complexity, the diversity, the transitory nature and fleeting character of city life; the fact that it is a meeting place for trade, for exchange, for different ideas, for varied ways of being; that the sensations and stimulations of the city are greater than that of country life, and thus, as Georg Simmel wrote in the early twentieth century, that the urbanite had to develop a corresponding sense of indifference to cope with the increased mental stimulation of the metropolis. Yet in another sense, the repetitive nature of both Soares's physical movements and his thoughts is the outcome of these very same social processes of urban modernity.

Simmel began his essay "The Metropolis and Mental Life" by stating that "the deepest problems of modern life flow from the attempt of the individual to maintain the independence and individuality of his existence against the sovereign powers of society, against the weight of the historical heritage and the external culture and technique of life" (2000, 157). *The Book of Disquiet* can be read as a chronicle of attempts—by Pessoa, by Guedes, by Soares—to maintain the independence and individuality to which Simmel refers. The drudgery to which their modern lives have been reduced in some sense diminishes each of them. Uninspired, they repeatedly tread the same streets. Day after day they perform the same banal and meaningless tasks. Urban life's sensory stimulations are kept at a distance, mediated, indirect, sounds heard through a window, or sunlight seen falling over the city's rooftops at dawn. They are quite far indeed from being exemplars of Simmel's adaptive urbanite. In lieu of an active or participatory indifference to urban life, they cultivate and nurture a retreat from it. Still, the heteronyms remain aware of this struggle, and of their relation to this strange modern urban age. As Guedes writes, "n'esta era metallica dos barbaros, só um culto methodicamente excessivo das nossas faculdades de sonhar, de analysar e de atrahir pode servir de salvaguarda á nossa personalidade, para que se não desfaça ou para nulla ou para identica ás outras" (frag. 118; "given the metallic, barbarous age we live in, only by methodically, obsessively cultivating our abilities to dream, analyze and attract can we prevent our personality from dissolving into nothing or into something identical to all the others"). It is not surprising that here Jull Costa opts to include the English word "obsessively" in what might otherwise be the literal translation of "methodically excessive cultivation." These narrators meet the challenge posed by Simmel's modern urban life to their individuality and independence through writing. To write is to cope. They turn obsessively to the written word in order to expiate and purge the monotony that has become a modern social condition.

On the Pointlessness of Walking: Pessoa and Cesário Verde

In *The Book of Disquiet*, what has shattered and fragmented the modern urban subject is not necessarily the earthquake that reduced the Baixa to rubble as much as it is the modern urban life that has formed in its wake. Pessoa's writing, the splintering off of his obsessive persona into different heteronyms and writerly selves, is paradoxically an attempt to rewrite himself as a connected and coherent being. This shattered self can be equally understood as a modern monad. Pessoa's obsessive thinking replicates the social interconnection that has been subjugated to the monotony of modern urban life. This creation is internal to the self. As his heteronyms struggle to overcome what Simmel called "the deepest problems of modern life"—in this case, modern urban alienation, or the tedium of living and working in Lisbon's Baixa— they engage in solitary walking and solitary writing.

To understand *The Book of Disquiet* and its relation to modern urbanism, these two activities need to be approached in tandem and within the tradition of the form of drifting urban stroll practiced as flânerie since Charles Baudelaire. In this tradition, walking itself is considered a form of expression, and it has been extensively theorized as such. In *The Practice of Everyday Life*, for instance, Michel de Certeau wrote of what he called "pedestrian speech acts." In his view, footsteps tell a story. "The act of walking is to the urban system what the speech act is to language or to the statements uttered" (1988, 97). He makes the argument that one can "write" patterns through the city streets via the practice of walking. This argument is grounded, of course, in an awareness of many earlier European traditions. These include not only Baude-laire's canonized celebration of flânerie but also Walter Benjamin's philosophical-historical meditations in *The Arcades Project* and the dérive practiced by the Situationists as a form of psychogeography. De Certeau means that pedestrian speech acts can inscribe spontaneity into an urban plan otherwise that is otherwise unsuited for "shadows and ambiguities." Thus the "long poem of walking manipulates spatial organizations" (101). Most frequently, however, the walking practiced by Bernardo Soares is not a long-form poetic practice but a short-form social fixation. He reaffirms monotony through his linear tracing of the Rua dos Douradores, and while he is not happy with it, he has accepted this as being part of his role to play in the urban social economy of modern Lisbon.

There is a contradiction surrounding walking for Pessoa. As his heteronym Soares notes, in order to write it is vitally important to walk. In one such fragment that recalls a drifting walk, some unknown urban stimulus prompts his imagination and he ends up at a café where he puts his meandering thoughts to paper. This is a marked departure from his obsessive retracings of a single street in the Baixa. The urban context seems, momentarily at least, to recover its links with spontaneity, change, and thought. During this fragment, the seeming indifference Soares fleetingly cultivates with regard to the city environment has a productive effect. The freedom embodied in the practice of urban drifting carries over also to his writing. Unfettered writing is in harmony with the notion of aimless urban wandering, and is described by the heteronym in a similar way: "Não sei onde ia conduzir os pensamentos, ou onde preferiria conduzil-os (frag. 280; "I don't know where I was going to lead those thoughts or where I would choose to lead them" [274]).

At other moments, however, walking is simultaneously an impediment to writing: "tenho construido em passeio phrases perfeitas, de que depois me não lembro em casa" (frag. 442; "while out walking, I have constructed perfect sentences that, once I'm home, I forget" [435]). Here readers might also distinguish two ways of walking that recur in *The Book of Disquiet*. The monotonous, functional, recursive, and brief walk from his home to office and back is strictly limited to one street in the Baixa. At other moments he expands beyond this street to a limited range of sites also within or on the border of the Baixa, for example, the Rua da Alfândega, Rua da Prata, Rua dos Fanqueiros, Igreja de São Domingos, Cais so Sodré, and Terreiro do Paço. Very rarely does he physically move beyond these confines—in one fragment, for instance, he does write of being exhausted upon crossing the Tejo river by boat and venturing from Terreiro do Paço to Cacilhas and back. Yet more often he escapes in his mind's eye or his writerly imagination. This ideation of escape through obsessive writing about travel or the countryside is explicitly noted as a product of the monotony of his urban work.

> Monotonizar a existencia, para que ella não seja monotona. Tornar anodyno o quotidiano, para que a mais pequena coisa seja uma distracção. No meio do meu trabalho de todos os dias, baço, egual e inutil, surgem-me visões de fuga, vestigios sonhados de ilhas longinquas, festas em aleas de parques de outras eras, outras paysagens, outros sentimentos, outro eu. (frag. 351)

> *One must monotonize existence in order to rid it of monotony. One must make the everyday so anodyne that the slightest incident proves entertaining. In the midst of my day-to-day work, dull, repetitive and pointless, visions of escape surface in me, vestiges off dreams of far-off islands, parties held in the avenues of gardens in some other age, different landscapes, different feelings, a different me. (frag. 344)*

The progressively clear delineation of work and leisure that can be observed in the modern city is also a byproduct of those same shifting urban conditions that shaped Lisbon's Baixa as a modern bourgeois space. The notions of private home life and public work life analyzed by Barreiros above have their complement in a whole tradition of European urban theory shaped by Henri Lefebvre. Leisure emerges as distinct from work, a comparatively private space of enjoyment juxtaposed with the drudgery of routinized modern labor. The figure of the flâneur is thus paradoxically both reacting against and also in step with urban modernity. To drift across the city is to enjoy the leisure time provided to those in a privileged class at the same time that it is an escape from the functional production and drudgery that now defines an increasingly regularized modern life.

To the degree that flânerie is implicit in Pessoa's depiction of Lisbon, it can be traced to the work of his predecessor and poetic hero Cesário Verde. Four of the fragments in the second part of *The Book of Disquiet* reference Verde, the first coming quite early on:

goso de sentir me coevo de Cesario Verde, e tenho em mim, não outros versos como os d'elle, mas a substancia egual à dos versos que fôram d'elle. Por alli arrasto, até haver noite, uma sensação de vida parecida com a d'essas ruas. De dia ellas são cheias de um bulicio que não quere dizer nada; de noite são cheias de uma falta de bulicio que não quere dizer nada. Eu de dia sou nullo, e de noite sou eu. Não ha differença entre mim e as ruas para o lado da Alfandega, salvo elas serem ruas e eu ser alma, o que pode ser que nada valha ante o que é a essencia das cousas. Ha um destino egual, porque é abstracto, para os homens e para as cousas — uma designação egualmente indifferente na algebra do mysterio. (frag. 169)

I like to imagine myself a contemporary of Cesário Verde and feel within myself not more verses like the ones he wrote, but the substance of his verses. The life I drag around with me until night falls is not dissimilar to that of the streets themselves. By day, they're full of meaningless bustle and, by night, full of an equally mean- ingless lack of bustle. By day, I am nothing, by night, I am myself. There's no difference between me and the streets around the Alfân- dega, except that they are streets and I am a human soul, and this, when weighed against the essence of all things, might also count for little. Men and objects share a common abstract destiny: to be of equally insignificant value in the algebra of life's mystery. (frag. 164)[30]

Pessoa's central themes reappear in this passage, now attached to the work of Verde and his reputation for extolling the virtues of noctambulism in his poetry: the drudgery of work, the saturation of the city streets by a monotony that stifles any possibility of human connection, and the reduction of humanity to the status of a mere object or thing. But there are key differences between the two chroniclers of Lisbon that become clear upon considering Verde in greater depth.

In "Pharmakopolis: Cesário Verde's Lisbon" (2017), Charles Rice-Davis characterizes the poet's legacy as that of "the aimless, somnambulist flaneur" (13) whose work leaves only "the traces of a purposeless, wandering gaze cast throughout the city" (14) of Lisbon. In tune with Walter Benjamin's analysis that "the idle- ness of the flâneur is a demonstration against the division of labor," the implication is that there is a positive aspect to Verde's aimless, purposeless drifting (Rice-Davis 2017, 17, citing Benjamin 1999, 427). This idleness is evident in the form, imagery, and themes of Verde's poems. In Rice-Davis's telling, the poet gives himself over to noctambulism, abandoning all other pursuits and submitting to the practice to the point of dependency. He specifically notes the relevance of stimulants such as coffee and cigarettes for Euro- pean flânerie and connects this theme with Verde and his work (20, 28, citing Schmidt 2003). The flâneur integrates into "the city's cyclical processes" with no other object than to catalyze a change of mood: "What 'happens' in the flâneur narrative is the very formation of the flâneur as subject" (28). Without saying so in such stark terms, the article makes clear that this nightly urban wandering is a self-perpetuating and thus also obsessive practice.

For Pessoa, however, the hallmark elements of Verde's urban wanderings are dulled, their catalyzing effects muted. The discourse of flânerie is there in *The Book of Disquiet*, but its humanizing aspirations are betrayed and ultimately snuffed out by the staid urban form and the monotony of modern city life. Spontaneity is not just fleeting but largely elusive in the Lisbon of Guedes and Soares. The positive quality of the idleness and pointlessness that Baudelaire and Verde extolled, that Benjamin and later de Certeau analyzed, is gone. The sensory connection with urban cycles, whether day or night, is absent. While Verde experienced and adapted to the ever-shifting and destabilized world of modern Lisbon, Pessoa experienced only its monotony. *The Book of Disquiet* is imprinted with this monotony, despite its aesthetic of rupture and shattered narrative structure. And it is arguably the obsessive, recurring fixation with this monotony that makes it such an enduring and quintessentially modern text.

Chapter 5
Bilbao Rebuilt: Urban Fixations and the After-Image

Bilbao is perhaps the Iberian city whose international reputation has changed most since the late twentieth century. While the Seven Streets or Zazpikaleak that comprise the city's medieval Casco Viejo continue to be the center of the city, the area along its segment of the Nervión river has been the focal point for sporadic modern urban planning. The plans drawn up in the eighteenth and nineteenth centuries—Nicolás Loredo's plan of 1786, the failed plan of 1861 crafted by Amado Lázaro, and the plan of 1876 by Alzola, Achúcarro, and Hoffmeyer—were largely ineffective, and in the 1990s the city was pushed into the global consciousness by the creation of highly symbolic, if limited, projects such as the construction of the Guggenheim Museum. Understanding the city's historical development along with a theoretical account of how urban images are detached from their referents in the twenty-first century provides the basis for approaching two Bilbao-centered graphic novels. Each is a visual meditation on urban obsession.

En segundo plano (2015), by Josep Busquet, Pedro J. Colombo, and Aintzane Landa, narrates a young man's obsession with a woman from a photograph, as the comic depicts Bilbao in line with a longstanding tradition of urban and architectural photography. Moreover, renowned Basque colorist Aintzane Landa makes compelling contributions to the urban-themed tale. The second example is *Morirse en Bilbao* (2018), by Kike Infame and Sr. Verde, a graphic novel that was first published in fanzine installments from 2011 through 2016. Here the creators imagine a post-apocalyptic Bilbao of the twenty-second century that is partially underwater and undergoing a zombie threat. Analysis here emphasizes specific city images from the comic and hinges on Joan Ramon Resina and Dieter Ingenschay's theorization of what they call the urban after-image.

The Seven Streets, the Bilbao Effect, and the After-Image

While the focus of this chapter will be more on twenty-first-century cultural production and the contemporary refashioning of the city as a global cultural capital, it is nonetheless useful to work swiftly through some historical details of Bilbao's urban planning. The changes that the largest Basque city experienced in the nineteenth century present many of the same characteristics already discussed in previous chapters. Bilbao's medieval city center, for instance, consisted of a rigid series of parallel streets situated on the east bank of the Nervión river. These streets included Somera (upper street), Artekale (middle street), and Barrenkale (lower street) and became known as "the seven streets," or in Basque, as the Zazpi-kaleak. Today these parallel lines metonymically denote the entire old quarter, or Alde Zaharra, of the city (Woodworth 2008, 130). Bilbao-born author Miguel de Unamuno knew them well, and used them as a setting for his early novel *Paz en la guerra* (see Salazar Arechalde 2008, 183–84, 190).

Like Catalonia, the Basque Country was an early industrial center in modern Spain. The courtly capital of Madrid, while populous, developed comparatively little productive capacity. As it did in Barcelona, too, the nineteenth century saw the destruction of Bilbao's medieval walls in support of the modern understanding of the open city as a hub for regional trade and commerce. The proximity of the city to the Nervión river was a clear industrial advantage, as it positioned Bilbao along the axis of a major maritime transportation network. Yet despite boasting such a prime location, the city was never subjected to sufficient urban planning.

A number of early plans for Bilbao were hatched only to fail. Nicolás Loredo's expansion plan of 1786 was never implemented. Architect Silvestre Pérez's idea for the Puerto de la Paz was abandoned in 1814. One meaningful advance was the creation of the city's Plaza Nueva, begun in 1821 and continued over a period of thirty years. Signifying a changing urban landscape with claims to modernization, the plaza has received continual poetic treatment by many figures from Miguel de Unamuno to Jon Juaristi.[1] Still, a more concerted effort to imagine the city as a whole proved elusive. In 1862, the Catalan planner Amado Lázaro, who had been given the responsibility by Bilbao's municipal government, submitted a plan based in urban research and influenced by the work of Ildefons Cerdà. By 1865, however, the plan was discarded completely due to local pressures.[2] A renewed expansion plan of 1876 envisioned a grid on the other side of the Nervión, to be constructed on the Abando plateau (see Cenicacelaya 2009, 17, 20).[3] This time Pablo Alzola, Severino Achúcarro, and Ernesto Hoffmeyer accounted for the previous local missteps of Lázaro's Cerdà-inflected plan

(Mas 2000, referring to Alzola, Achúcarro, and Hoffmeyer 1878).
Javier Cenicacelaya details the importance and ambition of the
plan by Alzola, Achúcarro, and Hoffmeyer and its elegant use of
curved streets to link important sites over the existing terrain, as
well as the functionality of its grid and diagonals. Yet his study also
chronicles the city's subsequent planning as a series of failures:
"de modo que Bilbao, después del magnífico Plan de Ensanche de
finales del XIX, ha renunciado a idearse como ciudad" (2009, 18;
thus Bilbao, after the magnificent Expansion Plan toward the end
of the nineteenth century, has given up thinking about itself as
a city). His judgment is applied even to the General Plan of 1994,
in effect noting the insufficiency of over one hundred years of
urbanistic thinking.

Urbanism is of course a social practice, and the lack of sustained
thinking about the city's form that Cenicacelaya criticizes was not
due solely to ineffective planning but also to social upheaval and
war. In 1937 the Basque Country was heavily bombed in a brutal
campaign early in the Spanish Civil War. During the regime of
Francisco Franco that followed, Basque cities suffered the common fate of other urban areas under the dictatorship. Francoist
urban planning was either neglected outright, as it was during the
decade following the end of the Civil War on April 1, 1939, or else,
as it was during the 1950s and '60s, handed over to speculators
with little foresight. Although certainly limited by such a context,
the idea of planning Greater Bilbao finally gained force with the
1964 Plan Comarcal del Gran Bilbao. This was a time in which
urbanization increased across Spain with many people migrating
to larger cities such as Madrid, Barcelona, and also Bilbao. These
rural dwellers sought opportunities after surviving the lean years
of the early dictatorship's period of autarky (Vegara 2001, 90). In
Cenicacelaya's view, the Basque city's 1964 plan was preoccupied
with zoning and building and promoted unorganized growth at the
expense of any real thinking about urbanity. The Bilbao plan was
supported by a technocratic turn in the dictatorship, designed to

superficially legitimate Spain in the eyes of liberal European governments, and thus it escaped any real criticism as it followed its course through the 1970s (Cenicacelaya 2009, 18).

Popular interest in participatory urbanism notably increased after Franco's death in 1975 and the Spanish constitution of 1978.[4] Even so, Bilbao's riverfront area in particular continued to be mired in a state of decay and obsolescence (Vegara 2001, 90). The need for systematic planning efforts that might be informed by existing topographical features was compounded in 1983 when the Nervión flooded old Bilbao, killing some one hundred people and causing excessive damage (Cenicacelaya 2009, 20). Cristina Diez Ridruejo's study of the post-1983 commercial revitalization of the zone provides illuminating context regarding what was at stake:

La zona comercial del Casco Viejo—que quedó totalmente destruida por las inundaciones—, la componen básicamente siete calles con cerca de un millar de comercios, pero además, el Casco Viejo inundado también cuenta con: 6.000 vecinos, 3 iglesias, la Catedral, la Biblioteca municipal, El Kiosko art-decó de la música, el Teatro Arriaga, el Mercado Central, 4 puentes, la Plaza Nueva, la primera sede del Banco de Bilbao, 2 estaciones de tren de cercanías, el primer hospital de Bilbao, las casas natales del escritor Unamuno y el músico Arriaga, la sede de Euskaltzaindia (Academia de la lengua vasca), el primer edificio de la Bolsa de Bilbao, el museo Histórico y Etnográfico, un árbol singular (tilo), etc. (2016, 56)

The commercial zone of the Casco Viejo—that was totally destroyed by the flooding–, is basically composed of seven streets with around one thousand businesses, but also, the flooded Casco Viejo also includes: six thousand residents, three churches, the Cathedral, the city library, the art-deco music Kiosk, the Arriaga Theater, the Central Market, four bridges, the Plaza Nueva, the first headquarters of the Bank of Bilbao, two commuter train stations, Bilbao's first hospital, the birth houses of the writer Unamuno and the musician

Arriaga, the headquarters of Euskaltzaindia (the Academy of the
Basque Language), the first building of the Bilbao Stock Exchange,
the Museum of History and Ethnography, a singular tree (tilo), etc.

Despite the historical and now urgent need for action, the plan
that developed in the wake of this catastrophic flooding would only
receive approval a decade later. Cenicacelaya's account suggests
that Ibon Areso's 1994 plan lacked the vision necessary to unite
such a neglected metropolitan area. Instead it circumscribed and
limited the positive effects such planning might have had: "el plan
estrangulaba el desarrollo de la ciudad con la proposición de un
cinturón de ronda, un cinturón de ronda, un anillo, en una estructura, la del Bajo Nervión, de carácter lineal" (2009, 21–22; the plan
strangled the city's development with the proposal of a beltway,
a beltway, a ring, on a structure, that of the Lower Nervión, of a
linear nature).[5] Moreover, contradictory aspects of the plan even
jeopardized public safety, as argued in Cenicacelaya's analysis of
the Gran Vía's ambiguity as pedestrian space that also permitted
busses and taxi traffic (26, 29). He concludes that in Bilbao's case,
urbanism was harnessed to create a city whose worth was determined by something other than the value it held for its inhabitants.
The resulting vision was one that played to what David Harvey
(1996) has called intercity competition: thus Bilbao was rebuilt
to be sold as a destination city that would attract fairs and invite
speculative markets.

Given the city's history of ineffective urban planning, it may
seem a surprise that people began talking of the "Bilbao effect"
as the twenty-first century approached. Also referred to as the
"Guggenheim effect" (Leira 2009, 36), the moniker recognized the
city's increased global visibility within a form of global capitalism
predicated on accumulation through exploitation of the urban service economy. This celebrated effect was the product of calculated
attempts to stimulate global interest in the city through selected
site-specific improvements. The inauguration of the Guggenheim

museum on the banks of the Nervión in 1997 was a catalyzing event. Once it was built, Eduardo Leira writes, the museum became "un 'motor' de cambio y un dinamizador sin igual del proceso de transformación urbana y de reactivación económica de Bilbao" (2009, 36; an "engine" of change and an unequalled driver of Bilbao's urban transformation and economic reactivation). While the Frank Gehry–designed Guggenheim provided an anchor for increased tourism, it was part of a broader strategy carried out in the 1990s. Other key elements included the creation of the Bilbao metro, inaugurated in 1995 and designed by British architect Norman Foster, and the Euskalduna Conference Center and Music Hall, inaugurated in 1999 and designed by Federico Soriano and Dolores Palacios.[6] Star architects were called in as a way of changing international perceptions of the city and using its built environment as a way to promote capital accumulation through the cultural and economic activity of selling place (Philo and Kearns 1993; see also Fraser 2011, 2015).

The singular representation of Bilbao as a spectacular success story—a model case or even a miracle—hides the ways the planning of the so-called creative city has been a much more widely used urbanistic approach (Rodríguez and Vicario 2005, 269). The global changes prompting the shift from an industrial economy to a service economy that has been analyzed in Bilbao's case can be observed in numerous other urban centers in the post-Fordist era of capital's flexible accumulation strategies (Leira 2009, 37).[7] The emergence of a city-region concept in the Basque Country in the twenty-first century illustrates how urban areas must leverage unique material and cultural landscape features to attract investment and spending. In this case, the city-region, or what Alfonso Martínez Cearra calls the "Euskadi ciudad-región global" (2005, 349; Basque global city-region) concept, is constituted by the close and complementary urban capitals of Bilbao, Donostia-San Sebastian. and Vitoria-Gasteiz, and leverages the cultural heritage and competitive advantages of some 160 rural communities for an emerging rural tourism market that relies on urban proximity (Vegara 2001, 88–89). As this example conveys, urban images are now routinely and carefully cultivated as cultural constructions in their own right with the potential to attract global capital. Joan Ramon Resina and Dieter Ingenschay's edited collection *After-Images of the City* (2003) builds off of the legacy of David Harvey's urban critique to advance an intriguing argument about the nature of contemporary urban images. Placing this argument within its proper context has the simultaneous advantage of suggesting connections with the modern history and language of obsession.

After-Images of the City zeroes in on one of the central ideas of Harvey's wider scholarly project. This is the Marxian notion that capital is a process, one that Harvey borrows more immediately from the post-war urban thinking of Henri Lefebvre. As a process, capital must make use of material forms and concrete places provisionally only to abandon them when greater potential for speculative accumulation presents itself in a different place and form. The kernel of this theory is Lefebvre's dictum—outlined in *The Production of Space* and *The Survival of Capitalism*—that capitalism has survived throughout the twentieth century by producing space in its own image. Harvey adapts this thinking to comment on what he calls capitalism's "spatial fix" (Lefebvre 1976, 1991; Harvey 1996). This fix cannot be understood as an obsession itself, even in the social sense, precisely because capital's social grip on a given place and time releases all too easily when it becomes unprofitable. There is no lingering addiction to a given space or place once that relationship, defined by profit and exchange-value, wanes. Capital is a process, not a person, and the ephemeral character of its attachment to place directs its accumulation practices only in the short-term. This is a superficial attachment. The real obsession of capital, if one can see value in its provisional personification, or of those who harness its accumulative power, is an addiction to profit. The urban image has become something quite profitable during the modern age. In *The Right to the City* (1996), Lefebvre suggests this shift begins to unfold during the nineteenth century as the exchange value of the city begins to eclipse its use-value. The practice of deriving exchange-value from the modern urban image relies on cultivating a certain obsession with place on the part of modern consumers. This obsession works both socially, at the large scale, and individually, in recurring patterns of consuming place.[8] While urbanites who live and work in a city still enjoy a certain access to its landscape as a use-value, it nonetheless operates as a clear exchange-value via patterns of travel and tourism and forms of cultural production and discourse—the growing regional and international market for the comic and graphic novel among them—that invoke Bilbao in the wider urban imaginary. It is here that the notion of the after-image proves a powerful tool.

Resina and Ingenschay's preface to the essays collected in *After-Images of the City* is characterized by a form of broad thinking that can be applied, in theory, to any global urban place, any modern time frame, and any literary genre or mode of cultural production with the power to channel the urban imaginary. The stated goal of their book is to explore "how the city becomes a fetishized object for a gaze that is caught in the symbolic conventions of cultural or ideological consumption" (2003, xvii). Though the volume does not include a chapter on Bilbao, two of the essays are devoted to the Iberian cities of Barcelona and Madrid, respectively: Resina's chapter explores how the Catalan capital has been "apprehended through acts of imagination" that cannot be fully severed from urban planning activity, social conflict, and specific aesthetic examples ranging from sculpture to film and the novel (2003b, 75); Ingenschay's chapter delves into literary production in even greater detail, reading Madrid's urban imaginary through the prose works of canonical nineteenth- and twentieth-century literary authors (2003, 123–38).[9] The notion of after-image both chapters share is not solely restricted to "the narrowly optic sense" of the word but instead conceived in broad terms as the more "general sense of 'visuality,' which includes tropes, mental arrangements of spatial information, and . . . the vanishing of 'the real'" (Resina and Ingenschay 2003, xii). Theirs is a call for "urban analyses that take into account the intrinsic instability of the image" (xvii).

What precisely is the nature of this instability? It is twofold. Resina and Ingenschay's intention is to highlight, as the volume's contributions do, "the moment (and movement) between the provisional 'freezes' in which an urban image comes to 'rest'" (xvii). After-images are unstable because they "depend on the ontological gap between perception and representation" (xiii), a constantly shifting realm. This instability means that cities thus become "a score for multiple self-projections, a space teeming with endless signification, a poly-palimpsestuous site"; they are subject to "endless" rewritings and reimaginings (xiv).[10] These invocations of multiplied meaning and endlessness can be taken—as Davis's modern history of obsession might suggest—as confirmations that being a specialized university scholar requires a degree of obsessive practice. But beyond the question of the vocabulary used and their singular analytical focus as specialists, what they are analyzing is itself an obsessive, modern social phenomenon. Though the editors do not explicitly frame it as such, the assertion of *After-Images of the City* is that a certain fixation with the idea of the city is pervasive in modern, urbanized social life. As Resina's generalized statement suggests, it is just not true today "that one transcends and leaves behind the imaginary," rather, there is a "visual sensation that lingers after the stimulus that provoked it has disappeared" (2003a, 1).

This very discussion of the urban after-image reveals quite an implicit connection with the obsessed modern thinking at the center of Lennard Davis's book-length history. This connection is established through what is at once both the trope and the reality of a persistent idea, a lingering thought. The malleability, the lingering nature, the potentially endless extension of the urban idea is made possible by the social and material conditions of modern life. The notion of the after-image is predicated on the fact that the modern consciousness imprinted with this urban image is vulnerable to stimulus. It is this vulnerability that is unstable, that looks for something solid to hold onto in a world of changing conditions and fleeting sensations. As Marx wrote, all that is solid melts into air in the modern age—a phrase whose meaning is explicitly urbanized by Marshall Berman. The ever-present "ontological gap," the persistence of the instability of the urban image, is connected to the variability with which the city image is harnessed in the interests of capital for various accumulative projects. One could argue that the obsessive elements of urban planning practice inaugurate an obsessive and endless thinking about the city that spreads from a specialized class of planners to the general population. Such an argument follows logically from, and is an urbanized retelling consistent with, Davis's work on what he called the democratization of partial madness. The forces of capital—human made and directed—not only shape the urban image and environment, they also are designed to cultivate and derive value from the modern obsessions of consumers who adopt a transactional understanding of the city in their own aesthetic production and consumption. While both of the graphic novels discussed in this chapter deal with the urban image of Bilbao, the first signifies a return to the obsessed modern specialist at the heart of Davis's history, while the second turns to the larger social scale of the urban after-image as an obsession in its own right.

Urban Shutter Bugs: The Banality of Photographic Obsession in *En segundo plano* (2015)

Baudelaire's celebration of flânerie is a clear point of reference for understanding urban modernity. The modern type of the flâneur, that of an aimless city stroller, is a touchstone for approaching a great number of Iberian literary practices, as has already been suggested through comments on the prose of Emilia Pardo Bazán (as discussed in Chapter 3) and the poetry of Cesário Verde (in

Chapter 4), for example. Simultaneously, the influence of flânerie can be observed in the enduring practice of urban photography. European interest in the photograph was of course being stoked during the very same decades in which Charles Baudelaire lived and wrote. The argument has often been made that the appeal of photographic representation, along with the influence of a range of scientific fields in development during the early and mid-nineteenth century, helped to shape and define forms of literary realism. There are natural affinities between the notion of someone who wanders the city, observing urban reality and capturing mental images, and someone who does the same but with camera in hand. The former may later record fleeting impressions in prose poems, for example, while the latter will later develop indexical images pointing back toward something just as ephemeral. Both activities tend to presume an attitude of cool detachment and relative disinterest, a class position sufficient to enjoy leisure time, and a fascination for urban life.

The cultural practice of urban photography spread throughout the twentieth century due to such factors as technological advancements in the construction of more powerful lenses and the mass-production of sensitive film, as well as the manufacture of affordable, easily portable, hand-held cameras. These developments arise in tandem with accelerating patterns of interurban tourism. Understood within this social context, the photographic representation of city scenes might itself be more extensively chronicled as an obsessive modern practice. There is no doubt that it has been approached in this way in prose and film. One famous example is the short story "Las babas del diablo" (1959, The devil's drool) by Belgian-born Argentine writer Julio Cortázar, and the film it inspired, Michelangelo Antonioni's *Blow-up* (1966). While the film differs in some respects from the prose story, common to both is an obsession with photographic representation. In each case, the central character develops a fixation with an individual photograph that inspires obsessive thinking and leads to the heightened drama of a mystery-like scenario. Photography thus assumes the status of a new device that nonetheless contributes to a preexisting form of modern urban storytelling. Take photography out of the equation and you are still left with the story of an obsessive pursuit that echoes the monomaniacal protagonist's movements in a mystery tale like Emilia Pardo Bazán's "La gota de sangre." Similarly, in Cortázar and Antonioni, the obsessive narratives all transform a relatively mundane observation into the anchor for an investigation that threatens to spiral out of control. As in the detective fiction models that also developed out of a fusion of the literary modes of realism and romanticism, the investigator's obsession is portrayed as a psychologically remarkable trait. His relative social marginality corresponds with a superior intellect, a discerning attention capable of seeing what others do not, and a potential for arriving at greater social knowledge.

While this sort of photographic obsession is dramatized to great effect by both the prose author and the filmmaker, it is nonetheless important to note that it has become so ingrained in modern urban culture that it is somewhat unremarkable. Today, obsessing over images is a clear social norm and even a value of sorts. Prior to the mass availability of digital cameras and the ubiquity of image-driven social media accounts, widespread interest in photography and patterns of modern tourism had already led to the habitual capturing of urban images by city residents and travelers alike. To follow the line of thinking suggested by Davis's history, photographic obsession was a modern value spurred on by a combination of technological advance and social expectation. No longer a socially marginal figure, an urban flâneur wandering the city with camera in hand soon in fact became emblematic of modernity. To understand precisely how banal, democratized, and institutionalized the practice of obsessive urban photography has become, one can turn to the Bilbao-situated graphic novel *En segundo plano* (2015).

Created by Josep Busquet, Pedro Colombo, and Aintzane Landa, the central plotline is constructed around a conventional boy-meets-girl urban love narrative. Its central character is Raúl, an urban photographer of the modern, specialized, and mildly depressive type. The opening page depicts the first time that Raúl, as a child, encountered a camera in three panels arranged in vertical succession. The very first panel approximates the ratio of a 3×5 photo image and depicts a scenic rural house following the rule of thirds, an element of basic photographic composition. The second is a narrow landscape panel depicting a close-up of the camera on the table. The lens and the top of the camera are ever-so-slightly cut out of the image by the panel border and white gutter space. In the third panel, the perspective shifts. The protagonist stares at the camera lens while facing readers, who now see the viewfinder on the back. He is amazed and totally focused on the object, which appears to be a manual 35 mm. The voice of an adult communicates to Raúl's sister that, although it is broken, it is a gift that should entertain the young child (5). The next page dramatizes Raúl reaching out to touch the camera and presents an extreme close-up of its lens. The third page effects a temporal jump and consists of a single image—a selfie taken by a young-adult Raúl using a bathroom mirror—taken with a more modern, and of course smaller, hand-held digital camera (67). The youngster is portrayed as completely enthralled by the representational power of the photographic image, and this state of fascination is quickly confirmed as continuing as he ages into adulthood.

Next, a full blank page effects what turns out to be a great shift not merely in temporal terms but in emotional terms. The protagonist now works in a photography store where he must carry out monotonous tasks on a daily basis. The immediate implication is that he has transitioned from the pursuit of leisure photography to the banal and uninspiring world of routinized work photography. The graphic novel confirms this with a visual example. In the store, Raúl asks an older woman to smile as a first-person narration in yellow-framed text has him reflecting on his lack of enthusiasm for the mechanical and repetitive job that requires him to take, print, and cut headshots (9–10). Outside of the store, he takes on other ad-hoc photography gigs through his network of contacts, for example, serving as a wedding photographer (12), or in another case—as a sort of paid dare—donning the jersey of the San Sebastián team known as La Real to take photos at a football match where local Bilbao team Atlétic plays against Barça (50–51). These gigs he also regards as uninspiring. When his sister suggests that he submit an image to a contest that pays 500 euros, his internal reflections reveal a disparagement of the banality of so much modern photography. He dismisses the kind of stock image that tends to win contests, "la típica foto facilona" (the typical easy photo), and as an example readers are shown a panel-photo of vegetation growing out from a crack in the concrete (28).

By contrast, photography still seems to hold his attention when disconnected from the monotony of work and the predictability of aesthetic urban cliché. Much of the graphic novel is devoted to Raúl's leisurely movements through Bilbao and to the photographs that result from his urban wanderings (see, for example, 13, 28). His reflections on the page reveal a consistent low-level interest in the mystery of photography, in what might be going on behind the scenes of a certain image: he wonders who each person he photographs really is, what motivates them, or where they are going. This is a mode of thought that is carried to an extreme in the spectacular narratives of "Las babas del diablo" and *Blow-up*, but here its cognitive energy is decidedly quotidian. The comic's depiction of low-level photographic obsession is relatively banal, even socially normative, and bears little in common with clinical categories of abnormality. That is, the protagonist's fixation on a certain photograph is presented more or less as the natural accompaniment to his generalized passion for photography, his vocation as an avid photographer.

There are two instances in which Raúl markedly obsesses over an individual image. The first is a photograph of a man with a mysterious package who is staring down into the Nervión river. When it is first introduced, it appears repeated in three vertical reframings on a single page. Each panel effects a subsequent zoom-out from what appears as a single image, progressively situating the man within a wider urban geography. In the second panel a row of urban buildings come into view, and the third panel offers a much more expansive horizontal panorama of constructions along the Nervión. This zoom-out movement is the very same conceit that drives the prose story "Las babas del diablo" and the film *Blow-up*. Raúl's inner meditations on this particular photograph and its subject quickly cover a range of ground: "¿Qué hace en el puente?" (What is he doing at the bridge?), "Está esperando a alguien?" Is he waiting for somebody?), "¿Ha venido a despedirse de este sitio?" (Has he come to say goodbye to this place?), "¿Lleva una nota de suicidio en el bolsillo?" (Does he have a suicide note in his pocket?), "¿O simplemente ha ido a comprar una escoba para casa y se ha parado un rato a ver la ría?" (15; Or has he simply gone out to buy a broom to bring home and stopped to look at the river for a bit?). Toward the end of the graphic novel, the same photo reappears, revealing just how long the protagonist has been obsessively fixated on it. At this point, Raúl imagines his own explanation for the man's presence at the river. The story he invents has the man once again returning to fishing after a long absence—the man has not been fishing even once during the twenty-three years, five months, and seven days an unnamed woman has been gone from his life (64-67). What Raúl has discovered is not how to investigate and uncover a sordid history, but instead that he enjoys fictionalizing the lives of those he has photographed: "He descubierto que no solo me encanta capturar momentos, sino que me encanta escribir esas historias" (67; I have found out that not only do I love capturing moments, I also love writing these histories). Instead of a spectacular narrative where the obsessed protagonist investigates a photograph and gets more than he bargained for, Raúl in effect uses photography as a way to retreat even further into his own mind, as a vehicle for his obsessive ruminations.

The second instance of an image that obsesses Raúl more than usual is the photograph that has motivated the title of the graphic novel. *En segundo plano* (In the background) refers to a single photograph Raúl had once taken in a bar of his friend Carlos. To the right of Carlos, in the background of the image, there appears a certain woman we later learn is named Nahia. Raúl's memory of this image is stimulated by his use of an online social media platform called flizkr where he uploads and blogs about his leisure photography. He traces a comment expressing interest in his photographs back to the flizkr site of a red-haired woman with green eyes who likes cats. He appears to immediately recognize her and goes to his extensive analog photo archive to find the bar photo of Carlos. It is the woman's gaze that had him hypnotized from the moment he printed that photo, and he becomes fixated on her presence in the photo's background. He reaches out to her through the internet and awaits a response. His pursuit of the behind-the-scenes reality of the woman captured in the photograph, however, forces him into social situations that prove challenging for him to navigate. Compared to "Las babas del diablo" and *Blow-Up*, the stakes are far lower, and despite his brief fixation, Raúl returns to rest in the state of mild depression in which he has been mired throughout the graphic novel. He remains aloof and alone, preferring his obsessive thinking to the company of others.

One single page in the book shows how the obsessive fixation with Nahia plagues him. At this point in the storyline he has reached out to her over flizkr and is anxiously awaiting her reply. Sixteen similar images, all framing Raúl's head and shoulders, are organized into four rows and columns (See Figure 5.1). He is wearing a different shirt in each photo, such that the series conveys the succession of various days spent waiting with no response from her. In each snapshot he sustains more or less the same facial expression, with only subtle changes visible around the eyes, in the muscles of the forehead, and in the line representing his mouth. In the last row, he becomes visibly disappointed and ends with his head down

FIGURE 5.1. A page from *En segundo plano* featuring sixteen similar images of Raúll; only his shirt is changed from one to the next, indicating time's passing, and his expression turns to a frown (Busquet, Colombo, and Landa 2015, 42).

on the keyboard in defeat (42). Nahia has not responded. The sixteen images function as a remarkable depiction of the monotony accompanying his fixation. This depiction is carried out in a way that foregrounds the theme and form of photographic representation. Each panel is cropped to suggest the headshot format Raúl shoots in his work at the photography store, thus further recalling the monotony of his repetitive job. Comics form here provides a further reinforcement of this theme. In prose fiction, the depiction of a character's physical characteristics would generally happen once, when the character is first introduced for example. Yet in comics, due to a property that theorists call iconic redundancy, quite frequently a character is repetitively, redundantly reintroduced to maintain continuity in action between one panel and the next. In the case of this sixteen-panel page, the comic's creators excessively exploit this visual property's potential to become repetitive as a way of emphasizing the theme of obsession. The gutters separating the panels do not convey action or changes of emotion as much as they do the banal monotony of time's passing and the fixity of Raúl's state of mind.

Raúl's does manage to meet up with Nahia as the graphic novel comes to its conclusion. He meets her at a party at his sister's place, later runs into Nahia and a friend on the street, and thereafter asks his sister to invite Nahia to a second party at her place where he succeeds in talking with her, albeit very briefly (71). Raúl's blog is then unexpectedly picked up for a book publication curiously bearing the identical title and cover of the graphic novel *En segundo plano* (78). At a book signing organized by the publisher, Nahia arrives with his book in hand and hands Raúl her number telling him to call her to get a drink. While until this point she has been depicted with green eyes, now her eyes are pink (78–79). Surprisingly, Raúl promptly tosses her number in the trash, leaving it to readers to speculate why. After a punctuating white page, the coda of *En segundo plano* includes a vision of events from Nahia's perspective: the photo where she appeared in the background, the first party, the encounter on the street, the second party, all quickly narrated in succession (81–92). Throughout, her eyes are pink. The one exception is when she appears in the photo with her cat that Raúl had found on flizkr, wherein she appears to have green eyes, which readers may conclude may be due to an accident of lighting or some form of digital augmentation. During the comic's coda, when Nahia awaits but does not receive Raúl's call, she puts his graphic novel back on her shelf and apparently moves on in her life (92). In retrospect, the reader may properly entertain some doubt about whether Raúl was obsessed with an idealized green-eyed woman who did not exist, whether he loses interest in Nahia because of his previous failures in striking up a conversation with her, or whether she was just a muse for the graphic novel we are reading—a vehicle for his internal fixation and his predilection for fictionalizing the lives of others rather than pursuing human relationships.

En segundo plano is notable for its page layout and composition, storyline, narrative pacing, formal innovation, and most of all for the work of colorist Aintzane Landa, who employs a range of color wash techniques throughout the comic. The theme of obsession is evident from the title of the work through its various plot elements and the techniques it uses to characterize its protagonist. Raúl's modern urban life is defined by repetitive drudgery and infused with a pervasive monotony that is only intermittently interrupted by moments that pique his interest and push him into a state of obsessive fixation. Raúl's activities as an urban flâneur are prompted by his obsessive interest in photographs, and these wanderings also serve to reinforce that original obsession with the camera that has originated in his childhood. As happens to the protagonists of "Las babas del diablo" and *Blow-Up*, his life is destabilized to some degree by his efforts to delve into the reality of what he sees in the photograph of Nahia. Yet rather than proving to be threatening to his person, this destabilization has only relatively banal effects for his romantic life. The realization that

he enjoys fictionalizing the lives of his photographic subjects ultimately leads to his further social disconnection. Even though the
urban references to Bilbao are specific and crop up in important
moments, including the photograph of the man at the Nervión
river that is central to establishing the theme and tone of the comic,
the urban image is largely implicit in what is an internally focused
urban tale. As the graphic novel's closing scenes suggest, Raúl's
monomaniacal obsession for taking, collecting, and speculating
about photographs can be understood as a form of self-protective
insulation against the unpredictable aspects of modern urban life.

The Unstable Urban Image in *Morirse en Bilbao* (2018) by Kike Infame and Sr. Verde

Providing quite a contrast with *En segundo plano*'s interior focus
on obsessive fixation, the city is invoked as a highly unstable but
persistent image in the action-oriented graphic novel *Morirse
en Bilbao*. The artist in this case is critic and journalist Enrique
Martínez-Inchausti Portu, who commonly signs as Kike Infame,
and the writer is Gorka Echevarría González, otherwise known as
Sr. Verde. Finally collected in a single volume in 2018, the story's
five installments were originally released from 2011 to 2016, with
covers drawn by Víctor Santos, Alex Orbe, Alberto Muriel, and
Raquel Alzate. During the final installment, the comic's two creators brought in other artists to design certain panels—José Carlos Torre, Roberto González, Amaia Ballesteros, Pi Ortiz, Oskar
Blanco, Dani Gojénola, and Mikel Bao. Each is attributed in the
panel frame itself, using the English phrase "Art by" followed by
the individual artist's name. This very fact reveals a self-awareness
regarding the international comics market. While the use of English
may draw attention here—overall, text zones are predominantly
composed in Spanish—the graphic novel also includes phrases
in French, German, and Basque. At one point, an extended dialogue in Russian is translated into Spanish text that is marked off

in brackets. Within the global panorama of the ninth art, such a pluri-linguistic approach can be understood as leveraging Bilbao's reputation to draw international attention.

Morirse en Bilbao borrows its title from a popular song recorded by the Bilbao band Doctor Deseo. Though that song is titled "De nuevo en tus brazos" (In your arms once again), it is more popularly known as "Morirse en Bilbao" due to its lyrics:

> Morirse en Bilbao
> No hay nada mejor
> Quemar la vida
> Para volver a nacer
> De nuevo en tus brazos
>
> *To die in Bilbao*
> *There's nothing better*
> *To call it quits*
> *In order to be reborn*
> *In your arms once again.*[11]

Love and longing, ever a standard theme of popular music, is here urbanized in nostalgic recollections of place. References to Bilbao's streets, bars, parties, and grey atmosphere pervade the song. Mentioning vice, defeat, knives, and a life lived too fast, the lyrics suggest there is something dangerous—destructive or self-destructive—embedded in the city's fabric. Bilbao's most persistent central geographical marker, the Nervión, is invoked early in the song as a way of channeling the city's paradoxical gritty beauty: "Y la ría en silencio / Susurra pecados" (And the quiet river / whispers of sin). The contradictions of this specific urban environment—one structured by loneliness, violence, and love, a listener might suppose—testify to the narrator's complex, visceral, and emotional attachment to this place. As described in the song, the hostile beauty of Bilbao's urban imaginary immediately brings

to mind the dour atmosphere and the theme of postponed or elusive redemption that pervade the modern detective or crime novel.
In borrowing from Doctor Deseo's song for their title, Kike Infame
and Sr. Verde seem to be consciously harnessing the very same
sorts of emotional attachments to Bilbao. A brief note penned
by Fernando Tarancón that is included at the beginning of the
graphic novel positions it in precisely this way, as an homage to
the creators' beloved city.

The graphic novel's narrative action is centered around a future
Bilbao, as confirmed in the first textual zone readers see: "Esta-
mos en el año 2136 y todo el norte de la península ibérica está
sumergida a causa del deshielo de los casquetes polares" (We are
in the year 2136 and the entire north of the Iberian peninsula is
underwater due to the melting of the polar icecaps).[12] Just as the
future city is now flooded with water, so, too are the pages of the
comic. On early pages, sharks and fish swim by and are superim-
posed over images of the tallest buildings. Readers learn that the
cities of Bilbao and Donostia are shielded by protective, translucent
bubbles that have also safeguarded their inhabitants from nuclear
detonations on the earth's surface. Sunken boats have emerged
as the ideal sites for prisons. Berlin is depicted as an island city
perched high atop a narrow plateau whose cliffs drop steeply into
the ocean, beneath which underwater areas of the city are pro-
tected by a glass enclosure. Later, as a battle scene unfolds in one
of the German city's underwater ballrooms, the glass enclosure
is broken and the area is flooded. In this future wasteland, water
is just as much of a threat as it is a resource.

The graphic novel's protagonist is a criminal and smuggler
known as Leire López Zumalakarregi. She is also known as Leire
Riscal—this nickname reflects the fact that she has stolen the last
thirty bottles of Marqués de Riscal wine known to exist. She is
accompanied by her loyal companion, a nameless three-eyed cat
who smokes, can drive a car, and at one moment carries a gun
and grenade to Leire deep inside an underwater prison complex

known as the 204. The comic is persistent in its allusions to Spain's twentieth-century political history, and these references are evident already in the text description of the protagonist's biographical data and possessions. For instance, she was born on April 14, the anniversary of the declaration of Spain's Second Republic, a fact that is specifically noted for readers who might otherwise have missed it. She is described as arming herself with both an AK-47—a hallmark Soviet weapon of the post-WWII era—and also a submachine gun that was manufactured in 1938 during the Spanish Civil War. These details suggest Leire's connection with the coalition of communist, Basque, and Republican identities that fought against the fascist troops of the Francoist uprising. The mention of 1938 is pertinent, as the gun's manufacture would have occurred after the widespread bombing of the Basque Country by Franco's troops in 1937. Leire Riscal and her three-eyed cat are thus positioned as politically redemptive figures. In a dramatic sense, readers who root for her to triumph over her adversaries are taking a stand also in the interests of a Civil War–era Basque, Republican identity. In fact, in the final appendices of the single-volume graphic novel, a brief ancillary comic depicts the high-ranking, later to be known as Francoist, generals of the uprising, the coordinated northern campaign of 1937 to conquer the Basque Country, and the continuing resistance of small groups of Basque fighters.

This historical and political invocation of Basqueness is further solidified by the fact that when readers first encounter Leire she has already met, befriended, and fought alongside Morgan Erzilurrugaztañazagogeaskoa Goiri, an ex-leader of the Basque government (*exlehendakari*). This is the man who declares to the protagonist that he would like to return to Bilbao to die, thus inspiring the comic's title. She pledges to help him with his goal, and once in the city, she shoots him in what might be considered a mercy killing, due to certain details of the storyline. Readers learn that in the twentieth century, Morgan had been diagnosed with an incurable disease—caused by the Gargantua virus—and cryogenically frozen. Only recently unfrozen, his disease had once again started to grow and his one desire was death in his beloved city. He had come into the possession of a mysterious briefcase, which the authorities want. Leire has hidden the briefcase and does not reveal its location to those authorities, who send her to a sunken prison boat. Given the nature of the alliances and the historical references that pervade the text, she might be considered a political prisoner, with her incarceration recalling that of dissidents held in Spain's fascist era prisons. While in the prison boat, she joins prisoners to regularly watch a form of cinematic newsreel referred to as *cinediario*, which itself suggests the NO-DOs (short for Noticiarios y Documentales [News and documentaries]) that the Francoist State used as a form of media propaganda beginning in the 1940s, during the early dictatorship.

As the action-based plot unfolds, there is an eclipse, a tsunami, a blackout, and a jailbreak, as well as multiple references to a fourth world war, all while building tension surrounding the location and contents of the mysterious briefcase. *Morirse en Bilbao*'s page layout and artistic style are as unstable and chaotic as its basic premise. Divisions between panels come and go. There are grids competing with full-page backgrounds. The comics gutter, never fixed and constantly alternating between black and white when present, is continually transgressed by images and onomatopoetic text in the course of battle scenes. Many pages lack panels or gutters of any kind. In these cases, the strategic placement of text boxes leads the reader's eyes across a sprawling and unique and muralistic landscape.[13] There is thus an instability inherent to the narrative emplotment of the graphic novel that also regularly impacts the page layout. Aesthetically, the work is, by design, a chaotic mess.

While *Morirse en Bilbao* might also be approached in the context of an emerging intensification of the market for stories acknowledging climate change (see for example *Dengue* (2015) by Rodolfo

Santullo and Matías Bergara, and Fraser [2019b]), it boasts connections to certain hallmarks of earlier science fiction. For example, the oft-repeated trope of a protective bubble famously attracted attention in Clifford D. Simak's *All Flesh Is Grass*, and the focus on a flooded dystopia appeared memorably in J. G. Ballard's *The Drowned World*. Extra-fictional urban history must also be taken into account. Given the catastrophic flooding experienced in Bilbao's center in 1983, the extreme vision of the Basque city presented by Sr. Verde and Kike Infame is consistent with the fears and anxieties of its past and present inhabitants. These fears and anxieties surrounding the impacts of excessive water on city life, grounded as they are in real urban history, are the foundational source of the narrative's tension.

This narrative tension is rendered in visible terms by the comic's art. Located just after Tarancón's introductory note and just before the initial text description of the climatological conditions in the year 2136, a two-page spread depicts a partially submerged Bilbao in great architectural detail. The scene conveys what appear to be two incompatible realities. On one hand, Bilbao is completely destroyed. The Nervión has risen to a permanent level of flooding much higher than the former street entrances to central buildings. In the left-bottom corner of the image, an electric streetcar is detached from its upper rail and seems to float along the water as a ghostly river vessel. In the same region of the page, the overhead suspension of a bridge spanning the river is broken off, and the streets in this part of the city center are below the water's surface. Yet signs of life persist. In the top-left and bottom-right regions of the spread, there are some lights on in the buildings. In the far-right upper quadrant, large towers send emissions out into the starry night, signaling that some degree of productive capacity has been retained. At middle-right, a lone bridge remains visible above the waterline, appearing to connect both banks of the river. The city's protective bubble cannot be seen, and one must wonder whether this image is transitional—conceived to push the twenty-first-century reader's image of Bilbao from the contemporary world toward that imaginary world of the narrative's twenty-second-century context.

This initial two-page comics spread is perhaps not by itself what Resina and Ingenschay would call an after-image. It is a specific and concrete city representation that does not itself shift. Yet it can nonetheless be taken as an urban image that both stems from and in turn contributes to the unstable after-image of Bilbao as a modern city. The represented urban scene reflects anxieties over the urban form that recall specific events of the city's past, and it catalyzes uncertainties about the sustainability of an urban population under the conditions governing late capitalism. The after-image is intended more as a mental concept, as something that cannot be reduced to being synonymous with visuality in the narrowly optic sense. Rather, according to Joan Ramon Resina in *After-Images of the City*, it is a "visual sensation that lingers after the stimulus that provoked it has disappeared" (2003a, 1). The formal and aesthetic properties of comics form replicate this sensation of lingering. In general, when readers turn the comics page, for instance, they see and take in both verso and recto in a glance. All the images therein are, in principle and in practice, simultaneously visible. This property of simultaneity can be harnessed for forms of page composition that are meant to be consumed holistically, all at once. The so-called gallery format of comics is one example, but even this familiar layout is merely one example of the property of iconostasis theorized by Andrei Molotiu (2012; for more about Molotiu, see Fraser 2019a).

The sprawling comics scene of a flooded Bilbao is one type of image where simultaneity and unified composition prove particularly meaningful. A comparison with cinema is useful here. While in urban cinema, a given film might group together a large-scale general shot of a city landscape and a series of establishing shots at closer distance to individual anchors of that landscape, all of these views can be suggested at once in comics in a single image. The comics reader does the work of scanning, focusing in on a given quadrant or aspect of the image. The very nature of this comics aesthetic presumes a fundamental instability in the way a comic is read. Here it is possible to speak of the reader's active and self-directed exploration as opposed to the relative passivity implied by the consumption of cinematic images. Engagement with distinguishable visual details, what might be called kinemes in the cinema, is not temporally restricted in any way. Yet just as interesting is what theorists such as Thierry Groensteen and Barbara Postema have written regarding co-presence in the comics text. On any given page, seemingly discrete images are not merely sequential, as they might be when considering reading as a linear movement of thought. Instead, they interact and co-mingle in an immediate and unregulated sense. This co-presence exists also, to some degree, across pages and chapters of a graphic narrative in what Thierry Groensteen has called the comics multiframe (2007, 22–24). A given image lingers in the mind of the visual comics reader even as the narrative progresses. It necessarily continues to exercise an influence, resonating with and being recalled by subsequent images.

The initial two-page spread that depicts Bilbao partially submerged continues to inform the subsequent pages of *Morirse en Bilbao* in precisely this way: it is a visual suggestion of urban instability that itself lingers and becomes unstable over the course of the comic. In 2136, the modern city is threatened not merely by catastrophic flooding but also by compounded apocalyptic threats. Even inside the bubbles protecting Bilbao and Donostia, for example, the dangerous Gargantua virus has been spreading among the population, and consequently a quarantine line has been established outside of Bilbao. Readers discover that the Confederación de Superestados de América (CSA) has spread the virus in Donostia and Bilbao through infected *txuletones*, large rib steaks prepared in the Astigarraga style. To the threats posed by flooding, nuclear detonations, and food-borne illness, one must add also widespread technological collapse. One of the military tactics of the CSA was to systematically prevent all technological advances in computing. During the Fourth World War, which took place prior to the first installment of the graphic novel, the CSA had used outdated but functional WWII-era weaponry in their invasion of Bilbao in order to maintain the upper hand in the absence of computerized arms. In the year 2136, their Round Man satellite has continued to prevent modern computing from working. This means that telepathic weapon links, and mind control of beasts such as dragons and dinosaurs is no longer possible. No weapons produced after the 1940s will function until Round Man is destroyed—thus the importance of Leire's pre-1940s weapons. (The mysterious contents of Morgan's briefcase are what will in fact undo the satellite's effect and restore technological capability.) The fact that these compounded apocalypses are fleshed out over the course of the graphic novel's five installments rather than detailed all at once lends the volume a continual feeling of anxiety and dread. As the primary destination suggested in the comic's title and the primary emotional attachment, Bilbao is constructed by the discourses of apocalypse as a fundamentally instable image. The graphic novel's sense of compounded danger further destabilizes the city's after-image.

The way urban architecture is represented—and perhaps more importantly not represented—in *Morirse en Bilbao* is connected with the destabilization of the after-image of the city. Beyond the initial two-page spread featuring a flooded Nervión, the most clear urban reference to Bilbao is the comic's representation of the Basílica de Begoña. This comes in a final sequence of the fifth installment. After failing to cross the Deusto bridge, Leire and crew manage to arrive at the Basílica, where the mysterious briefcase is hidden along with a bottle or two of Riscal wine. It turns out that a rocket is stored under the Basílica de Begoña, and that by launching the rocket through the cupula with the briefcase contents on board, the Round Man satellite might finally be destroyed (spoiler: new information comes to light and Leire does not destroy it).

Here, credited with the phrase "Art by Dani Gojénola," are three panels with full-page vertical extension that are allocated unevenly across another two-page spread. Each panel effects a shift in perspective in advance of the rocket's path. The ground-level perspective of the first panel depicts the towering grandeur of the basilica from a distance and a low-angle, crowding the open sky and solid foreground with onomatopoetic rumbling noise. Here what Groensteen calls the text zone and the image zone are merged (2007, 69). Text takes on the quality of a textured graphic item. To the right, the second panel portrays a high-angle shot from an altitude on level with the basilica's cupula. The point of view is much closer to the building, which allows a three-dimensional rendering of its architectural features.

Onomatopoetic text rushes from the fissured ground as if it were taking the form of rocket emissions escaping from below the surface of the earth and rushing skyward. At far right, the rocket has launched, breaching the surface and catapulting the Basilica upward. The perspective of this final panel tilts further downward, a hint that the sequences to follow will dramatize a battle in space (See Figure 5.2). This Basílica de Begoña launch sequence functions as a comics dramatization of the unstable urban image. One of the symbolic anchors of Bilbao's urban environment is uprooted and sent spinning into the air. To dispense with this symbolic anchor is at once to dispense with the idea that "the city is primarily a visual object" (Resina 2003a, 5). This is such a powerful sequence because it represents the instability of architecture, and by extension, of the monumental city.

Citing J. B. Jackson, Joan Ramon Resina writes that the modern urban image is "a blend of cartographic abstraction and aerial view" (2003a, 5, qtg. Jackson 1980, 55). Resina's elaboration suggests how the above sequence in the graphic novel might be interpreted: "The perceptual change does not mean simply that a previously dominant architectural image has been displaced by a more abstract aviator's view. A downward-looking, remote perspective has not

FIGURE 5.2. A two-page spread from *Morirse en Bilbao*, by Kike Infame and Sr. Verde, with Dani Gojénola (2019, n.p.).

taken the place of an upward-looking, more absorbed one. The mutation, rather is that architecture has become obsolete as the sole or even primary medium for visualizing the city" (5–6). The shift of perspective carried out in the Basilica de Begoña sequence in *Morirse en Bilbao* is consistent with the way the city image has shifted in urban modernity. Resina's point is that cartographic abstraction and the view from above have prompted modern urbanites to see their city abstractly, as something in principle separable from everyday living practices and ground-level sensory impressions of the city (5).[14] There are two things to note here. First, Resina keeps the discussion focused on the visual apprehension of the city without delving into the history of urban planning too explicitly. Nonetheless, the abstracted vision that drives modern city planning is a coeval force in producing this contemporary urban image—as is evident in Resina's own research into Ildefons Cerdà and Barcelona (2008). Second, although he does not mention the history of aerial photography specifically in aiding with this modern change of perspective, that is also crucial for the shift he outlines. The proliferation and consumption of overhead views of the city fundamentally changed the modern urban image, beginning with those that Gaspard-Félix Tournachon, otherwise known as Nadar, took of Paris in the mid-nineteenth century.

The most crucial assertion made by Resina is that architecture is no longer privileged as a way of approaching the city image. Applying this insight to the graphic novel's Basílica launch sequence imbues it with an allegorical weight. Architecture is viscerally and visually cast aside. This also can help explain the relative lack of architectural references in the comic. For a story that is so concerned with the urban imaginary—prominently in its title and repeatedly in its city-centric storyline—the appearance of the Basílica in the fifth installment is too little, too late. Most interesting, in this respect, is *Morirse en Bilbao*'s refusal to capitalize on the iconic urban sites that have attracted international attention through the "Bilbao effect" or "Guggenheim effect." Other recent Iberian graphic novels have indulged in seemingly endless repetition of iconic urban sites. *El fantasma de Gaudí / The Ghost of Gaudí*, for example, features architectural depictions of Barcelona on a vast number of its pages, and even organizes its chapters around Gaudí's famed creations (See Fraser 2019a, and forthcoming). Yet here in *Morirse en Bilbao*, as Resina would put it, the city image "floats free" from the built environment (2003, 6; citing Kevin Robbins 1993).

Taken together, the initial two-page spread of Bilbao partially submerged and the culminating sequence of the Basílica de Begoña launch thus constitute the two major coordinates of the abstracted approach to the urban that comes to define the modern afterimage. While *En segundo plano* adapted a single-minded mode of cognition from the nineteenth-century context to the twenty-first-century city, here Kike Infame and Sr. Verde's graphic novel showcases a complementary form of obsession. This is not an obsessive fixation on a single photograph, but an obsession with the very malleability of the urban image. The first is a clear example of simple attachment, while the second may seem to be a detachment of sorts. Yet the latter example is a fixation nonetheless. Understood as a social practice, the invocation of such a free-floating urban after-image is subject to the same sort of endless rumination and continual reassertion that obtains in more classical depictions of nineteenth-century monomania. The diminishment of everyday urban experience has become itself a social value as the city is invoked as exchange-value. It is a product to be endlessly recreated, reproduced, recycled and consumed. The urban image is in principle a mutable concept.

This unmooring of the city idea from the reality of urban life has been extensively chronicled by Marxist urban theorists focusing on the exchange-value implicit in interurban competition. The fact is that, whether in the graphic novel form or not, urban-themed cultural products are a social and urban obsession. Distancing Bilbao's image from the architectural specificity of the city and the historical specificity of its urban past, from everyday experiences and sensory impressions as they are lived on the ground has a number of consequences. To return to and extend Resina's observation, it is not just that the visual perspective on the city has mutated from an upward- to a downward-looking, aerial view. It is rather that the city image has acquired social value as an object of contemplation for an obsessive, abstracted, disembodied form of cognition. This form of cognition is not just that of the cultural creator, but also that of the modern urbanist. Urbanistic thinking itself evolved in its own way as an obsessive practice carried out by specialist planners in a milieu where endless, unfettered, and recursive imagination was seen as a normative social value. The case of Bilbao shows just how self-involved urbanism has been. As critic Cenicacelaya has written, "La verdadera visión de futuro de Bilbao no está, como pudiera parecer, en su urbanismo. La opción que el urbanismo ha tomado, tal y como he referido, está carente de planificación y repleta de enormes contradicciones" (2009,

29; The true future vision of Bilbao, does not lie, as it might seem, in its urbanism. The path that urbanism has followed, as I have asserted, is lacking in planning and full of enormous contradictions). The dystopic tale of *Morirse en Bilbao* is so compelling for readers precisely because it carries the legacy of inadequate planning to its extremes.

CONCLUSION

While the idea of urban culture may more often call to mind images of skylines, buildings, crowds, and traffic, it can also be seen as a way of thinking. This latter perspective is, in fact, one of the core insights offered by urban theory throughout the twentieth century. This is more than evident in the work of figures such as Georg Simmel, Jane Jacobs, David Harvey, Manuel Delgado Ruiz, and most extensively Henri Lefebvre, critics who analyze and critique the central ideas and the very social foundations of the modern practice of city building. Lefebvre's point of view has always been, for me, decisive. As urban planning emerged as a modern bourgeois science in nineteenth-century Europe, the city became one more exchange-value in modern social life. This is the very time period in which the urban image, in the modern sense used by Joan Ramon Resina, is forged. While cities have perhaps long been thought of in aesthetic terms, the analyses carried out in

Obsession, Aesthetics, and the Iberian City suggest a much more narrow linkage between cognition and the urban.

The vaguely defined mental conditions appearing in urbanized nineteenth-century life, having gone by the names monomania, neurasthenia, obsession, or partial madness, can be approached as reactions to the values of a newly modern social reality as much as they can be understood as individual states of mind. This book has not attempted to tie these mental states to a single root cause, but has instead pointed to the modern urban social conditions in which obsession arises as such and through which it is expressed. Culled from Lennard J. Davis's *Obsession: A History*, and complemented by insights from urban theory, there are many urban conditions that set the coordinates for the modern recognition and classification of obsessive states of mind. Boundaries of the urban and the rural are blurred as European urban planners break through medieval city walls; the breached citadel becomes an urbanized metaphor for partial madness; illness is democratized to wider segment of the population than ever before. Along with urbanization, cultures of mechanization and industrialization lead to widespread forms of repetitive labor; these repetitive tasks threaten to reduce humans to mere machines, and cognition—intellectual labor— follows suit, becoming similarly routinized. Single-minded thinking is praised and institutionalized through discrete bodies of disciplinary knowledge and university structures. The urban environment is regularized through repeated patterns—the straight line, the grid—and decorated with geometrical flourishes. Specialized urban planners become fascinated by ideas of the infinite growth and the infinite linear extension of cities. Such endless thinking emerges as a much more widespread social value in an urbanized culture that lauds excess in multiple forms: excessive production, excessive accumulation, excessive writing, excessive thinking.

It is in this modern urban context that obsession—as it is defined by Davis—emerges "as a known category involving doing or thinking one thing too much, being aware of that activity, but being unable to stop it" (2008, 32). In Europe's cities, artists, writers, and scientists—with or without Cesário Verde's access to stimulants such as coffee and cigarettes—indulge a single-minded obsession. This is a cultural and social obsession as much as it is an individual one, one that has yielded prolific writers such as Emilia Pardo Bazán—who wrote over six hundred stories, not counting other works such as novels, criticism and theater—and Fernando Pessoa— whose twenty-five thousand unorganized manuscript pages were later found among his possessions. Santiago Ramón y Cajal's obses- sion for the microscopic imaging of the neuron earned him a Nobel prize. What is so interesting is that the social obsession with spe- cialized thinking coincides with an obsession for the city itself. We have seen that Pardo Bazán, Pessoa, and Cajal turn to the urban as not just a context or backdrop, but as the source, muse, and focus of their creative endeavors. The modern urban fabric is to a large degree inseparable from their aesthetic production. Disaffected and obsessed characters such as Selva in "La gota de sangre," Juan in "El pesimista corregido," and Soares in *Livro do desassossego* can exist as such only in a modern urban environment.

These and other texts treated in this book also suggest that fur- ther research connect the notion of a specifically urbanized form of obsession with gender. In what way, for example, are the urban freedoms enjoyed by males in nineteenth- and early twentieth- century European society and the rectilinear, geometrical, repet- itive patterning of the socially instituted, masculine practice of urban planning connected with gendered categories regarding the practice of flânerie? Moreover, there is an opportunity here for research that much more concertedly delves into the archives of late nineteenth-century medicine and psychology, that incorpo- rates more clinical sources from the health sciences or culls from social psychoanalytic theory. It is possible that this book may have raised more questions than it has answered. In a sense, this is only natural given that its goals have been, first, to bring Davis's insights more fully into the realm of urban theory and, second, to map them across the uneven cultural geography of Iberian cities.

The original provocations of Davis's argument remain central to this book. Some readers who remain unconvinced may decide that obsession is solely an individual trait or characteristic, or that it is a subject that should be studied only by the clinical sciences. I continue to believe that there is value in considering how some forms of obsessive thinking acquire social prestige of a sort— whether in the intellectual, scientific, or artistic realms of modern life—while others have been stigmatized and medicalized as a problem in need of a solution. This is one of the contradictions that, if fully taken on board, may help to broaden the social critique advanced by disability studies and push it farther into the interdisciplinary terrain of urban cultural studies.

It bears repeating that this study is neither an urban studies project nor a disability studies project, but rather something in between. It has avoided the tendency to rely overtly on clinical language, description, and diagnosis. This is not merely because the distance between late nineteenth-century and contemporary diagnosis is so great, but also because the disability studies critique of the medical model is so powerful. Disability does not reside in the individual but is instead a social construction. This social construction is reshaped as time and history move on. In addition, however, I find it a compelling idea, as investigated by Henri-Jacques Stiker in *A History of Disability*, that the social changes brought on by modern, industrial, urban life would at once have been tied up with a sea-change in the emergence of disability as a social category.

If obsessive thinking becomes a modern social value of sorts, it follows that this value would be expressed in modern urban aesthetics. While the precise role the urban has played in the maladies explored in this book is not specifically addressed in these texts, there is a strong suggestion that the boredom, tedium, and pessimism such protagonists experience is both partially caused by and partially alleviated by modern urban life. The city is a contradiction in itself: it can be a joy, a place to walk through, and a wondrous sensorial experience. At the same time that it is a visual wonder, the city is also an overstimulating cacophonous assault. The modern city taxes the nerves as it stimulates the senses. The routinization and social alienation encoded into modern urban life and the modern urban grid itself nonetheless finds complement in the spontaneity that the city can still promise for some. Selva finds this spontaneity and rejuvenation in obsessive wandering through his own mystery tale, Juan in obsessive scientific investigation, Soares in endless writing, which is to say for him, endless thinking. These analyses, offered up in Chapters 3 and 4, might be considered closest to the kinds of examples that Lennard Davis himself explored. Yet they differ in that they explicitly urbanize his approach.

Obsession manifests in the urban experience in two ways—as the monomaniacal drive for a single, repeated form and as the endless flight from convention and normative expectation into unregulated creativity. Chapter 5's discussion of Josep Busquet, Pedro J. Colombo, and Aintzane Landa's comic evinces this duality in capturing the split between the protagonist's monotonous work photography and the leisure photography that for him is synonymous with the pleasures of urban wandering. One can also consider this duality at a broader scale. While there is a modern urban aesthetics of regularization, there is also a modern urban aesthetics of irregularity. As Chapter 2 argued through the revered architecture created by Antoni Gaudí, not to mention the entrancingly obsessive qualities of Hiroshi Teshigahara's documentary, it is arguably this aesthetics of irregularity that allows a work of architecture to endure. At the same time, our contemporary urbanized society's obsession with regularization threatens to subjugate human participation to a series of speculative acts controlled by the economic market. Also covered in Chapter 2, Mercedes Álvarez's documentary illustrated how human figures and what are considered nonproductive minds are the neglected and forgotten background of this urban modernity. Her contemplative film stages a confrontation between two competing visions of urban life: as exchange-value and as use-value. Chapter 5's discussion of Kike Infame and Sr. Verde's comic returned to this same antagonistic relationship, noting how the ground-level human experience of the city has ceded discursive space to a free-floating urban after-image. As an aesthetic marker, the urban image is unstable and infinitely malleable to suit the needs of capital accumulation at a given space and time. In truth this may be considered yet another urban social form that obsession takes—the monomaniacal drive for capital accumulation that ignores human experience and sells the city as an aesthetic idea rather than a living space. The obsessive aspects of wealth creation can be observed in the fact that this drive, as David Harvey has explored, leads as a matter of course to periodic crises in capitalism that can tend—in the short-term at least—to be quite unfavorable to the interests of capitalists themselves.

Another way to write this book would have been to delve further into the lives and struggles of its central figures—to approach the modern planner, the scientist, the writer, and the artist, not through culture, not through aesthetics, but through individual biography. This path was neither appealing nor possible.[1] The very approach I have selected suggests that cognitive difference—whether one calls it obsession, cyclical thinking, depression, mania, monomania, mood disorder, neurasthenia, or academic specialization—is a broader value of modern urban society and not solely an individual trait. Why pursue such an approach? At the end of *Obsession: A History*, Lennard J. Davis suggests that for many there may be comfort in knowing that obsessions are not merely individual but social phenomena. But there is another reason. The through line of this book has been to specify that obsession is inseparable from urbanization. Richard Sennett has distilled an entire tradition of urban theory into a statement he included in his book *The Crafts-man*: that in creating the city, humankind has been creating itself. To apply this notion to Davis's book, the partial madness of modern urban culture is one in which we all participate to one degree or another. It should be no surprise to think that the cultivation and reproduction of an inherently unstable, urbanized social forma-tion has induced a comparatively unstable consciousness, or to put this another way, that an unstable social consciousness has produced an unstable, urban social reality. The point is to under-stand the potential opportunity offered by this instability. If our modern urban society can acknowledge obsession as a social value that impacts aesthetic production—including the aestheticized city image and form—then perhaps this acknowledgment can impact urban planning and lead, ultimately, to the creation of a more human city, a more spontaneous, less normative city—one to which all enjoy an equal right of access and use.

NOTES

INTRODUCTION

1. It would be possible and, more-over, enlightening to frame the modern urban planning tradition as it developed in Europe and in Spain as a project of normative liberalism, melding the perspective of Lennard Davis with Iberian studies scholar Richard Cleminson's assertion (2016) that toward the end of the nineteenth century in Spain "the individual was also brought into the limelight by a cluster of social concerns pinpointed by specialist bodies and political analysts" (28); "deviance from prescribed models, whether gendered, sexual, or political (in particular anarchism and socialism, but also periphery nationalisms were designated "teratological" or monstrous, another naturalised category) . . ., was articulated in medical and psychiatric terms in the context of the individual as the store of new subjectivities and the fount of criminality, perversity, and immorality" (34–35). Cleminson explores there the oft-discussed relation of genius to madness, and the social perception that geniuses were said to embody a benign form of abnormality or degeneracy.

2. For example *Visible Cities, Global Comics* (University Press of Mississippi, 2019), *Toward an Urban Cultural Studies: Henri Lefebvre and the Humanities* (Palgrave, 2015), *Antonio López García's Everyday Urban Worlds* (Bucknell University Press, 2014), and *Henri Lefebvre and the Spanish Urban Experience* (Bucknell University Press, 2011).

3. As reflected in a complementary list of my book-length publications, *Cognitive Disability Aesthetics: Visual Culture, Disability Representations and the (In)Visibility of Cognitive Difference* (University of Toronto Press, 2018), *Cultures of Representation: Disability in World Cinema Contexts* (Wallflower/Columbia University Press, 2016), *Disability Studies and Spanish Culture* (Liverpool University Press, 2013), and *Deaf History and Culture in Spain* (Gallaudet University Press, 2009).

4. The most important book-length publications in this area, written over the past two decades, are arguably those written by Edward Baker and Malcolm Compitello, Mari Paz Balibrea, Monica Degen, Daniel Frost, Rebecca Haidt, Oliver Hochadel and Agustí Nieto-Galan, Edgar Illas, Susan Larson, Araceli Masterson-Algar, Leigh Mercer, Diana Palardy, Carlos Ramos, Joan Ramon Resina, Nathan Richardson, Jon Snyder, and Stephen Vilaseca. The full list would include a number of relevant volumes published in the Hispanic Urban Studies book series. Susan Larson (Texas Tech University) and I serve as editors of that series, whose titles include *Urban Spaces in Contemporary Latin American Literature* (González and Robbins 2019), *The Dystopian Imagination in Contemporary Spanish Literature and Film* (Palardy 2018), *Gender in Spanish Urban Spaces* (DiFrancesco and Ochoa 2017), *Politics of Architecture in Contemporary Argentine Cinema* (Holmes 2017), *The Sacred and Modernity in Urban Spain* (Córdoba and García-Donoso 2016), *Ecuadorians in Madrid* (Masterson-Algar 2016), *Poetics of Opposition in Contemporary Spain* (Snyder 2015), and my own *Toward an Urban Cultural Studies: Henri Lefebvre and the Humanities* (Fraser 2015). Edward Baker and Malcolm Compitello's collection *Madrid. De Fortunata a la M–40: Un siglo de cultura urbana* (2003) was a pathbreaking volume, and this tradition can be traced through to contemporary texts such as *Cartographies of Madrid: Contesting Urban Space at the Crossroads of the Global South and Global North* (2019), edited by Silvia Bermúdez and Anthony Geist.

5. This was my approach in *Toward an Urban Cultural Studies* (Fraser, 2015).

6. See the book edited by Julio Enrique Checa Puerta and

Susanne Hartwig, *¿Discapacidad?: Literatura, teatro y cine
hispánicos vistos desde los
disability studies* (2018), and
especially Hartwig's (2018a,
2018b) introduction and essay
in that book, which are notable
exceptions.

7. Texts like Titchkosky's *The
Question of Access* (2011), which
situates its critique in Toronto,
Canada, are critical landmarks
in their own right. In Chapter 1, I discuss the Anglophone
approach evident in the nonetheless valuable work of Rob
Imrie (e.g. 1996).

8. Here I am thinking of *Madness and Modernism. Insanity in the Light of Modern Art,
Literature and Thought* (Sass
1992), *Paranoid Modernism:
Literary Experiment, Psychosis
and the Professionalization of*

English Society (Trotter 2001),
or more recently, *Madness and
the Romantic Poet: A Critical
History* (Whitehead 2017), and
*Modernism and the Machinery
of Madness. Psychosis, Technology and Narrative Worlds*
(Gaedtke 2017).

9. Works by such scholars as
Akiko Tsuchiya (*Marginal Subjects: Gender and Deviance in
Nineteenth-Century Spain*, 2011)
and Richard Cleminson ("Liberal Governmentality in Spain:
Bodies, Minds, and the Medical
Construction of the 'Outsider,'
1870–1910," 2016) are relevant
to the themes and time period
discussed here, particularly in
Chapter 3. See also Aramburu
(2019).

10. Regarding the phobia of the
everyday, see van Zuylen
(2005, 2).

CHAPTER 1

1. Lefebvre outlined in *The Production of Space* a triadic model
of space: space as conceived, as
perceived, and as lived. In brief,
whereas Imrie is focused on
lived space, this book is focused
on conceived space.

2. I constructed this argument
more carefully in the introduction to my *Cognitive Disability
Aesthetics* (2018) and rather than
rehash those details here, I refer
interested readers there for a
more thorough accounting.

3. Illness and the urban social
body is discussed more fully in
Chapter 2.

4. Here I refer to the argument
that we are all dependent on
others, and the myth of the
independent modern subject as
it has been challenged by Licia
Carlson (2010, 2001) and others.

5. For this definition, I also rely on
a statement by Davis from *The
Disability Studies Reader* (1997,
1).

6. See Harvey, Lefebvre, and
Mumford on ties between
industrialization and
urbanization.

7. For a primer on Lefebvrian
thinking, see Elden (2004)
and Merrifield (2006). His

influence on David Harvey and Edward Soja is particularly notable, and Barcelona-based theorist Manuel Delgado Ruiz has explicitly and repeatedly acknowledged his debt to Lefebvre in his work.

8. Jane Jacobs similarly reaffirms this conceptual distance of the planner in *The Death and Life of Great American Cities*, a work that had international resonance. Significantly, given the aims of the present study, she does this by mixing the discourse of science and art: "the pseudo-science of city planning and its companion, the art of city design, have not yet broken with the specious comfort of wishes, familiar superstitions, oversimplifications, and symbols, and have not yet embarked upon the adventure of probing the real world" (1992, 13).

9. Imrie is culling from E. Hall 1995 and Birkenbach 1993 here.

10. This provides a key insight into how both disability and normalcy work as a social relationship. Imrie is focused on how the ideology of ableism operates through the environment, once produced, in that the built environment is "actively discriminating" (1996, 2), while I want to show how the ideology of ableism is already active in the social understanding of what planning is and what it is not.

11. Though never completely, say Titchkosky and Michalko—see the discussion of visual impairment and passing in Michalko's work.

CHAPTER 2

1. These issues receive more careful consideration in previous books, including *Toward an Urban Cultural Studies* (Fraser 2015).

2. "The making of any object, out of any substance, by a human being is also in some way a making and remaking of the human. If aesthetics and the human are inseparable, it is because art is the process by which human beings attempt to modify themselves—and this process is a crucial factor in human history. The object of human craft is the human being, and the most immediate sign of the human and the material out of which we craft it is the human body" (Siebers 2010, 136).

3. See sources cited in the introduction to Fraser (2018).

4. Such talk is all too easily accepted and repeated by generations of urbanites who were born well after social shifts prompted the exchange-value of the city to triumph over its use-value, aggrandizing the city as commodity over the city as a living space.

5. Auerbach is aware of this, and notes it himself: "I said above that the Homeric style was 'of the foreground' because, despite much going back and forth, it yet

causes what is momentarily being narrated to give the impression that it is the only present, pure and without perspective" (1957, 9); also Homer "knows no background" (2).

6. For more detailed discussions, see Fraser (2011, 2015).

7. Though arguably motivated by different aims, both planners contributed to what Henri Lefebvre calls the bourgeois science of modern urban planning. On both Haussmann's Paris and Cerdà's Barcelona see chapters in Thomas Hall (1997).

8. Cerdá's account of this evolution moves from *locomoción pedestre* (pedestrian locomotion) to *locomoción ecuestre* (equestrian locomotion) to *locomoción rastrera* (locomotion by dragging) to *locomoción rodada* (wheeled locomotion—both *ordinaria* [ordinary] and later *perfeccionada* [perfected]).

9. "The scalpel had permitted anatomists to study the circulation of the blood: that knowledge, applied to the circulation of movement in streets, suggested that streets worked like arteries and veins" (Sennett 2008, 204); "To wit: the seventeenth century had seen the discovery of the circulation of blood (commonly attributed to the Englishman William Harvey), and to a certain degree the subsequent large-scale urban renovations of the nineteenth–century (by Haussmann, Cerdà and others) did little more than map this discovery onto existing cities through the rational, geometrical and even algebraic redesign of urban spaces" (Fraser 2011b, 185).

10. Significantly, it is Cerdà who is often credited with coining the word *urbanización* (urbanization). For more on Cerdà and Barcelona's urbanistic changes see Epps (2001, 2002), Fraser (2011), Goldston (1969), and Resina 2008. Regarding changes due to preparations for the 1929 World's Fair, see Epps (2001) and Vázquez Montalbán (1990); about effects from the creation of the Olympic City for the 1992 games, see Degen (2008) and McNeill (1999, 2002). Also see Corominas i Ayala (2010), T. Hall (1997), and Hughes (1992, 2004).

11. Not unique to Cerdà, this underlying organic metaphor was pervasive in the history of modern urban planning and was later borrowed by thinkers whose re-appropriation of the term functioned as a critique of the destruction of contemporary urbanistic practice pioneered by Cerdà and others.

12. My usage here is intended to recall Siebers (2010, 126).

13. There is of course a larger Marxian argument here concerning alienation in work, human relationships, and everyday life.

14. The term is Garland-Thomson's (1997) and relevant also to Davis (2013).

15. Boys (2017) follows up on these references and pushes further what Siebers says about architecture, yet both instances emphasize an understanding of

disability symbolism that is a bit
different than the approach that
Siebers himself applies to other
visual art and that Straus applies
to music. It is that notion of disability aesthetics I seek to apply
to urban disability aesthetics.

16. "These and other aesthetic dictates represent architecture
itself as providing a transcendental expression of human perfection, situating in the crafting
of concrete, wood, plastic, and
steel the ability to overcome
limitations of the human body
and mind, but they also use the
built environment to maintain
a spatial caste system at the
expense of people with disabilities. This caste system not only
targets individual disabled bodies for exclusion but also rejects
any form of appearance that
symbolizes disability" (Siebers
2010, 72).

17. Le Corbusier published this idea
in 1925; see Siebers (2010, 73).

18. Siebers's comments on Le Corbusier are in synch with the
analysis of Cerdà just offered:
"Ironically, Le Corbusier wanted
to tie buildings to the human
beings living in them, but his
theories privilege form over
function and establish one basis
for what Rob Imrie has called
the 'design apartheid' of modernist architectural practices"
(2010, 72).

19. The literature on this is vast.
Start, for example, with Davidson (2017): "Barcelona's arrival
as a sought-out destination—an
'in' city—on the world's map,

though, has been a mixed bless-
ing. Among its valued attrac-
tions Gaudí and his contemporaries' *modernista* architecture
has helped confer upon Barcelona 'must-see' status for travel-
lers to Europe. At the same time,
the celebrated urban renewals
have brought the holiday beach
experience to within steps of
the city proper. Similarly, the
image of Barcelona has become
one not of a specifically Catalan
conurbation but rather of a cos-
mopolitan/sensorial experience
that one consumes. As a result
of these multiple dynamics, the
city is a local city less and less
and a 'world' metropolis more
and more: a style, a surface to be
admired or a brand, as Andrew
Smith has suggested" (22).

20. Contrasting Gaudí with his
modernist architect contemporaries (and not with Cerdà,
though the contrast is equally
valid for the present purposes),
Robert Hughes wrote, "others
were moved by the grid; Gaudí
didn't give beans for it." (2004,
135). Van Hensbergen does contrast Cerdà and Gaudí directly,
however (2001, 146). Gaudí's
work was commissioned for, and
along with the work of other
architects, was instrumental in
promoting the urban development of the Eixample's Pas-
seig de Gràcia, which Davidson
refers to as the main artery for
a wave of mercantilization and
speculation (2017, 26). Davidson
also reflects on the problematic legacy of development in

Barcelona from the perspective of the twenty-first century: "real estate speculation, top-down urban planning and the promise of a unique urban experience projected by the postmodern brand image have all had deleterious consequences" (22).

21. van Hensbergen calls Batlló's balconies skull-shaped (2001, 157).

22. Note that a respect for what might be called "the diversity and extravagance of natural form" (Ashton 2008, 11) is common to both Gaudí and Teshigahara.

23. Gaudí once expressed his belief that Catalans, as opposed to Castilians, had "that sense of plasticity that gives the perception of objects as a whole" (van Hensbergen 2001, 117).

24. This rejection was led by Eugeni d'Ors and other prominent intellectuals (see van Hensbergen 2001; also Hughes 1992).

25. Based on Marcos P. Centeno Martín's analysis, the film *Antonio Gaudí* seems to share an aesthetic with *Tokyo 1958*, an earlier film by a group of collaborators, including Teshigahara.

26. Centeno Martín (2019) writes of Teshigahara that "He draws on the discussion developed by the post-war cultural circles about the necessity of redefining the document through a 'synthesis of arts' or *sōgō geijutsu*".

27. See for example, the performance piece *Los encargados* (2011), staged by Santiago Sierra and Jorge Galindo in Madrid's Gran Vía, and the 15M graphic novel *Lo que (me) está pasando: Diarios de un joven emperdedor* (2015), created by comics artist Miguel Brieva. On Miguel Brieva see Fraser (2018b); on Sierra and Galindo see Snyder (2015).

28. As Jane Jacobs wrote in *Cities and the Wealth of Nations* (1984) of agriculture and rural development as well.

29. This brings up the central tension of the present book. *The Biopolitics of Disability* is attentive to the problems of "universalizing" disability, and calls into question Lennard Davis's concept of "dismodernism" along with certain arguments advanced by other disability theorists such as James Berger, Tom Shakespeare, and Nicholas Watson. The idea in question is concisely expressed in an assertion that can be found somewhat easily in a survey of existing disability studies scholarship: the idea that "we are all disabled or, at least, potentially disabled" (Mitchell and Snyder 2015, 28). Mitchell and Snyder comment that "while the apparent promise of this acceptance often appears all to the good—after all a little acknowledgment of shared vulnerability can only be helpful—the analyses to come explore how such contentions also undermine an ability to pay more serious attention to crip/queer populations and the alternative perspectives that their differences bring into the

world" (2015, 28–29). While
I understand and agree with
this perspective, I am hesitant
to agree that "undermine" is
the best word to use here. As
Mitchell and Snyder's own
interrogation of the nuances
of the inclusion-driven form of
contemporary disability identity
politics in *The Biopolitics of Disability* bears out, radical social
change is at times postponed,
limited or co-opted in the social
process of assimilating previously marginalized subjectivities. This is not an argument
against disability identity politics, but rather an awareness
on the part of Mitchell, Snyder,
and others that multiple strategies are needed. In my reading,
their own afterword returns, by
another course, to the notion of
"shared vulnerability" broached
in passing in the introduction.
But most important is how
an explicit focus on cognitive
disability changes the central
problematic here. The fact is
that Davis's thesis regarding
obsession both acknowledges
the social construction of cognitive difference and accepts that
cognition is affected by biological factors. What his argument
does so well is show how social
stigma is applied unevenly to
cognitive difference across a
spectrum of behaviors and
activities. This unevenness is
part of what this book seeks to
highlight.

30. Admitting, too, the importance
of José Luis Guerín's *Innisfree*

(1990) (Riambau 2010, 30, see
also 11).

31. Notably, the UPF led the resur-
gence of the documentary form
in Catalonia, as noted in De
Pozo and Oroz (2010, 67).

32. As Jordi Balló notes, that first
full-length film is concordant
with the broader aims of the
documental de creación, in that
with *El cielo gira* "se ratificaba
que la frontera entre documental y ficción era solo una
cuestión nominal y de drama-
turgia, y que en este cine de lo
real anidaba una nueva poética
y un nuevo sentido de la emo-
ción" (2010, 115; it was confirmed that the border between
documentary and fiction film
was only a matter of terms and
of artifice, and that this cinema
of the real created a space that
welcomed a new poetics and
a new sense of emotion). Note
that García Roure was the assistant director on Álvarez's first
film (Balló 2010, 113).

33. Critics have noted her admira-
tion for Víctor Érice (Torreiro
2010a, 48), and his for her (Érice
2005) and her film's resonance
with Guerín's aesthetics (see
Torreiro 2010a, 46, also De Pozo
and Oroz 2010, 69).

34. On *En construcción* see Loxham
(2006); on *El sol del membrillo*
see Fraser (2010, 177–87).

35. Note that Nichols categorizes
modes of documentary filmmaking in *Representing Reality*
(1991), but that the poetic mode
was added later in his *Introduction to Documentary* (2001).

36. Nichols continues, noting that "This anonymous but surrogate voice arose in the 1930s as a convenient way to describe a situation or problem, present an argument, propose a solution, and sometimes to evoke a poetic tone or mood . . . a poetic tone that made the transmission of information secondary to the construction of a deferential, somewhat romanticized mood" (2001, 13–14).

37. Both examples from Nichols (2001, 90).

38. Picornell notes the presence of "carteles y maquetas como paisajes" (2017, 186; posters and paste-ups as landscape) but does not sufficiently explore how these are used filmically or symbolically.

39. This scene is also meaningfully discussed by Picornell (2017).

40. "El uso del *trompe l'oeil*, un mecanismo que permite a Álvarez dibujar fisuras en la superficie de la hiperrealidad" (Picornell 2017, 185; the use of *trompe l'oeil*, a device that allows Álvarez to inscribe fissures onto the surface of hyperreality); "El uso de formas diversas de *trompe-l'oeil* cinematográfico sirve para situar al espectador en una posición interrogante, desde donde puede aprender a mirar más allá de la superficie de lo que el poder—económico, político, periodístico—le pone ante los ojos" (Picornell 2017, 189; The use of many forms of cinematographic *trompe l'oeil* serves to place spectators in a position of asking questions, from which they can learn to look beyond the surface of what power—economic, political, journalistic—places before their eyes).

41. See also Henri-Jacques Stiker's *The History of Disability* ([1982] 1997).

CHAPTER 3

1. While it has not been feasible to include a chapter on Santiago de Compostela in this book, readers should see Bermúdez (2018) for an insightful analysis of architecture, monumentality, and cityscape in that city, which also draws on the ideas of Henri Lefebvre. A future project might extend the urbanized version of Lennard Davis's premise regarding obsession and modernity through investigation of cultural production in a city of Pardo Bazán's native Galicia.

2. Numerous other writings on the subject followed, including the foundation of the publication dedicated to the theme, in 1896 or 1897, titled *La ciudad lineal* and recognized as "la primera revista de urbanismo del mundo" (Navascués Palacios 1969, 52; De Terán 1999, 110–11; the first magazine dedicated to urbanism in the world).

3. This comes from Compañía Madrileña de Urbanización

(2011, 19); henceforth abbreviated as CMU.

4. The plan's reliance on the railway recalls Lewis Mumford's remarks on the paleotechnic city, which had essentially been an outgrowth of mining towns made possible by the railroad's material links with the mine itself (Mumford 1970, 150, 159).

5. For reasons that are themselves worthy of extended consideration; see Boileau (1959, 237), Collins and Flores (1968, 47), CMU 2011.

6. Given the brevity of the *Reader*'s reference to the Madrilenian planner, it would hardly seem necessary to have included a plate or any information on the subject at all. Yet this seeming contradiction may speak more to the lack of sustained interest in Spain by contemporary urban scholars than to the historical legacy and enduring influence of Soria y Mata's project itself.

7. The moral aspects of the design are also explicitly highlighted in the guide published by CMU (2011, 3–8). As a side note, the article connects Soria y Mata's use of the notions "ruralize the urban" and "urbanize the rural" with English garden planning traditions instead of connecting it with Cerdà's own work in Spain. See Cerdà (1867) and Resina (2008).

8. Using the expression grano de trigo (grain of wheat)—"El grano es la ciudad lineal, formulada de una sola calle" (Soria y Mata 1892, 49; The grain is the linear city, formulated from a single street).

9. Translations of Soria y Mata in this section by the author unless noted otherwise.

10. This represents the inverse of Gaudí's urban/architectural aesthetics, discussed in the previous chapter. See Collins and Flores (1968, 40) and Soria y Mata (1892, 49).

11. On biological evolution in Soria y Mata, see De Terán (1999, 106).

12. Her own *La cuestión palpitante* (1882) conveys in broad strokes her adoption and critique of Zola's deterministic, psychological and social naturalism, which—criticism has often had chance to establish—she appropriated and imbued with both a sense of messiness (no tidy resolutions or morals) and a Catholic sensibility.

13. The observation of Ariza's nervous hand at the theater (27), later the reading of the judge's facial expressions (35).

14. The end of chapter I (32–33) and beginning of numbered chapter IV (49).

15. Chapter VII, 69–75, is Julia telling the whole story.

16. Such specific toponyms are mentioned in Pardo Bazán (2001, 26, 28, 30, 33, 42). Gone today, the Apolo was established on the site of what was previously the Convento de San Heremenegildo. The Apolo was in operation for some fifty years dating from 1873.

17. See, for example, Bernebeu-Mestre et al., "Aunque se observaba en todas las clases sociales, para muchos autores su frecuencia era mayor entre la clase 'rica o desahogada' y

entre las profesiones con tensión cerebral" (2008, 96; Even though it was observed in all social classes, for many authors its frequency was greater among the 'rich or comfortable' class and among the professions of more intellectual bent).

18. The latter, in fact, is often in short supply in Pardo Bazán's works.

19. "Traeré al descubrimiento de los crímenes elementos novelescos e intelectuales" (Pardo Bazán 2001, 82; I will bring dramatic and intellectual elements to the discovery of crimes); "Después de esta aventura, he comprendido que, desde la cuna, mi vocación es la de policía aficionado" (81; After this adventure, I have realized that, since birth, my vocation has been that of amateur detective); the intensity of the experience is what attracts him, a fact that he explains with recourse to "mis condiciones y aptitudes, o, si se quiere, mis inspiraciones atrevidas y geniales" (81; my skills and abilities, or, if one prefers, my daring and splendid inspirations)

20. As Diana Aramburu asserts, "Chulita Ferna's [Julia's] evasion of the law is made possible through parody because Pardo Bazán sets the stage for the unmasking of the male detective myth. . . . [Selva] is revealed for what he is—an amateur sleuth manipulated by the femme fatale to become her accomplice" (2019, 46).

21. See also Manera, "Selva comete un doble delito: facilita la fuga de una cómplice y empuja al suicidio al culpable" (2001, 20; Selva commits a double fault: he facilitates the accomplice's escape and pushes the criminal to suicide).

22. "¿Cuándo empecé a no sentir el peso del fastidio? ¿Cuándo solté el yugo de plomo?" he continues (40; When did I begin to not feel the weight of this burden? When did I let go of the leaden yoke?).

23. See the doctoral thesis that Violeta Ruiz Cuenca (2020) has written on these linkages. Also interesting is her assertion that while in France, Charcot "'democratised' neurasthenia by presenting the case of a working-class neurasthenic man in his Tuesday lectures, thus demonstrating that it was not restricted to the upper-middle-classes. . . . Spanish physicians continued to present neurasthenia as a disease of the urban bourgeoisie" (46).

24. Bernabeu-Mestre cites from sources of the time such as Bassols i Villa (1912), A. Díaz de la Quintana y Sánchez Remón (1893), and J. Suárez-Figueroa Cazeaux (1909): "Coincidiendo con la época de mayor impacto de la Clorosis, en las últimas décadas del siglo XIX, la Neurastenia se convirtió en una dolencia que alcanzó una gran prevalencia en los países occidentales. Para muchos autores se trataba de una auténtica pandemia o peste nerviosa, siendo calificada como la enfermedad del siglo o la enfermedad de moda" (Bernabeu-Mestre et

al. 2008, 91; Coinciding with the time of greatest impact of Chlorosis in the last decades of the 19th century, Neurasthenia became a disease that reached high prevalence in Western countries. For many authors it was an authentic pandemic or nervous plague, being classified as the disease of the century or the fashionable disease).

25. Bernabeu-Mestre cites Bassols i Villa (1912, 5–6): "se habría vuelto más frecuente . . . con las modernas condiciones de vida" (had become more frequent . . . with the conditions of modern life).

26. Suárez-Figueroa Cazeaux (1909, cited in Bernabeu-Mestre et al. 2008, 95n54): "el hombre ignorante se hace culto; el obrero lee y oye; el obrero aprende y por eso se pone en condiciones para ser neurasténico . . . el hombre de hoy difiere del hombre de ayer que tenía una vida más vegetativa" (the ignorant man becomes learned; the worker reads and hears; the worker learns and therefore puts himself in a position to be neurathesenic . . . the man of today differs from the man of yesterday who had a more vegetative life).

27. "En realidad la variabilidad clínica era tan grande que se conocía a la Neurastenia como la enfermedad aristocrática que no se privaba de nada" (Bernabeu-Mestre et al. 2008, 93; In reality the clinical variability was so great that Neurasthenia was known as the aristocratic illness that knew no bounds).

28. "De nuevo llamé en mi auxilio a la extraña facultad de semiadivinación que sobre una base insignificante en lo real, me había guiado a través del laberinto del sombrío crimen, como tantos otros que en Madrid se cometen" (Pardo Bazán [1911] 2001, 77; Again I called to my aid the strange faculty of semidivination that, without a significant grounding in the real, had guided me through the labyrinth of the dark crime, like so many others that are committed in Madrid); "Sus ojos llameaban en la semioscuridad de la calle, cual los ojos eléctricos de los gatos" (79; His eyes blazed in the semidarkness of the street, like the electric eyes of cats).

29. "Según el gran especialista Salvador Vázquez de la Parga, *La gota de sangre* (1911) es una imitación de Arthur Conan Doyle, que quiere utilizar la estructura y el estilo del enigma británico, pero peca al mezclar el puro azar con las reglas de la lógica" (Manera 2001, 18; According to the renowned specialist Salvador Vázquez de la Parga, *La gota de sangre* (1911) is an imitation of Arthur Conan Doyle, that seeks to use the structure and style of the British mystery, but sins by mixing pure chance with the rules of logic).

30. He describes the kiss in the story titled "La casa maldita"; see Pratt (1995, 2001), and Otis (1999); the microbes of the city are in the story "El pesimista corregido," discussed in this section. Given that the novel

he wrote has been lost forever, the *Cuentos* remain today the best representation of his literary exploration of the microbial underworld (Otis 1999, 68).

31. Juan is called a misanthrope in *Cuentos* ([1905] 1999, 165); Ramón y Cajal, in Durán Muñoz and Burón (1960, 53).

32. His own body is a "ruin comedero de gérmenes" (vile trough of germs) and his soul a "vivero de pensamientos tristes y sentimientos deprimentes" (Ramón y Cajal [1905] 1999, 170; nursery garden of thoughts and depressing feelings).

33. Here I use the classic phrase excerpted from Fray Luis de León's poem "Vida retirada."

34. See Ramón y Cajal (1999, 212) for an extended meditation on this quality of the urban park focalized through Juan's consciousness.

35. Van Zuylen is quoting from Lefebvre's *Everyday Life in the Modern World* (1984, 13). Davis mentions Janet in passing (2008, 101).

36. This is intended as a Bergsonian philosophical position, evident in his analyses from *Time and Free Will, Matter and Memory, Creative Evolution*, and in particular, *The Two Sources of Morality and Religion.*

CHAPTER 4

1. See Chester (2001), who claims the number to be greater than one hundred thousand. Barreiros (2008) puts the number of dead more conservatively at ten to twenty thousand, including that among these were "only eight 'persons of quality'" (217). Note that the earthquake has been more frequently studied from the perspective of seismology than urbanism.

2. Barreiros is writing of Da Maia specifically.

3. "The *Baixa* (downtown) district of post-1755 Lisbon consists of a regular grid demarcated to the north by a rectangular square (*Rossio*), successor to the commercial and popular square, and to the south by another square open on one side to the Tagus estuary: *Real Praça do Comércio* (Royal Trade Square), replacing the existing vast *platea* next to the Royal Palace (*Terreiro do Paço*)." (Barreiros 2008, 218)

4. "In Lisbon's renewed areas public and private spheres were no longer commingled but very sharply separated, urban layout and architecture as well as urban behaviours were turned into public affairs and regulated as such, apartment buildings for rent spread out and became the realm of bourgeois private life—at the same pace as specific fragments of urban areas were transformed into the stage for bourgeois public life" (Barreiros 2008, 206).

5. "The social settlement of new Lisbon had three convergent themes. One was Da Maia's plan to place businessmen

upstairs in his buildings, near the port, the customs house, and the exchange, all on the new *Real Praça do Comércio*. Another was the move to preserve, on ground level, the pre-earthquake trades, each in its own street. A third was the versatility and variety of allotments in the single blocks. This versatility ensured, in fact, a great variety in the number and surfaces of commercial/residential plots in the blocks. Social composition, thus, was mixed, bourgeois and trades-folk intermingling" (Barreiros 2008, 224).

6. "The collective buildings of the 16th, 17th and early 18th centuries differed sharply from their medieval predecessors because they delimited with greater rigor 'inside' and 'outside,' private space and public space, as they rose in height and detached the dwellers from the urban soil; and because they negated the poly-functionality and relative autonomy of the medieval urban house" (Barreiros 2008, 215).

7. Though many of the fragments of *The Book of Disquiet* are unattributed to a specific heteronym, throughout this chapter I follow the spirit of the organization offered by Jerónimo Pizarro and Margaret Jull Costa in their 2017 edition of Pessoa's work. This has the effect of attributing the first part or phase of the book to Guedes, and the second part or phase of the book to Soares.

8. The Latin *nulla dies sine linea* appears on page 106 of Davis (2008); Davis notes that "people in the nineteenth century had a range of opiates, barbituates, stimulants, and other drugs available to them without prescription" on 105; and the point about factory work and intellectual labor is made on 106.

9. Jull Costa dates Pessoa's remark to 1928.

10. It is pertinent, too, that in fragment 340 Soares feels "a strange feeling of doubt" about being a character in a novel. But again, he both is and is not a character in a novel. He is the narrator and a character, while by contrast, Unamuno's Augusto Pérez is a character and not a narrator.

11. This passage is quoted and discussed by Stevens (2007, 39–40); in Jull Costa's translation this is fragment 83; the Portuguese in the text is from Pizarro fragment 83. Stevens quotes from the 1998 Portuguese edition by Richard Zenith and notes that she has modified the English translation of the 2001 Penguin edition. The sentences quoted here are rendered thus by Stevens: "My obsession with creating a false world still accompanies me, and will until my death. Today I don't line up spools of thread and chess pawns in my dresser drawers (with an occasional bishop or knight sticking out) but I regret that I don't . . . I line up figures in my imagination, that dwell in my inner being and are alive

and dependable, and I feel cozy, like someone sitting by a warm fire in winter. I have a world of friends inside me, with their own real, individual, imperfect lives." The original Portuguese begins, "A minha mania de criar um mundo falso acompanha-me ainda, e só na minha morte me abandonará." Stevens nonetheless treats the heteronyms as "autonomous writing selves" in a way that ignores their purposeful ambiguities (2007, 43); and Jull Costa's introduction also does the same, in her insistence that the heteronyms enjoy a "stylistic and intellectual independence from him" (2017, ix). Independence, just as autonomy, seems too strong of a word, given Pessoa's statement and literary approach.

12. See earlier note, this is precisely what can be seen in Stevens (2007, 40).

13. "As I see it, the landscape of *The Book of Disquiet* is not exactly the city of Lisbon, which so disquiets the protagonist; rather, it is Pessoa's own malaise or tedium that becomes the book's landscape" (Pizarro 2017, xviii).

14. When citing from Pessoa in the body text and the notes, I give not the page numbers but the fragment numbers (indicated by the abbreviation "frag."). Since these fragment numbers do not align across versions published in Portuguese, or across translations from Portuguese into English, it is necessary to use two sets of numbers. I have chosen to cite the English fragment number from Jull Costa's 2017 translation (which is derived from Pizarro's 2013 Portuguese edition but not always identical), while the Portuguese fragment number corresponds to the version of Pizarro's edition freely available through the collaborative Arquivo LdoD (https://ldod.uc.pt), a number that does not always seem to correspond with Pizarro 2013. On the structure of the work see Gomes and Willitanea de Oliveira (2017), and on digital Pessoa see Portela and Silva (2016).

15. "The mania for the absurd and the paradoxical is the animal joy of the sad. Normal men tell jokes and clap each other in the back out of sheer zest for life, while those incapable of enthusiasm or joy can only indulge in intellectual somersaults, and their cold manner takes the place of any warm, friendly gestures" (frag. 146); "The idea of any social obligation—going to a funeral, discussing something with someone at the office, going to meet someone (whether known or unknown) at the station—the mere idea blocks that whole day's thoughts and sometimes I even worry about it the night before and sleep badly because of it. Yet the reality, when it comes, is utterly insignificant, and certainly doesn't justify so much fuss, yet it happens again and again and I never learn" (frag. 201).

16. Frag. 59 in Pizarro and frag. 59 in Jull Costa.

218   *Notes to Pages 145–147*

17. For examples of anxious and obsessive thinking, see fragments 275, 289, 320, 402 409 (Jull Costa).

18. See, for example, fragments 8, 12, 36, 206, 291, 312, 336 (Pizarro); 336 especially contains a markedly long meditation on the nature of tedium.

19. This preface is unnumbered and blends Pizarro fragments 122, 136, 142, and 146; the quotation is from page 5 of Jull Costa's translation, which corresponds to Pizarro frag. 142.

20. See also Sónia da Silva Pina (2007), who approaches *o tédio* in the *Livro do Desassossego* as an existential element of modernity.

21. "In modern life the world belongs to the stupid, the insensitive and the disturbed. The right to live and triumph is today earned with the same qualifications one requires to be interned in a madhouse" (frag. 136); "When seized by a fit, epileptics are extraordinarily strong; paranoiacs have reasoning powers beyond those of most normal people: religious maniacs in their delirium attract larger crowds of believers than (almost) any demagogue and give an inner strength to their followers that demagogues never can. But all this proves nothing except that madness is madness" (frag. 191); also see fragments 197, 246, 317.

22. "or like someone freed by an earthquake from the feeble light of the prison to which he had become accustomed" (frag.

221); "A sudden splintering, a blaze of light, exploding inside minds and thoughts. Everything stopped. Hearts stopped. Like sensitive souls. The silence terrifies as if a death had just occurred. The sound of the rain growing louder brings a sense of relief like tears copiously shed. The air is leaden" (frag. 269); "As far as I can see, plagues, storms and wars are all products of the same blind force, which sometimes operates through unconscious microbes, sometimes through unconscious lightning bolts and floods, sometimes through unconscious men. I see no difference between an earthquake and a massacre, except in the way that murdering someone with a knife and murdering someone with a dagger can be considered different" (frag. 349).

23. "Mas eu quero crêr que a vida seja meio luz meio sombras" (frag. 21; "I like to believe that life is half-light, half-shade"); "os privilegios da penumbra" (frag. 201; "the privileges of the penumbra" [205]); "A manhã, meio fria, meio morna" (frag. 213; "the morning, half-cold, half-warm" [208]); "ao pé da janella entreaberta" (frag. 223; "outside a half-open window" [218]); "accordo de dentro do meio-somno em que estagnei" (frag. 223; "I wake within the half-sleep in which I lie stagnating" [218]); "por traz dos vidros meio-limpos da janella fronteira" (frag. 227; "behind the half-cleaned window" [222]); "Toda a vida da alma humana é

um movimento na penumbra"
(frag. 239; "The whole life of the
human soul is just a movement
in the half-light" [233]); "Vive-
mos, num lusco-fusco da cons-
ciencia" (frag. 239; "We live
in a twilight of consciousness"
[233]); "Sou metade somnam-
bulo e a outra parte nada" (frag.
294; "I am half somnambulist
and half nothing" [288]); "estas
meias reflexões" (frag. 366;
"these semi-reflections" [359]);
"tudo isso se me tornou numa
vaga penumbra" (frag. 432; "all
this has become for me a vague
penumbra" [425]).

24. Also see frag. 306: "My writing
is just like the reverie in which
someone avoiding thought
would naturally immerse himself"; and Jull Costa (2017, xii–
xiii). The suggestion in fragment
326 that words are tangible
bodies returns to the metaphors
discussed by Siebers in *Disability Aesthetics* (2010; see Chapter
2 of the present book).

25. "Installed on the upper floors
of certain respectable taverns
in Lisbon can be found a small
number of restaurants or eating
places, which have the stolid,
homely look of those restaurants you see in towns that lack
even a train station" (Jull Costa
2017, 3).

26. See also fragments 301, 304, 305,
309, 338.

27. The slash marks are in the original Portuguese version but
do not appear in Jull Costa's
translation.

28. Also see, for example, frags. 318,
322, 360.

29. "Mais que uma vez, ao passear
lentamente pelas ruas da tarde,
me tem batido na alma, com
uma violencia subita e estonteante, a extranhissima presença
da organização das coisas. Não
são bem as coisas naturaes que
tanto me affectam, que tam
poderosamente me trazem esta
sensação: são antes os arruamentos, os lettreiros, as pessoas
vestidas e fallando, os empregos,
os jornaes, a intelligencia de
tudo. Ou, antes, é o facto de que
existem arruamentos, lettreiros,
empregos, homens, sociedade,
tudo a entender-se e a seguir e
a abrir caminhos" (Frag. 272;
"More than once, while out
strolling in the evening, the
strange presence of things and
the way they are organized in
the world has often struck my
soul with sudden, surprising
violence. It's not so much the
natural things that affect me,
that communicate that feeling so powerfully, it's rather
the arrangement of the streets,
shop signs, the people talking
to one another, their clothes,
jobs, newspapers, the intelligence underlying everything.
Or, rather, it's the fact of the
very existence of streets, shop
signs, jobs, men and society, all
getting on together, following
familiar routes and setting out
along new ones" [266]).

30. Verde also reappears in fragments 191, 248, 265 in Pizarro,
and 186, 242, 259 in Jull Costa.

CHAPTER 5

1. See Kortazar (2008), who analyzes Unamuno's "Las magno-
lias de la Plaza Nueva de Bilbao,"
Juaristi's "MCMLIV," and Blas
de Otero's "Lejos." Other analyses in the article look at poetry
written in Basque that center on
Bilbao but not specifically on
the Plaza Nueva, such as Gabriel
Aresti's "Bilbaoko kaleak."

2. Mas (2000, 161–62) establishes
the connection between Lázaro
and Cerdá; on the Puerto de
la Paz see Mas (2000, 157–59).
See also José María Beascoechea's description in "Plan de
ensanche de 1862," on Bilbao-
pedia, www.bilbaopedia.info/
plan-ensanche-1862 (accessed
July 21, 2021) and Beascoechea
(2007).

3. Cenicacelaya considered the
plan's elegance to have been
discarded by twentieth-century
planners.

4. See the foundational study by
Manuel Castells (1983).

5. Vegara concurs with Cenicacelaya and provides detail: "the
industrial development in the
past two centuries has converted the river into a great
physical and psychological
barrier. The Nervión River has
come to represent both the
physical and social division of
the metropolitan region. Historically, the principal port facilities and shipyards were located
almost to the heart of the city.
Since the ships needed to reach

these facilities, low-level or
pedestrian bridges connecting
the two sides of the river could
not be built" (2001, 90).

6. See Vegara (2001, 91–92) and
Rodríguez and Vicario (2005,
270). Leira (2009) discusses
twenty-first-century plans such
as Bilbao 2000 / Bilbao Ría 2000
/ BR2000 and Metrópoli 30. See
also Urrutia (2009) on the wider
context and social conflicts
informing urban life and planning in contemporary Bilbao.

7. Leira's general premise follows
from the work of Harvey 1989,
1996.

8. This obsession cannot be fully
separated from our real attachments to place that are shaped
by relational personhood, by
community, shared experi-
ences and senses of belonging; and even these attachments, of course, are exploited
by capital, see Harvey (1996)
and his discussion on militant
particularism.

9. The primary reference of Ingenschay's chapter's title is *La colmena* by Camilo José Cela. See
also Resina (2001b) on Madrid.

10. These quotations appear during
a summary of Jürgen Schlaeger's
London-focused contribution to
the volume.

11. See these lyrics and the discussion of their use in the graphic
novel in Javier Torrezno's post
"Morirse en Bilbao – Reseña
cómic," on La comicteca,

https://lacomicteca.com/
morirse-en-bilbao, (accessed 24,
July 2021). The song "De nuevo
en tus brazos (Morirse en Bilbao)" is the tenth and final song
on the Doctor Deseo album
titled *Rómpeme con mil caricias,
Cielo* (2004).

12. The pages of the graphic novel
are unnumbered.
13. An excellent example of the latter is two-page introduction of
the character Daigoro.
14. Resina uses these terms in a
discussion mentioning theorist
Kevin Lynch.

CONCLUSION

1. Nassir Ghaemi's historical
approach in his *New York Times*
bestseller *A First-Rate Madness:
Uncovering the Links between
Leadership and Mental Illness* seeks to diagnose historical
figures, and while not wholly
unconvincing, still has the effect
of framing mental illness as an
identifying trait of an individual.

REFERENCES

Álvarez, Mercedes, dir. 2011. *Mercado de futuros*. Spain: IB Cinema.

Alzola, Pablo, Severino Achúcarro, and Ernesto Hoffmeyer. 1878. *Memoria del Proyecto de Ensanche de Bilbao*. Bilbao: Juan E. Delmás.

Andres Barquin, Pedro J. 2001. "Ramón y Cajal: A Century after the Publication of His Masterpiece." *Endeavor* 25, no. 1: 13–17.

Aramburu, Diana. 2019. *Resisting Invisibility: Detecting the Female Body in Spanish Crime Fiction*. Toronto: University of Toronto Press.

Ashton, Dore. 2008. "Border Crossings." DVD booklet accompanying *Antonio Gaudí*, directed by Hiroshi Teshigahara (1984). Criterion Collection.

Aslanov, Cyril. 2012. "Pessoa's Heteronymy between Linguistics and Poetics." *Partial Answers: Journal of Literature and the History of Ideas* 10, no. 1: 121–32.

Auerbach, Erich. 1957. *Mimesis: The Representation of Reality in Western Literature*. Garden City, NY: Doubleday Anchor.

Baker, Edward, and Malcolm Alan Compitello, eds. 2003. *Madrid: De Fortunata a la M-40: Un siglo de cultura urbana*. Madrid: Alianza.

Balibrea, Mari Paz. 2017. *The Global Cultural Capital: Addressing the Citizen and Producing the City in Barcelona*. London: Palgrave Macmillan.

Ballard, J. G. 1966. *The Drowned World*. New York: Berkley Medallion.

Balló, Jordi. 2010. "Cronología de una transmisión (El Máster de Documental de la UPF)." In Torreiro, *Realidad y creación*, 105–21.

Barreiros, Maria Helena. 2008. "Urban Landscapes: Houses, Streets and Squares of 18th Century Lisbon." *Journal of Early Modern History* 12, no. 3–4: 205–32.

Bassols i Villa, J. 1912. *Neurastenia*. Barcelona: Imprenta Inglada y Cia.

Beascoechea Gangoiti, José María. 2007. "Abando, el lugar del nuevo Bilbao." In *Bilbao y sus barrios: Una mirada desde la historia*, I, edited by F. Martínez Rueda, 47–65. Bilbao: Ayuntamiento de Bilbao; BilbaokoUdala.

Benjamin, Walter. 1999. *The Arcades Project*. Translated by Howard Eiland and Kevin McLaughlin. Cambridge, MA: Belknap Press.

Bergua, Antonio, and Wolfgang Skrandies. 2000. "An Early Antecedent to Modern Random Dot Stereograms—'The Secret Stereoscopic Writing' of Ramón y Cajal." *International Journal of Psychophysiology* 36, no. 1: 69–72.

Bermúdez, Silvia. 2018. "Santiago de Compostela and the Spatial Articulation of Power: From the Cathedral to the *Cidade da Cultura*." *Abriu*, no. 7: 47–58.

Bermúdez, Silvia, and Anthony L. Geist, eds. 2019. *Cartographies of Madrid: Contesting Urban Space at the Crossroads of the Global South and Global North*. Nashville, TN: Vanderbilt University Press.

Bernebeu-Mestre, Josep, Ana Paula Cid Santos, Josep Xavier Esplugues Pellicer, María Eugenia Galiana-Sánchez. 2008. "Categorías diagnósticas y género: Los ejemplos de la clorosis y la neurastenia en la medicina española contemporánea (1877–1936)." *Asclepio: Revista de Historia de la Medicina y de la Ciencia* 60, no. 1: 83–102.

Birkenbach, J. 1993. *Physical Disability and Social Policy*. Toronto: University of Toronto Press.

Boileau, Ivan. 1959. "La Ciudad Lineal: A Critical Study of the Linear Suburb of Madrid." *Town Planning Review* 30, no. 3: 230–38.

Borja, Jordi, and Zaida Muxí, eds. 2009. *Urbanismo en el siglo XXI*, 2nd ed. Barcelona: Edicions UPC, Escola Tècnica Superior d'Arquitectura de Barcelona.

Bou, Enric, and Jaume Subirana, eds. 2017. *The Barcelona*

Reader: Cultural Readings of a City. Liverpool, UK: Liverpool University Press.

Boyde, Alan. 1992. "Three-Dimensional Images of Ramón y Cajal's Original Projections, As Viewed by Confocal Microscopy." *Trends in Neurosciences* 15, no. 7: 246–48.

Boys, Jos, ed. 2017. *Disability, Space, Architecture: A Reader.* New York: Routledge.

Burke, Lucy, ed. 2008. "Thinking about Cognitive Impairment." Special issue, *Journal of Literary & Cultural Disability Studies* 2, no. 1 (May).

Busquet, Josep, Pedro J. Colombo, and Aintzane Landa. 2015. *En segundo plano.* Madrid: Diábolo Ediciones.

Butler, Ruth, and Hester Parr, ed. 1999. *Mind and Body Spaces: Geographies of Illness, Impairment and Disability.* New York: Routledge.

Cameron, Bryan, ed. 2014. "Spain in Crisis: 15-M and the Culture of Indignation." Special issue, *Journal of Spanish Cultural Studies* 15, no. 1–2.

Caparrós Lera, José María. 2001. "Cataluña y su historia, en la pantalla." *Cuadernos de Historia Contemporánea,* no. 23: 103–24.

Carlson, Licia. 2010. *The Faces of Intellectual Disability: Philosophical Reflections.* Bloomington: Indiana University Press.

Carlson, Licia. 2001. "Cognitive Ableism and Disability Studies: Feminist Reflections on the History of Mental Retardation." *Hypatia* 16, no. 4: 124–46.

Castanon-Akrami, Brice. 2014. "*Mercado de futuros* (2011) de Mercedes Álvarez ou la société du Spectacle et la crise du développement." In "Actes choisis du colloque de Strasbourg 'Crise(s) dans le monde ibérique et ibéro-américain,'" edited by E. Fisbach and P. Rabaté. Special issue, *HispaniSme,* no. 4 (July 2014): 248–60. http://www.hispanistes.org/images/PDF/HispanismeS/Hispanismes_4/19-shf%20hispanismes%204%20castanon%20obrice.pdf.

Castells, Manuel. 1983. *The City and the Grassroots: A Cross-Cultural Theory of Urban Social Movements.* Berkeley: University of California Press.

Cenicacelaya, Javier. 2009. "Bilbao y la urgencia de un urbanismo sostenible." In Borja and Muxí, *Urbanismo en el siglo XXI,* 17–33.

Cerdà, Ildefons. 1867. *Teoría general de la urbanización.* 2 vols. Madrid: Imprenta Española.

Centeno Martín, Marcos P. 2019. "Legacies of Hani Susumu's Documentary School." *Arts* 8, no. 82: no page.

Checa Puerta, Julio Enrique, and Susanne Hartwig, eds. 2018. *¿Discapacidad?: Literatura, teatro y cine hispánicos vistos desde los disability studies,* vol. 1. Berlin: Peter Lang.

Chester, David K. 2001. "The 1755 Lisbon Earthquake." *Progress in Physical Geography: Earth and Environment* 25, no. 3: 363–83.

Choay, Françoise. 1969. *The Modern City: Planning in the 19th Century*. Translated by Marguerite Hugo and George R. Collins. New York: George Braziller.

Chueca Goitia, Fernando. 2011. *Breve historia del urbanismo*. Madrid: Alianza.

Cleminson, Richard. 2016. "Liberal Governmentality in Spain: Bodies, Minds, and the Medical Construction of the 'Outsider,' 1870–1910." *Journal of Iberian and Latin American Studies* 22, no. 1: 23–40.

Collins, George, and Carlos Flores, eds. 1968. *Arturo Soria y la Ciudad Lineal*. Madrid: Revista de Occidente.

Compañía Madrileña de Urbanización (CMU). 2011. *Guía de la Ciudad Lineal*. Valladolid, Spain: Maxtor.

Connor, David J. and Beth A. Ferri, eds. 2010. "Learning Disabilities." Special issue, *Disability Studies Quarterly* 30, no. 2 (Spring).

Córdoba, Antonio, and Daniel García-Donoso, eds. 2016. *The Sacred and Modernity in Urban Spain*. New York: Palgrave.

Corominas i Ayala, Miquel. 2010. *Los orígenes del Ensanche de Barcelona: Suelo, técnica e iniciativa*. Barcelona: Edicions UPC.

Davidson, Robert. 2017. "Barcelona: The Siege City." In *The Barcelona Reader: Cultural Readings of a City*, edited by Enric Bou and Jaume Subirana, 21–42. Liverpool, UK: Liverpool University Press.

Davis, Lennard J. 2013. *The End of Normal: Identity in a Biocultural Era*. Ann Arbor: University of Michigan Press.

Davis, Lennard J. 2008. *Obsession: A History*. Chicago: University of Chicago Press.

Davis, Lennard J. 2002. *Bending Over Backwards: Disability, Dismodernism and Other Difficult Positions*. New York: New York University Press.

Davis, Lennard J. 1997a. "Universalizing Marginality: How Europe Became Deaf in the Eighteenth Century." In *Disability Studies Reader*, edited by Lennard J. Davis, 110–27. New York: Routledge.

Davis, Lennard J., ed. 1997b. *Disability Studies Reader*, 1st ed. New York: Routledge.

Davis, Lennard J. 1995. *Enforcing Normalcy: Disability, Deafness and the Body*. London: Verso.

De Certeau, Michel. 1988. *The Practice of Everyday Life*. Berkeley: University of California Press.

DeFelipe, Javier. 2002. "Sesquicentenary of the Birthday of Santiago Ramón y Cajal, the Father of Modern Neuroscience." *Trends in Neurosciences* 25, no. 9: 481–84.

Degen, Monica M. 2008. *Sensing Cities: Regenerating Public Life in Barcelona and Manchester.* New York: Routledge.

Degen, Monica M. 2004a. "Barcelona's Games: The Olympics, Urban Design and Glocal Tourism." In *Tourism Mobilities: Places to Play, Places in Play*, edited by John Urry and Mimi Sheller, 131–42. London: Routledge.

Degen, Monica M. 2004b. "Passejant per la passarel·la global: Ciutats i turisme urbà." *Transversal*, no. 23: 30–32.

Degen, Monica M. 2001. "Book Review: Capturing Public Life." *Space and Culture* 4, no. 1–9: 265–66.

De la Fuente, Manuel. 2017. "Documenting the Indignation: Responses to the 2008 Financial Crisis in Contemporary Spanish Cinema." *Romance Quarterly* 64, no. 4: 185–95.

Delgado García, Gregorio. 2006. "Don Santiago Ramón y Cajal (1852–1934), figura máxima de las ciencias españolas." *Cuadernos de Historia de la Salud Pública*, no. 103: 1–8.

Delgado Ruiz, Manuel. 2010. "La ciudad levantada: La barricada y otras transformaciones radicales del espacio urbano." In *Hacia un urbanismo alternativo*, Architectonics, Mind, Land and Society, no. 19/20, 137–53. Barcelona: UPC.

Delgado Ruiz, Manuel. 2007a. *La ciudad mentirosa: Fraude y miseria del 'modelo Barcelona.'* Madrid: Catarata.

Delgado Ruiz, Manuel. 2007b. *Sociedades movedizas: Pasos hacia una antropología de las calles.* Barcelona: Anagrama.

Delgado Ruiz, Manuel. 2001. *Memoria y lugar: El espacio público como crisis de significado.* Valencia, Spain: Ediciones Generales de la Construcción.

Delgado Ruiz, Manuel. 1999. *El animal público.* Barcelona: Anagrama.

De Pozo, Gonzalo, and Elena Oroz. 2010. "Centralización y dispersión (Dos movimientos para cartografiar la 'especificidad' del documental producido en Cataluña en la última década)." In Torreiro, *Realidad y creación*, 61–86.

De Terán, Fernando. 1999. *Historia del urbanismo en España III: Siglos XIX y XX.* Madrid: Cátedra.

De Terán, Fernando. 1968. *Antecedente de un urbanismo actual: La Ciudad Lineal.* Madrid: Cuadernos Ciencia Nueva.

Díaz de la Quintana y Sánchez Remón, A. 1893. *Contribución al estudio de la Neurastenia.* Madrid: La Nacional.

Diez Ridruejo, Cristina. 2016. "Marketing sensorial y su aplicación en la revitalización del Casco Viejo de Bilbao tras las inundaciones de 1983." Grado en Administración y Dirección de Empresas, Universidad de

Valladolid, Facultad de Ciencias Empresariales y del Trabajo de Soria, May 9, 2016.

DiFrancesco, Maria C. and Debra
J. Ochoa, eds. 2017. *Gender in
Spanish Urban Spaces*. New
York: Palgrave.

Doctor Deseo. 2004. "De nuevo en
tus brazos (Morirse en Bilbao)."
*Rómpeme con mil caricias,
cielo*. Pamplona: Gor Diskak.

Dolmage, Jay. 2017. "From Steep
Steps to Retrofit to Universal
Design, from Collapse to Aus-
terity: Neo-liberal Spaces of
Disability." In Boys, *Disability,
Space, Architecture*, 102–15.

Donaldson, Elizabeth and Catherine
Prendergast, eds. 2011. "Disabil-
ity and Emotion." Special issue,
*Journal of Literary & Cultural
Disability Studies* 5, no. 2 (July).

Doxiadis, C. A. 1967. "On Linear
Cities." *Town Planning Review*
38, no. 1: 35–42.

Durán Muñoz, García, and Fran-
cisco Alonso Burón. 1960.
*Ramón y Cajal: Tomo I. Vida y
obra*. Prologue by Pedro Laín
Entralgo. Zaragoza: Institución
Fernando el Católico.

Elden, Stuart. 2004. *Understanding Henri Lefebvre: Theory
and the Possible*. New York:
Continuum.

Epps, Brad, ed. 2002. "Special section: Barcelona and the Projection of Cataluña." *Arizona
Journal of Hispanic Cultural
Studies* vol. 6: 191–287.

Epps, Brad, ed. 2001. "Modern
Spaces: Building Barcelona." In
Iberian Cities, edited by J. R.
Resina, 148–97. New York:
Routledge.

Érice, Víctor. 2005. "A propósito
de *El cielo gira*," *El País*,
May 13, 2005. https://elpais.
com/diario/2005/05/13/
cine/1115935209_850215.html.

Estrada, Isabel. 2017. "'Democrazy'
In Spain: Cinema and New
Forms of Social Life in the
Twenty-First Century." *MLN*
132, no. 2: 386–406.

Fernández Santarén, Juan, Pedro
García Barreno, and José
Manuel Sánchez Ron. 2006.
"Santiago Ramoón y Cajal, su
vida y su mundo." In *Santiago
Ramón y Cajal: Premio Nobel
1906*, edited by Juan Fernán-
dez Santarén, 51–85. Madrid:
Museo Nacional de Ciencias
Naturales/Sociedad Estatal de
Conmemoraciones Culturales.

Foucault, Michel. 2006. *History
of Madness*. Edited by Jean
Khalfa. Translated by J. Khalfa
and Jonathan Murphy. London:
Routledge.

Foucault, Michel. 1994. *The Birth of
the Clinic: An Archaeology of
Medical Perception*. Translated
by A. M. Sheridan Smith. New
York: Vintage.

Fraser, Benjamin. Forthcoming.
*Barcelona, City of Comics.
Urbanism, Architecture and
Design in Postdictatorial Spain*.
Albany: State University of
New York Press.

Fraser, Benjamin. 2019a. *Visible
Cities, Global Comics: Urban*

Images and Spatial Form. Jackson: University Press of Mississippi.

Fraser, Benjamin. 2019b. "On Polysemiotic Interactions, Visual Paratexts and Image-Specific Translation in Comics: The Case of Rodolfo Santullo and Matías Bergara's *Dengue.*" *Studies in Comics* 10, no. 2: 277–93.

Fraser, Benjamin. 2018a. *Cognitive Disability Aesthetics: Visual Culture, Disability Representations and the (In)Visibility of Cognitive Difference.* Toronto: University of Toronto Press.

Fraser, Benjamin. 2018b. "Miguel Brieva, *quincemayista*: Art, Politics and Comics Form in the 15-M Graphic Novel *Lo que (me) está pasando* (2015)." *Transmodernity: Journal of Peripheral Cultural Production of the Luso-Hispanic World* 8, no. 1: 42–62.

Fraser, Benjamin. 2016a. "Battling Voices: Schizophrenia as Social Relation in Abel García Roure's *Una cierta verdad* [A Certain Truth] (2008)." *Disability Studies Quarterly* 36, no. 2: n.p.

Fraser, Benjamin, ed. 2016b. *Cultures of Representation: Disability in World Cinema Contexts.* New York: Wallflower/Columbia University Press.

Fraser, Benjamin. 2015. *Toward an Urban Cultural Studies: Henri Lefebvre and the Humanities.* Backingstoke, UK: Palgrave Macmillan.

Fraser, Benjamin. 2014. *Antonio López García's Everyday Urban Worlds: A Philosophy of Painting.* Lanham, MD: Bucknell University Press.

Fraser, Benjamin. 2013. *Disability Studies and Spanish Culture.* Liverpool, UK: Liverpool University Press.

Fraser, Benjamin. 2011. *Henri Lefebvre and the Spanish Urban Experience: Reading the Mobile City.* Lanham, MD: Bucknell University Press.

Fraser, Benjamin. 2010, *Encounters with Bergson(ism) in Spain: Reconciling Philosophy, Literature, Film and Urban Space.* Studies in Romance Languages and Literatures #295. Chapel Hill: University of North Carolina.

Fraser, Benjamin, ed. 2009. *Deaf History and Culture in Spain.* Washington, DC: Gallaudet University Press.

Fraser, Benjamin. 2008. "What Is Liberal Learning?: Lessons on Pedagogy from Spain's Institución Libre de Enseñanza." *Proteus: A Journal of Ideas* 25, no. 1: 9–17.

Frost, Daniel. 2008. *Cultivating Madrid: Public Space and Middle-Class Culture in the Spanish Capital 1833–1890.* Lewisberg, PA: Bucknell University Press.

Garland-Thomson, Rosemarie. 1997. *Extraordinary Bodies: Figuring Physical Disability in American Culture and Literature.* New York: Columbia University Press.

Gaedtke, Andrew. 2017. *Modernism and the Machinery of Madness. Psychosis, Technology and Narrative Worlds*. New York: Cambridge University Press.

Ghaemi, Nassir. 2011. *A First-Rate Madness: Uncovering the Links between Leadership and Mental Illness*. New York: Penguin.

Gleeson, Brendan J. 2001. "Disability and the Open City." *Urban Studies* 38, no. 2: 251–65.

Gleeson, Brendan J. 1997. "Disability Studies: A Historical Materialist View." *Disability & Society* 12 (2): 179–202.

Goldston, Robert. 1969. *Barcelona: The Civic Stage*. London: Collier-Macmillan Ltd.

Gomes, Edivam Pereira, and Maria Wellitanea de Oliveira. 2017. "O *Livro do desassossego*: Aspectos estruturais de uma narrativa fragmentada." *Revista Cereus* 9, no. 2: 142–53.

González, José Eduardo, and Timothy R. Robbins, eds. 2019. *Urban Spaces in Contemporary Latin American Literature*. New York: Palgrave.

Groensteen, Thierry. 2007. *The System of Comics*. Jackson: University Press of Mississippi.

Haidt, Rebecca. 1998. *Embodying Enlightenment: Knowing the Body in Eighteenth-Century Spanish Literature and Culture*. New York: St. Martin's Press.

Haidt, Rebecca. 2012. *Women, Work and Clothing in Eighteenth-Century Spain*. Oxford, UK: The Voltaire Foundation-University of Oxford.

Hall, Ed. 1995. "Contested (Dis)abled Identities in the Urban Labour Market." Paper presented at the Tenth Urban Change and Conflict Conference, University of London, Egham, Surrey, September 5–7, 1995.

Hall, Peter. 2002. *Cities of Tomorrow*, 3rd ed. Oxford: Blackwell.

Hall, Thomas. 1997. *Planning Europe's Capital Cities: Aspects of Nineteenth-Century Urban Development*. London: E and FN Spon.

Hamburger, Viktor. 1991. Foreword to *Cajal's Degeneration and Regeneration of the Nervous System*, edited by Javier DeFelipe and Edward G. Jones, vii–xi. Translated by Raoul M. May. New York: Oxford University Press.

Hamraie, Aimi. 2012. "Universal Design Research as a New Materialist Practice." *Disability Studies Quarterly* 32, no. 4. https://dsq-sds.org/article/view/3246.

Hartwig, Susanne. 2018a. "Introducción." In Checa Puerta and Hartwig, *¿Discapacidad?*, 7–22.

Hartwig, Susanne. 2018b. "Positions of Partiality: Acercamientos a la diversidad funcional cognitiva." In Checa Puerta and Hartwig, *¿Discapacidad?*, 187–210.

Harvey, David. 2012. *Rebel Cities*. New York: Verso.

Harvey, David. 2006. *Paris, Capital of Modernity*. New York: Routledge.

Harvey, David. 2005. "The New Urbanism and the Communitarian Trap: On the Social Problems and the False Hope of Design." In *Sprawl and Suburbia*, edited by William S. Saunders, 21–26. Minneapolis: University of Minnesota Press.

Harvey, David. 1996. *Justice, Nature and the Geography of Difference*. London: Blackwell.

Harvey, David. 1989. *The Urban Experience*. Baltimore: Johns Hopkins University Press.

Hellman, Hal. 2001. *Great Feuds in Medicine: Ten of the Liveliest Disputes Ever*. New York: John Wiley and Sons.

Hochadel, Oliver, and Agustí Nieto-Galan, eds. 2016. *Barcelona: An Urban History of Science and Modernity, 1888–1929*. New York: Routledge.

Holden, Stephen. 1998. "Film Review: A Musical Tour of Architecture as an Ode to Fertility." *New York Times*, February 27, 1998, 23.

Holmes, Amanda. 2017. *Politics of Architecture in Contemporary Argentine Cinema*. New York: Palgrave.

Hughes, Robert. 2004. *Barcelona: The Great Enchantress*. Washington, DC: National Geographic Society.

Hughes, Robert. 1992. *Barcelona*. New York: Knopf.

Illas, Edgar. 2012. *Thinking Barcelona. Ideologies of a Global City*. Liverpool, UK: Liverpool University Press.

Imrie, Rob. 2017. "The Body, Disability and Le Corbusier's Conception of the Radiant Environment." In Boys, *Disability, Space, Architecture*, 22–32.

Imrie, Rob. 2007. "The Interrelationships between Building Regulations and Architects' Practices." *Environment and Planning B: Planning and Design* 34, no. 5: 925–43.

Imrie, Rob. 2003. "Architects' Conceptions of the Human Body." *Environment and Planning D: Society and Space* 21, no. 1: 47–65.

Imrie, Rob. 2000a. "Disability and Discourses of Mobility and Movement." *Environment and Planning A* 32, no. 9: 1641–56.

Imrie, Rob. 2000b. "Disabling Environments and the Geography of Access Policies and Practices." *Disability & Society* 15, no. 1: 5–24.

Imrie, Rob. 1996. *Disability and the City: International Perspectives*. London: Paul Chapman.

Infame, Kike, and Sr. Verde. 2018. *Morirse en Bilbao: Las aventuras de Leire Riscal y Gato*. 3rd ed. Bilbao: Infame&Co.

Ingenschay, Dieter. 2003. "Bees at a Loss: Images of Madrid (before and) after *La colmena*." In Resina and Ingenschay, *After-Images of the City*, 123–38.

Jacobs, Jane. 1992. *The Death and Life of Great American Cities*. New York: Vintage.

Jacobs, Jane. 1984. *Cities and the Wealth of Nations: Principles of Economic Life*. New York: Random House.

Jackson, John Brinckerhoff. 1980. *The Necessity for Ruins and Other Topics*. Amherst: University of Massachusetts Press.

Jull Costa, Margaret. 2017. "Introduction." *The Book of Disquiet* by Fernando Pessoa, edited by Jerónimo Pizarro, vii–xv. Translated by Margaret Jull Costa. New York: New Directions.

Kafer, Alison. 2013. *Feminist Queer Crip*. Bloomington: Indiana University Press.

Kortazar, Jon. 2008. "Bilbao en la poesía del País Vasco." *Bidebarrieta* no. 19: 223–45.

Lafuente, Antonio, and Tiago Saraiva. 2004. "The Urban Scale of Science and the Enlargement of Madrid (1851–1936)." *Social Studies of Science* 34, no. 4: 531–69.

Laín Entralgo, Pedro. 1957. "Estudios y apuntes sobre Ramón y Cajal." In *España como problema*. Madrid: Aguilar.

Larson, Susan. 2011. *Constructing and Resisting Modernity: Madrid 1900–1936*. Madrid: Vervuert/Iberoamericana.

Lefebvre, Henri. 2003. *The Urban Revolution*. Translated by Robert Bononno. Minneapolis: University of Minnesota Press.

Lefebvre, Henri. 1996. *The Right to the City*. In *Writings on Cities*, edited and translated by Eleonore Kofman and Elizabeth Lebas, 63–181. Oxford, UK: Blackwell.

Lefebvre, Henri. 1995. *Introduction to Modernity*. Translated by John Moore. New York: Verso.

Lefebvre, Henri. 1991a. *The Production of Space*. Translated by Donald Nicholson–Smith. Oxford, UK: Blackwell.

Lefebvre, Henri. 1991b. *Critique of Everyday Life*. Vol 1. Translated by John Moore. New York: Verso.

Lefebvre, Henri. 1984. *Everyday Life in the Modern World*. New Brunswick, NJ: Transaction Books.

Lefebvre, Henri. 1982. *The Sociology of Marx*. Translated by N. Guterman. New York: Columbia University Press.

Lefebvre, Henri. 1976. *The Survival of Capitalism: Reproduction of the Relations of Production*. Trans. Frank Bryant. New York: St. Martin's Press.

LeFrancois, Brenda A., Robert J. Menzies, and Geoffrey Reaume, eds. 2013. *Mad Matters: A Critical Reader in Canadian Mad Studies*. Toronto: Canadian Scholars' Press.

LeGates, Richard T. and Frederic Stout, eds. 2005. *The City Reader*, 3rd ed. New York: Routledge.

Leira, Eduardo. 2009. "Bilbao: Balance provisional de una

importante transformación urbana." In Borja and Muxí, *Urbanismo en el siglo XXI*, 35–49.

López-Muñoz, Francisco, Jesús Boya, and Cecilio Alamo. 2006. "Neuron Theory, the Cornerstone of Neuroscience, on the Centenary of the Nobel Prize Award to Santiago Ramón y Cajal." *Brain Research Bulletin* 70, no. 4–6: 391–405.

Loxham, Abigail. 2006. "Barcelona under Construction: The Democratic Potential of Touch and Vision in City Cinema as Depicted in *En construcción* (2001)." *Studies in Hispanic Cinemas* 3, no. 1: 35–48.

Manera, Danilo. 2001. "Introducción." *Cuentos policiacos*, by Emilia Pardo Bazán, 11–20. Madrid: Bercimuel.

Martínez Cearra, Alfonso. 2005. "Ciudades y valores." *Ekonomiaz* 58, no. 1: 348–72.

Mas, Elías. 2000. "Los nuevos Bilbao del Ensanche." *Bidebarrieta*, no. 8: 155–74.

Masterson-Algar, Araceli. 2016. *Ecuadorians in Madrid*. New York: Palgrave.

McNeill, Donald. 2002. "Barcelona: Urban Identity 1992–2002." *Arizona Journal of Hispanic Cultural Studies* vol. 6: 245–62.

McNeill, Donald. 1999. *Urban Change and the European Left: Tales from the New Barcelona*. New York: Routledge.

McRuer, Robert. 2017. "No Future for Crips: Disorderly Conduct in the New World Order; or, Disability Studies on the Verge of a Nervous Breakdown." In *Culture – Theory – Disability: Encounters between Disability Studies and Cultural Studies*, edited by Anne Waldschmidt et al., 63–78. Bielefeld: Transcript Verlag.

McRuer, Robert. 2010. "Disability Nationalism in Crip Times." *Journal of Literary and Cultural Disability Studies* 4, no. 2: 163–78.

McRuer, Robert. 2006. *Crip Theory: Cultural Signs of Queerness and Disability*. New York: New York University Press.

McRuer, Robert, and Anna Mollow, eds. 2012. *Sex and Disability*. Durham, NC: Duke University Press.

Mercer, Leigh. 2013. *Urbanism and Urbanity: The Spanish Bourgeois Novel and Contemporary Customs (1845–1925)*. Lewisburg, PA: Bucknell University Press.

Merrifield, Andy. 2006. *Henri Lefebvre: A Critical Introduction*. New York: Routledge.

Miles, Steven, and Malcolm Miles. 2004. *Consuming Cities*. New York: Palgrave MacMillan.

Mitchell, David T., and Sharon L. Snyder. 2015. *The Biopolitics of Disability: Neoliberalism, Ablenationalism and Peripheral Embodiment*. Ann Arbor: University of Michigan Press.

———. eds. 2010. "The Geo-Politics of Ablenationalism." Special issue, *Journal of Literary and Cultural Disability Studies* 4, no. 2.

_____.2000. *Narrative Prosthesis: Disability and the Dependencies of Discourse.* Ann Arbor: University of Michigan Press.

Molotiu, Andrei. 2012. "Abstract Form: Sequential Dynamism and Iconostasis in Abstract Comics and in Steve Ditko's *Amazing Spider-Man.*" In *Critical Approaches to Comics: Theories and Methods*, edited by Matthew J. Smith and Randy Duncan, 84–100. New York: Routledge.

Moreno-Caballud, Luis. 2015. *Cultures of Anyone: Studies on Cultural Democratization in the Spanish Neoliberal Crisis.* Liverpool, UK: Liverpool University Press.

Morris, Adam. 2014. "Fernando Pessoa's Heternymic Machine." *Luso-Brazilian Review* 51, no. 2: 126–49.

Mullin, John R. 1992. "The Reconstruction of Lisbon Following the Earthquake of 1755: A Study in Despotic Planning." *Journal of the International History of City Planning Association*, no. 45: n.p.

Mumford, Lewis. 1970. *The Culture of Cities.* New York: Harcourt, Brace Jovanovich.

Murray, Stuart, and Clare Barker, eds. 2010. "Disability Postcolonialism." Special issue, *Journal of Literary and Cultural Disability Studies* 4, no. 3.

Navascués Palacios, Pedro. 1969. "La Ciudad Lineal de Arturo Soria." *Villa de Madrid*, no. 28: 49–58.

Nichols, Bill. 2001. *Introduction to Documentary.* Bloomington: Indiana University Press.

Nichols, Bill. 1991. *Representing Reality: Issues and Concepts in Documentary.* Bloomington: Indiana University Press.

O'Connor, D. J. 1985. "Science, Literature and Self-Censorship: Ramón y Cajal's *Cuentos de vacaciones* (1905)." *Ideologies and Literature* 1, no. 3: 98–122

Olsen, Donald J. 1986. *The City as a Work of Art: London, Paris, Vienna.* New Haven, CT: Yale University Press.

Ostrander, Noam and Bruce Henderson, eds. 2013. "Disability and Madness." Special issue, *Disability Studies Quarterly* 33, no. 1 (Winter).

Otis, Laura. 2001. "Introduction." *Vacation Stories: Five Science Fiction Tales*, by Santiago Ramón y Cajal. Translated by L. Otis. Urbana: University of Illinois Press.

Otis, Laura. 1999. *Membranes: Metaphors of Invasion in Nineteenth-Century Literature, Science and Politics.* Baltimore, MD: Johns Hopkins University Press.

Palardy, Diana. 2018. *The Dystopian Imagination in Contemporary Spanish Literature and Film.* New York: Palgrave.

Pardo Bazán, Emilia. (1911) 2001. "La gota de sangre." In *Cuentos policiacos*, 25–82. Madrid: Bercimuel.

Pessoa, Fernando. (1982) 2017. *The Book of Disquiet: The Complete Edition*, edited by Jerónimo Pizarro. Translated by Margaret Jull Costa. New York: New Directions.

_____.2013. *Livro do desassossego*. Edited by Jerónimo Pizarro. Lisbon: Tinta-da-China.

_____.n.d. *Livro do desassossego: Edição de Jerónimo Pizarro*. Edited by Arquivo LdoD, collaborative digital project. https://ldod.uc.pt

Pessoa, Fernando. 2008. *Lisbon: What the Tourist Should See*. Exeter: Shearsman.

Philo, Chris, and Gerry Kearns, eds. 1993. *Selling Places: The City as Cultural Capital Past and Present*. Oxford, UK: Pergamon.

Picornell, Mercè. 2017. "Abriendo fisuras en el escenario de lo hyperreal: Una lectura del documental Mercado de futuros de Mercedes Álvarez." *Confluencia: Revista Hispánica de Cultura y Literatura* 32, no. 2: 178–91.

Pina, Sónia da Silva. 2007. "O Tédio: O grito do Eu no seu paradoxo. Configuracão do Tédio no *Libro do Desassossego* de Fernando Pessoa." Repository of the Universidade de Lisboa. https://repositorio.ul.pt/handle/10451/46699.

Pizarro, Jerónimo. 2017. "Editor's Note." *The Book of Disquiet: The Complete Edition*, by Fernando Pessoa, edited by Jerónimo Pizarro, xvii–xix. Translated by M. Jull Costa. New York: New Directions.

Portela, Manuel, and António Rito Silva. 2016. "Encoding, Visualizing, and Generating Variation in Fernando Pessoa's *Livro do Desassossego*." *Variants: The Journal of the European Society for Textual Scholarship*, no. 12/13: 189–210.

Postema, Barbara. 2013. *Narrative Structure in Comics: Making Sense of Fragments*. Rochester, NY: RIT Press

Pratt, Dale. 2001. *Signs of Science: Literature, Science and Spanish Modernity*. West Lafayette, IN: Purdue University Press.

Pratt, Dale. 1995. "Literary Images of Spanish Science since 1868." Ph.D. diss., Cornell University.

Puar, Jasbir. 2007. *Terrorist Assemblages: Homonationalism in Queer Times*. Durham, NC: Duke University Press.

Ramón y Cajal, Santiago. (1905) 1999. "El pesimista corregido." In *Cuentos de vacaciones: Narraciones seudocientíficas*, 165-222. Madrid: Espasa-Calpe.

Ramón y Cajal, Santiago. (1905) 1999. *Cuentos de vacaciones: Narraciones seudocientíficas*. Prologue by José M. R. Delgado. Madrid: Espasa-Calpe.

Ramón y Cajal, Santiago. 1901. "Recreaciones estereoscópicas y binoculares." *La Fotografía*, no. 27: 41–48.

Ramos, Carlos. 2010. *Construyendo la modernidad: Escritura y arquitectura en el Madrid moderno (1919–1937)*. Leida, Spain: Edicions de la Universitat de Leida.

Ramos Brieva, J. A., A. Gutiérrez-Zotes, and J. Sáiz Ruiz. 2002. "Escala de Control de los Impulsos 'Ramón y Cajal' ECIRyC: Desarrollo, validación y baremación." *Actas Españolas de Psiquiatría* 30, no. 3: 160–74.

Resina, Joan Ramon. 2008. *Barcelona's Vocation of Modernity: Rise and Decline of an Urban Image*. Palo Alto, CA: Stanford University Press.

Resina, Joan Ramon. 2003a. "The Concept of After-Image and the Scopic Apprehension of the City." In Resina and Ingenschay, *After-Images of the City*, 1–22.

Resina, Joan Ramon. 2003b. "From Rose of Fire to City of Ivory." In Resina and Ingenschay, *After-Images of the City*, 75–122.

Resina, Joan Ramon, ed. 2001a. *Iberian Cities*. New York: Routledge.

Resina, Joan Ramon. 2001b. "Madrid's Palimpsest: Reading the Capital against the Grain." In *Iberian Cities*, edited by Joan Ramon Resina, 56–92. New York: Routledge.

Resina, Joan Ramon, and Dieter Ingenschay, eds. 2003. *After-Images of the City*. Ithaca, NY: Cornell University Press.

Resina, Joan Ramon, and Dieter Ingenschay. 2003. "Preface." In Resina and Ingenschay, *After-Images of the City*, ix–xvii.

Riambau, Esteve. 2010. "Cuando los monos aún no eran como Becky (El documental catalán antes de 1999)." In Torreiro, *Realidad y creación*, 11–31.

Rice-Davis, Charles. 2017. "Pharmakopolis: Cesário Verde's Lisbon." *Journal of Urban Cultural Studies* 4, no. 1–2: 13–29.

Richardson, Nathan. 2011. *Constructing Spain: The Reimagination of Space and Place in Fiction and Film, 1953–2003*. Lewisburg, PA: Bucknell University Press.

Robbins, Kevin. 1993. "Prisoner of the City: Whatever Could a Postmodern City Be?" In *Space and Place: Theories of Identity and Location*, edited by Erica Carter, James Donald, and Judith Squires, 303–30. London: Lawrence and Wishart.

Rodríguez, Arantxa, and Lorenzo Vicario. 2005. "Innovación, Competitividad y Regeneración Urbana: Los espacios retóricos de la "ciudad creativa" en el nuevo Bilbao." *Ekonomiaz* 58, no. 1: 262–95.

Ruiz Cuenca, Violeta. 2020. "Medicine, Modernity and Masculinity: A History of Neurasthenia in Spain, c. 1890-1920." PhD diss., Universitat Autònoma de Barcelona, Institut d'Història de la Ciència.

Salazar Arechalde, José Ignacio. 2008. "Historia y paisaje de

Bilbao en *Paz en la guerra*." *Bidebarrieta*, no. 19, 181–201.

Sambricio, Carlos. 2004. *Madrid, Vivienda y Urbanismo: 1900–1960*. Madrid: Akal.

Santullo, Rodolfo, and Matías Bergara. 2015. *Dengue*. Los Angeles: Humanoids.

Sarfati, Georges-Elia. 2012. "Fernando Pessoa's Lisbon: Toponymy vs. Heteronymy." *Partial Answers: Journal of Literature and the History of Ideas* 10, no. 1: 149–61.

Sass, Louis A. 1992. *Madness and Modernism: Insanity in the Light of Modern Art, Literature and Thought*. New York: Basic Books.

Savarese, Emily Thornton, and Ralph James Savarese, eds. 2010. "Autism and the Concept of Neurodiversity." Special issue, *Disability Studies Quarterly* 30, no. 1 (Winter).

Schivelbusch, Wolfgang. 1986. *The Railway Journey: The Industrialization of Time and Space in the Nineteenth-Century*. Berkeley: University of California Press.

Schmidt, Roger. 2003. "Caffeine and the Coming of the Enlightenment." *Raritan* 23, no. 1: 129–49.

Sennett, Richard. 2008. *The Craftsman*. New Haven: Yale University Press.

Sennett, Richard. 1994. *Flesh and Stone: The Body and the City in Western Civilization*. New York: W. W. Norton.

Sennett, Richard. 1992. *The Conscience of the Eye: The Design and Social Life of Cities*. New York: W. W. Norton.

Serlin, David. 2012. "On Walkers and Wheelchairs: Disabling the Narratives of Urban Modernity." *Radical History Review*, no. 114: 19–28.

Serlin, David. 2006. "Disabling the Flâneur." *Journal of Visual Culture* 5, no. 2: 193–208.

Serrano, Javier. 2012. "*Mercado de futuros*, entre el suelo y el humo." *La República Cultural*, March 19, 2012. https://larepublicacultural.es/article5533.html.

Siebers, Tobin. 2017. "Disability Aesthetics." In Boys, *Disability, Space, Architecture*, 57–66.

Siebers, Tobin. 2010. *Disability Aesthetics*. Ann Arbor: University of Michigan Press.

Simak, Clifford D. 1965. *All Flesh Is Grass*. New York: Avon.

Simmel, Georg. 2000. "The Metropolis and Mental Life." In *Readings in Social Theory: The Classic Tradition to Post-Modernism*, 3rd ed., edited by James Farganis, 149–57. New York: McGraw Hill.

Snyder, Jon. 2015. *Poetics of Opposition in Contemporary Spain: Politics and the Work of Urban Culture*. New York: Palgrave.

Sobrer, Josep Miquel. 2002. "Against Barcelona? Gaudí, the City, and Nature." *Arizona Journal of Hispanic Cultural Studies*, vol. 6: 205–19.

Soria y Mata, Arturo. 1894. *El origen poliédrico de las*

especies. Madrid: Sucesores de Rivadeneyra.

Soria y Mata, Arturo. 1892. *Ferrocarril-tranvía de circunvalación de Madrid á Canillas, Hortaleza, Funcarral, Vicálvaro, Vallecas, Villaverde, Carabanchel y Pozuelo. Datos y noticias referentes á su construcción y explotación.* Madrid: Sucesores de Rivadeneyra.

Soria y Puig, Arturo, ed. 1996. *Cerdá: Las cinco bases de la teoría general de la urbanización.* Barcelona-Madrid: Fundació Catalana per a la Recerca-Sociedad Editorial Electa España.

Sotelo, Constantino. 2003. "Viewing the Brain through the Master Hand of Ramón y Cajal." *Nature Reviews Neuroscience,* no. 4: 71–78.

Stahnisch, Frank W., and Robert Nitsch. 2002. "Santiago Ramón y Cajal's Concept of Neuronal Plasticity: The Ambiguity Lives On." *Trends in Neurosciences* 25, no. 11: 589–91

Stiker, Henri-Jacques. (1982) 1997. *A History of Disability.* Translated by William Sayers. Foreword by David T. Mitchell. Ann Arbor: University of Michigan Press.

Straus, Joseph N. 2018. *Broken Beauty: Musical Modernism and the Representation of Disability.* Oxford, UK: Oxford University Press.

Straus, Joseph N. 2013. "Autism as Culture." In *Disability Studies Reader,* 4th ed., edited by Lennard Davis, 460–84. New York: Routledge.

Straus, Joseph N. 2011. *Extraordinary Measures: Disability in Music.* Oxford, UK: Oxford University Press.

Stevens, Dana. 2007. "To Pretend Is to Know Oneself." In *Embodying Pessoa: Corporeality, Gender, Sexuality,* edited by Anna M. Klobucka and Mark Sabine, 39–51. Toronto: University of Toronto Press.

Suárez-Figueroa Cazeaux, J. 1909. "La Neurastenia y los trabajos mentales." Doctoral Thesis, Universidad Central de Madrid, November 16, 1908. Madrid: Tortosa, Imp. De Sucesores de L. Bernis.

Teshigahara, Hiroshi. (1984) 2008. *Antonio Gaudí.* Toho Co. and Criterion Collection.

Teshigahara, Hiroshi. 2008. "My First Trip to the West." DVD booklet accompanying *Antonio Gaudí,* directed by Hiroshi Teshigahara (1984). Criterion Collection.

Titchkosky, Tanya. 2011. *The Question of Access: Disability, Space, Meaning.* Toronto: University of Toronto Press.

Titchkosky, Tanya, and Rod Michalko. 2017. "The Body as a Problem of Individuality: A Phenomenological Disability Studies Approach." In Boys, *Disability, Space, Architecture,* 67–77.

Torreiro, Casimiro. 2010a. "De tendencias y autores (La

configuración artística del documental catalán contemporáneo)." In Torreiro, *Realidad y creación*, 33–59.

Torreiro, Casimiro, ed. 2010b. *Realidad y creación en el cine de no-ficción (El documental catalán contemporáneo, 1995–2010)*. Madrid: Cátedra.

Trotter, David. 2001. *Paranoid Modernism: Literary Experiment, Psychosis and the Professionalization of English Society*. New York: Oxford University Press.

Tsuchiya, Akiko. 2011. *Marginal Subjects: Gender and Deviance in Nineteenth-Century Spain*. Toronto: University of Toronto Press.

Tzitsikas, Helene. 1988. *El quijotismo y la raza en la Generación de 1898*. Buenos Aires: Plus Ultra.

Unamuno, Miguel de. 1914. *Niebla*. Madrid: Renacimiento.

Urrutia, Víctor. 2009. "Bilbao, el peso de un contexto." In Borja and Muxí, *Urbanismo en el siglo XXI*, 51–61.

van Hensbergen, Gijs. 2001. *Gaudí: A Biography*. New York: Harper Perennial.

Van Zuylen, Marina. 2005. *Monomania: The Flight from Everyday Life in Literature and Art*. Ithaca, NY: Cornell University Press.

Vázquez Montalbán, Manuel. 1990. *Barcelonas*. Translated by Andy Robinson. London: Verso.

Vegara, Alfonso. 2001. "New Millenium Bilbao." In *Waterfronts in Post-industrial Cities*, edited by Richard Marshall, 86–94. New York: Spon.

Velez, Diana. 1983. "Late Nineteenth-Century Spanish Progressivism: Arturo Soria's Linear City." *Journal of Urban History* 9, no. 2: 131–64.

Vilaseca, Stephen. 2020. *Anarchist Socialism in Early Twentieth-Century Spain: A Ricardo Mella Anthology*. New York: Palgrave.

Vilaseca, Stephen. 2013. *Barcelonan Okupas: Squatter Power!* Lanham, MD: Fairleigh Dickinson University Press.

Viveros, Carmen, and Josep M. Català. 2010. "La nueva ecología del documental (El Máster de Documental Creativo de la UAB)." In Torreiro, *Realidad y creación*, 123–41.

Whitehead, James. 2017. *Madness and the Romantic Poet: A Critical History*. Oxford, UK: Oxford University Press.

Woodworth, Paddy. 2008. *The Basque Country: A Cultural History*. Oxford, UK: Oxford University Press.

Young, Iris Marion. 1990. *Justice and the Politics of Difference*. Princeton, NJ: Princeton University Press.

INDEX

AUTHOR BIO

Benjamin Fraser is Professor of Hispanic Studies in the College of Humanities at the University of Arizona. He is former head of the Department of Spanish and Portuguese at the University of Arizona, and former chair of the Department of Foreign Languages and Literatures at East Carolina University. Fraser's publications on disability themes include *Cognitive Disability Aesthetics* (U of Toronto P, 2018), *Cultures of Representation: Disability in World Cinema Contexts* (Wallflower P/Columbia University Press, 2016), *Disability Studies and Spanish Culture: Films, Novels, the Comic and the Public Exhibition* (Liverpool University Press, 2013), and *Deaf History and Culture in Spain* (Gallaudet University Press, 2009). His work on urban topics includes *Visible Cities, Global Comics* (University Press of Mississippi, 2019), *Toward an Urban Cultural Studies* (Palgrave, 2015), *Antonio López García's Everyday Urban Worlds* (Bucknell University Press, 2014), and *Henri*

Lefebvre and the Spanish Urban Experience (Bucknell University Press, 2011). His most recent book projects are *The Art of Pere Joan* (University of Texas Press, 2019), *Beyond Sketches of Spain: Tete Montoliu and the Construction of Iberian Jazz* (Oxford University Press, forthcoming), and *Barcelona, City of Comics* (State University of New York Press, forthcoming). Fraser is editor-in-chief of *Hispania*, executive editor of the *Journal of Urban Cultural Studies*, a senior editor of the *Arizona Journal of Hispanic Cultural Studies*, and founding co-editor of the Hispanic Urban Studies book series. He serves on the editorial board of *Disability Studies Quarterly* and his articles have been published in *Hispanic Review, Cultural Studies, Journal of Spanish Cultural Studies, Social and Cultural Geography, Journal of Literary and Cultural Disability Studies, Disability Studies Quarterly, Arizona Journal of Hispanic Cultural Studies, Dieciocho* and *Bulletin of Spanish Studies.*

www.ingramcontent.com/pod-product-compliance
Lightning Source LLC
Chambersburg PA
CBHW030732280326
41926CB00086B/1169